MW00810541

THE

EDGAR CAYCE

BIBLE COMPANION

THE

EDGAR CAYCE

BIBLE COMPANION

Biblical Treasure from the Edgar Cayce Readings

by Dick Daily

ARE PRESS

ASSOCIATION FOR
RESEARCH AND
ENLIGHTENMENT

A.R.E. Press • Virginia Beach • Virginia

Copyright © 1998
· by Dick Daily
2nd Printing, December 1998

Printed in the U.S.A.

All rights reserved. No part of this book may be reproduced or trans-
mitted in any form or by any means, electronic or mechanical, including
photocopying, recording or by any information storage and retrieval system, without permission in writing from the Publisher.

A.R.E. Press
215 67th Street
Virginia Beach, VA 23451-2061

Library of Congress Cataloging-in-Publication Data
   Daily, Dick.
   The Edgar Cayce Bible companion : biblical treasure from the Edgar Cayce
readings / by Dick Daily.
       p.   cm.
   ISBN 0-87604-398-8
   1. Bible—Criticism, interpretation, etc. 2. Cayce, Edgar, 1877-1945—Edgar
Cayce readings. 3. Bible—Indexes. I. Cayce, Edgar, 1877-1945. Edgar Cayce read-
ings. Selections. II. Title.
BS534.D25   1998
220.7—dc21   97-33437

Edgar Cayce Readings © 1971, 1993, 1994, 1995, 1996
by the Edgar Cayce Foundation.
All rights reserved.

Cover design by Richard Boyle

Dedicated in memory of my parents
Estelle and **Henry Daily**
who gave me my first Bible when
I was ten years old

Contents

Acknowledgments

My study of the Edgar Cayce Bible references was originally undertaken as a thesis project for a master of arts degree from Atlantic University. I would like to express my gratitude to the members of my thesis committee: Dr. Bob Danner, Dr. Scott Sparrow, and Kieth VonderOhe for their guidance and assistance. In addition, I want to give special thanks to Dr. Charles Thomas Cayce for his comments, support, and encouragement. Also, I want to give special thanks to Bill Kirklin for his patient and expert assistance with my many computer challenges and opportunities.

" ... more time must be given to
the study of the Holy Word and
more expression of the self must
be spent in manifesting these
truths before men." (3981-1)

FOREWORD

Many times I heard people ask my father, Hugh Lynn, what aspect of his father's readings he found most meaningful. He would always answer that it was the material on prayer and meditation, or it was how the readings made the Bible take on new meaning and come alive for him. My grandfather's secretary, Gladys Davis Turner, always had one answer to the same question: It was the Bible material in the readings along with Edgar Cayce's Bible study classes. Clearly, the Bible was a major source of inspiration for Edgar Cayce, himself, and for his readings.

Dick Daily has done what many students of the Edgar Cayce readings have dreamed of doing, or at least wish that someone would do. He has collected all of the Bible references in the readings and grouped them by subject. These subjects which comprise his Table of Contents are forty-seven of the most important nonmedical topics in the readings. One can scan the index and immediately find topics of personal interest, turn to those, and see how the readings related Bible passages to those topics. I just spent thirty minutes, for example, on "Ideals," "Relationships with Others," and "Aim for Perfection," and had new insights about both the subjects and the Bible passages that were cited.

In addition, he summarizes the specific suggestions for Bible study that were made for those getting readings from Edgar Cayce. For those of us who have been curious about which Bible passages were most frequently quoted and recommended in the readings, those tabulations are available in Appendices.

I am especially pleased to be given the opportunity to introduce this new volume for two reasons. First, I think Edgar Cayce would nod and smile when he saw it. I have known the author for years as A Search for God study group member, a successful businessman who grew up with the Bible and the Boy Scouts, and has asked the hard questions of life that many of us try to ask. He has found the readings helpful in that search and is sharing what he has found to be helpful. There is not much lengthy philosophizing, just Bible quotes, readings, and brief commentary arranged in a way I found to be helpful, too. I hope you will find the book interesting and stimulating, as I have.

Charles Thomas Cayce, Ph.D.
President, Edgar Cayce Foundation

INTRODUCTION

It is said that Edgar Cayce read the entire Bible once for each of the sixty-seven years that he lived. The decision to do this was made when he was ten years old, and for the first few years he had to read it more than once in order to catch up. The Bible that he read was the King James Version and the language used in the readings seems to reflect this influence.

In 1944 a woman wanted to know, "What present printed version of the Bible gives the nearest to the true meaning of both the Old and New Testaments?" Here is Cayce's answer: "The nearest true version for the entity is that ye apply of whatever version ye read." (2072-14)

The psychic readings of Edgar Cayce include more than 16,300 Bible references and quotations. I have separated the quotations from the Bible by theme and subject into chapters, which are arranged in order of the frequency these verses were quoted in the readings. For example, the eleven verses used in Chapter 1—"Ideals"—were quoted a combined total of 885 times, while the seven verses used in Chapter 47—"His Way"—were quoted a combined total of only thirty-nine times.

In our last chapter we discuss the Bible study recommendations contained in the readings. This is followed by Appendix A which lists the Bible study recommendations by book, chapter, and verse. It also shows the number of times each reference was recommended. This is followed by Appendix B which identifies and lists the page location of the thirty-four Bible verse interpretations included in this book. Appendix C lists some questions of special interest and the page location of the answer.

Appendix D summarizes all of the Bible verses used in this book. It reflects the number of times each verse was quoted in the readings and the page location.

This book includes 470 Bible verses and 590 quotations from the Edgar Cayce readings that quote or relate to these verses. Over half of these quotations, 330 to be exact, come from either the 262 Series or the 281 Series of readings. Many of you may know that the 262 Series of 130 readings was given to the original A.R.E. study group which I identify as simply "Study Group 1." The 281 Series of 65 readings was given to a prayer group known as the Glad Helpers which I identify as the Prayer Healing Group. Reading this book may well give you a feeling of what it was like to be a member of these early groups.

Chapter 7 is entitled "Soul Growth." In a sense, this is what the entire book is concerned with. Chapter 1 is about "Ideals." The purpose of establishing and working with ideals is, clearly, to help insure that soul growth occurs as rapidly as possible during our earthly sojourn.

The Bible quotations have been set in bold type and the Edgar Cayce readings have been set in bold italic type to help the reader and because I feel that the bold italic helps to bring out the inherent boldness and beauty of the readings.

I hope that reading the book will be as joyful and rewarding to you as its compilation has been for me.

Dick Daily
Virginia Beach, Va.
December 1997

1

IDEALS

The Bible verse most frequently quoted in the Edgar Cayce readings is II Timothy 2:15: **Study to shew thyself approved unto God, a workman that needeth not to be ashamed, rightly dividing the word of truth**. This verse was quoted 638 times. In some cases the wording was changed to: *Study to show thyself approved unto thy ideal.*

The Cayce readings, on a number of occasions, stress the importance of setting ideals. Here is a portion of reading 5489-1: *Ideals...must be set as high as the heavens themselves - then work! making self a channel...*

The readings recommend that each individual select their own spiritual ideal, mental ideal, and physical ideal. A firm commitment to our ideals can be one of the most important things we can do for our physical health, mental ability, and spiritual growth. The readings suggest that our ideals be reviewed from time to time and be revised when we are prepared to establish a higher level of commitment.

Many years ago, after joining the Boy Scouts, I pledged to be physically strong, mentally awake, and morally straight. While these were not referred to as ideals, for those of us who took this pledge seriously, that's what they became. Looking specifically at the spiritual ideal, a pledge to be morally straight would seem to obligate one to be completely fair with others and never take advantage of them. When a scout is prepared to do so, he might want to pledge himself to be loving and helpful to others rather than just being fair with them, thus raising his spiritual ideal to a higher level. Of course, the scouting principle of "doing a good deed daily" seems to go beyond being just "morally straight."

We should set ideals that are realistic. Ideals to which we are entirely prepared to make a commitment. Next, we need to periodically, perhaps at the end of each day, review our experiences to determine how well we have lived up to our ideals. Thus, this Bible verse to, **Study to shew thyself approved unto God**, should, perhaps, be seen as directing us to set aside specific periods to review how well we are living up to our ideals.

A second verse that seems to relate to living up to our ideals is Matthew 5:16: **Let your light so shine before men that they may see your good** works and glorify your Father which is in heaven. Here reading 2545-1 ties together letting our light shine with living up to our ideals: *Let thy light so shine, day by day, that ye fail not in that standard thou hast set to thyself...For, thou art high indeed in thy ideals. Do not lessen them, but let thy prayer be daily:* "Lord, here am I - thy servant, seeking to be a greater expression of thee among my fellow men. Show me the way..."

Luke 6:45 seems to relate to living up to those ideals that have been established in our heart: **A good man out of the good treasure of his heart bringeth forth that which is good...for of the abundance of the heart his mouth speaketh.** In the following of reading, 262-51, we find reference to this verse and our ideals: *...the activity of each soul should be...to show forth in its actions that* [which] *it professes to believe. For, from the abundance of the heart the mouth speaketh truth...that...found as a tinkling cymbal may come only from that held as a tenet or as an ideal.*

Here is Micah 6:8 which was quoted several times in the readings: **...what doth the Lord require of thee, but to do justly, and to love mercy, and to walk humbly with thy God?** Some advise on ideals is given in reading 2205-1 which also quotes from this verse: *First, know self and self's ideal. Know...that the ideal must be of spiritual import, - and thus may bring into the experience of the entity those things that bring harmony. For, know that to live justly, to love mercy, to walk humbly before the Lord thy God is the whole duty of man.*

One might raise the question of what takes place if we do not have an ideal or what happens if we loose our ideal. Proverbs 29:18 seems to speak to this: **Where there is no vision, the people perish...** Reading 5754-3 tells us what occurs when we loose our ideal: *...as has been so well pointed out in Holy Writ, if the ideal of the individual is lost, then the abilities for that...individual to contact the spiritual forces are gradually lost...*

The readings relate John 10:10 to our ideals. **...I am come that they might have life, and that they might have it more abundantly.** A 46-year-old housewife asked Cayce how she could gain a better understanding of her conflicting emotions and urges. His response, in reading 997-1, includes the following: *...the sources may be seen. For it is only* [self] *meeting self...to overcome same, set thine standard* [ideal]. *The choice may be in Him...who has...given a way for all; that in Him ye may know life, may have life, may have life more abundantly; more joy, more harmony, more peace.*

Here is another verse which the readings relate to our ideals, Romans 12:1: **...present your bodies in living sacrifice, holy acceptable unto God, which is your reasonable service.** In this portion of reading 262-87 Cayce discusses the meaning of sacrifice: *...you each should present yourselves as channels of blessings to others; in* [order] *that others may receive a bet-*

ter concept of the necessity of presenting their bodies as a living sacrifice, as a living example. Each should understand that sacrifice does not necessarily mean a giving up; [but] rather, a glorifying of the body for a definite purpose...for an ideal, for a love.

A 20-year-old student asked if he were holding the right ideals. Cayce's reply makes reference to Matthew 6:21: **Where your treasure is, there will be your heart also.** Here is a portion of reading 488-6: *...hold that same attitude, that same willingness to be shown...*[and the right ideals] *will be presented...will be gradually builded; for that* [which] *we think upon, that we become - "for, where the treasure is, the heart is also."*

In a reading for a 41-year-old housewife Cayce speaks of the need to know our ideals and makes reference to Romans 12:9: **Let love be without dissimulation. Abhor that which is evil; cleave to that which is good.** Here is reading 2845-2: *...analyze self, self's purposes. And know thy ideals, spiritually, mentally,* [and] *materially...Let thy love be without dissimulation. Abhor evil. Cleave to that which is good; showing thyself approved to Him who is the way, the truth, the light.*

John 4:23 speaks of our worship of God as follows: **...the true worshippers shall worship the Father in spirit and in truth: for the Father seeketh such to worship him. God is Spirit and they that worship him must worship him in spirit and in truth.** Cayce quotes from this Scripture in reading 816-10 for a 54-year-old man: *Spirit is the natural, the normal condition of an entity. For hath it not been given, God is Spirit and seeketh such to worship Him in spirit and in truth?...Today...There is the opportunity to make manifest that which is* [the] *ideal, in the experience of* [each] *entity.*

Romans 14:8 speaks to the issue of life and death as follows: **Whether we live, we live unto the Lord; and whether we die, we die unto the Lord: whether we live therefore, or die, we are the Lord's.** Reading 262-29 discusses changes that may be needed to comply with our ideal and relates this to Romans 14:8 as follows: *Know ye not that whether ye live or die ye live or die in the Lord...When one has set the ideal, and knows what the ideal represents, and then knows self measured by the ideal, one sees, is aware of that lacking or that overdone in self, and plucks it out...*

First, set your ideals. Then, each day compare your life experiences with your ideal. Finally, and most importantly, change your behavior as needed to measure up to your ideal.

2

KARMA

One of the most frequently quoted Bible verses in the Edgar Cayce readings is Galatians 6:7...**whatsoever a man soweth, that shall he also reap.** The typical quotation from the readings is: *As ye sow, so shall ye reap.* This principle is sometimes referred to as karmic law or the law of cause and effect. The Cayce readings say that reincarnation and karmic law, sowing and reaping, is a common way that soul growth takes place. The readings also discuss moving from the law of karma to the law of grace as an alternative path for soul development. The key to moving to the law of grace is to make our will one with that of our Creator. As we do this we become cocreators with the Universal Consciousness which we call God.

The operation of karmic law is discussed in the following portion of reading 3660-1: *...the law is perfect - that ye sow, ye reap. If ye sow it to the flesh, in the flesh, ye must reap. If ye sow it in the mind, to the mind it must be made straight. For it depends upon what spirit ye entertain. For it is only with the spirit of truth as manifested in that light, that knowledge of God deep within self, that ye may make thy paths straight.*

The principle of karmic law is also evident in Matthew 7:2 ...**with what measure ye mete, it shall be measured to you again.** In many places the readings quote these words verbatim and in some instances the individual was asked to keep this in mind in their conversations and activities with others. In reading 3240-1, this Bible verse was followed by the question, when you analyze a neighbor do you use the same standard that you desire to be measured by.

In Luke 6:37 we find karmic law expressed in these words: **Judge not, and ye shall not be judged; condemn not, and ye shall not be condemned...** Cayce quotes from this verse in 262-109: *Let mercy and justice be thy watchword rather than judgment upon others. For "Judge not that ye be not judged" is the same as saying show mercy to those that are wayward, to those that are awkward, to those that are unkind, to those that are rude... For in thy awkwardness, in thy stumbling, ye oft find fault in thine self. Do not judge thyself. Let God's mercy and love rule thee.* In some readings the focus was on **condemn not** rather than **judge not.** For example, in reading 3022-1 the individual was advised to: *Condemn not, if ye would not be condemned.*

Reading 262-82 makes reference to karma and the law of grace in connection with Matthew 5:18: **...Till heaven and earth pass, one jot or one tittle shall in no wise pass from the law, till all be fulfilled.** Here is a portion of 262-82: *Have ye not read as He gave, that he who is guilty of one jot or tittle is guilty of it all? Have ye not read that ye shall pay to the uttermost farthing? Yet it is not the same as considered by some, that ye have builded thine own karma - and that the blood...the law of grace is of* [no] *effect. But as He has given, if thine activity is* [done so] *that ye may be seen of men, or if thine purpose, thine aim, thine desire is for self-glorification, then ye are* [not one] *of His.*

In reading 281-38 Cayce relates Exodus 20:5 to the operation of karmic law. Here is Exodus 20:5: **...I the Lord thy God am a jealous God, visiting the iniquity of the fathers upon the children unto the third and fourth generation...** And here is a portion of 281-38: *How is it given in our Word? That the sins of the fathers are visited unto the children of the third and fourth generation...This is not saying that the results are seen only in the bodily functions of the descendants, as is ordinarily implied; but that the essence of the message is given to the individual* [father] *respecting the activity of which he may or must eventually be well aware in his own being. That is, what effect does it have upon you to...get mad, to laugh, to cry, to be sorrowful? All of these activities affect not only yourself* [and] *your relationships to your fellow man, but your next experience in the earth!*

In reading 281-4 a member of the Prayer Healing Group asked this question: "When one is working out a karma, is it right to try to help that one?" In his reply Cayce refers to John 9:3 which is as follows: **Jesus answered, Neither hath this man sinned, nor his parents: but that the works of God should be made manifest in him.** These words by Jesus were in response to this question. **Master, who did sin, this man, or his parents, that he was born blind?** Here is the relevant portion of 281-4: *This may be answered...as was... "Who sinned, this man or his parents?" "That the works of God might be manifest before you!" When there are karmic conditions in the experience of an individual...those that have the Christ-like spirit* [are] *not only in praying for them, holding meditation for them, but aiding, helping, in every manner* [so] *that the works of God may be manifest in their lives, and* [they include in] *every meditation or prayer:* **Thy will, O God, be done in that body as thou seest best.**

In discussing karma and reincarnation in reading 262-99, Cayce makes reference to Ecclesiastes 11:3 which includes these words: **...if the tree fall toward the south, or toward the north, in the place where the tree**

falleth, there it shall be. Here is a portion of reading 262-99:*...each experience in the earth is as a schooling, is as an experience for the soul...As the tree falls so does it lie.* There *it begins* [again] *when it has assimilated...in* [the] *spiritual...that* [which] *it has gained.* Thus, under the law of karma, habits, both good and bad, are carried over from one life experience to the next. Knowledge of this law can, perhaps, help us to overcome a habit such as smoking. Once we understand that we will be wanting to smoke from here to eternity unless we overcome the addiction, then we may somehow find the motivation necessary to overcome the problem. It has helped me!

In reading 262-14 Cayce was asked "Is the faith of a man in Buddha or Mohammed equal, in the effect on his soul, to faith in Jesus Christ?" His reply refers to Matthew 10:41: **He that receiveth a prophet in the name of a prophet shall receive a prophet's reward...** Here is 262-14: *As He gave, he that receiveth a prophet in the* name *of a prophet* receives *the prophet's reward, or that* ability *that that individual spiritual force may manifest in the life of that individual...each* [prophet] *in their respective spheres are but stepping stones to that* [which] *may awaken in the individual the knowledge of the Son in their lives.* My perspective on this reading is that a follower of Buddha or Mohammed will progress spiritually to the extent that true "Christ Consciousness" is awakened during that lifetime.

Matthew 7:16 **Ye shall know them by their fruits...** While neither this verse, nor the related reading make direct reference to karmic law, it appears to me that we are dealing here with "cause and effect" which is a basic principle of karmic law. Reflect upon reading 262-18: *Keep the way open. Do not become a stumbling block to any.* Know *in what thou has believed, and* where *thy faith has been placed. By the works ye shall know them...by their fruits; for as virtue is a fruit of faith, so does the* understanding *come - as the full-grown seed ready for planting.*

Here is a second Bible verse and related reading which seem to have karmic implications. Luke 17:1: **...It is impossible but that offenses will come; but woe unto him, through whom they come.** Reference to this verse is included in the following message for a 30-year-old man in reading 262-109: *The way is narrow, yet it is the Happy Way...He was Happy even* [on the way] *to the Cross. Not that moments of discouragement do not arise in thine experience, for as He gave... "It must indeed be necessary that offenses come, but woe to him by whom they come!" Then never be...an offense to anyone. Let mercy and patience keep thee.*

When we think of karma, many of us may, somewhat automatically, think of current negative situations or experiences and their relationship to past deeds and choices. While looking back may provide some insight on the present, we should not dwell on the past. Instead, we need to simply respond to every situation as constructively as possible, with our attention fixed firmly on the future.

3

TRUE PROSPERITY

True prosperity is related to our spiritual gifts. Here is a verse about our gifts. James 1:17: **Every good and perfect gift is from above and cometh down from the Father...** In reading 3053-3 Cayce says: *...who is the Giver of all good and perfect gifts, and who is hurt when such gifts are used for indulgence, for gratification* [of self]... A somewhat similar reference to this verse is found in reading 2919-1:*...use* [your gifts] *to the glory of Him who is the Giver of all good and perfect gifts, and not to the satisfying or gratifying of self...* Here is a third comment about gifts from reading 1646-1:*...as has been given of old; ...to some there is the gift of healing, to some the gift of speech, interpreting of tongues, to ministering. Yet all are of the same Spirit.* Whatever our individual gifts may be, we must cultivate, develop, and use them in such a way as to be helpful to others. We should be grateful to the Source of all life for our gifts, whatever they may be.

Initiative is another principle of prosperity. Luke 11:9 speaks to this:**...ask and it shall be given you; seek and ye shall find; knock and it shall be opened unto you.** Reference to this verse is included in 4905-57 for a man seeking business advice: *"Ask and ye shall receive, knock and it shall be opened." Ask for the money. Keep hammering, and it will open...*The following is from 3051-2 for a 45-year-old housewife: *Seek and ye shall find; ask and it will be given thee - if ye have chosen aright.* God listens to our prayers and He cares for us. He gives to us joyously that which we need. It is interesting to note that both of the Cayce readings specify that something over and above just knocking, seeking, and asking is required to get results. One reading emphasizes persistence, *keep hammering*, and the other reading promises success if the individual's choice is correct.

In a prosperity seminar a few years ago, the leader said that we select *what* we desire and God will provide the answer as to *how*. My personal reaction was that my God will supply the how only if the what is correct for me. The seminar leader talked at length about the need for proper programming of our subconscious mind, giving detailed instructions for doing this. I think it is true that we can obtain some assistance from this subconscious/unconscious level of mind activity for anything we desire. However, the highest level that can provide assistance is the superconscious level or true God level of mind activity. At this level the things we are seeking must be for our highest good in order for assistance to be granted.

A third principle of prosperity involves faithfulness over what we have, no matter how few or small our resources may appear. Here is Matthew 25:21: **His lord said unto him, Well done, thou good and faithful servant, thou hast been faithful over a few things, I will make thee ruler over many things: enter thou into the joy of thy lord.** Edgar Cayce makes reference to this verse in the following portion of 262-25: *Be faithful to that which is given in thy charge day by day, for he that is faithful over the little things will be made the ruler over the many.*

In order to achieve material well-being, we need, first, to prepare the way mentally and spiritually. In Haggai 2:8 we find these words: **The silver is mine, and the gold is mine saith the Lord of hosts.** In reading 877-29 a 48-year-old lawyer asked how he could clear his debts. Here is Cayce's reply: *These can be met only by measuring up to that which brings the promise...from the sources of supply - materially, physically. For the earth is indeed the Lord's, and the fullness thereof. The silver and the gold are his. When ye measure [up] to that standard [that] is needed...for the best mental and soul development, such is - will be - supplied.*

Psalm 84:11 tells us that God rewards those who walk uprightly: **The Lord is a sun and a shield; the Lord will give grace and glory: no good thing will be withheld from them that walk uprightly.** Here is a reference to this verse from reading 281-61 for a 52-year-old housewife: *In joy, in patience, run the race that is set before thee; knowing He is faithful and keeps His promise to those who are faithful in purpose, in aim, in desire, and will not withhold anything good from the righteous.*

Look to Him, for, indeed, He is our source. Here is Psalm 50:10: **Every beast of the forest is mine, and the cattle upon a thousand hills.** Reading 2900-2 for a 55-year-old masseuse includes the following reference to this verse: *...the earth is the Lord's and the fullness thereof, the silver and the gold are his, the cattle on a thousand hills. And though ye may be far afield, far astray, His promises are sure...Then, let not the anxieties of the moment deter thee. Look to Him, and ye will find that changes will come about...that in thine own heart may be manifested in thy life...if ye will but serve the Lord.*

Malachi 3:10 tells us the Lord will pour out a great blessing: **Bring ye all the tithes into the storehouse, that there may be meat in my house, and prove me now herewith, saith the Lord of hosts, if I will not open you the windows of heaven, and pour you out a blessing, that there shall not be**

room enough to receive it. Here is a reference to this verse from 262-121: *...doubts* [and] *fears in the material things* [have] *come into thy experience...* [These are] *today a portion of thy lot. As ye have trusted wholly in Him, these fears* [and] *doubts have faded away. For His promises are, "Rely ye on the Lord, and see if He will not open even the windows of heaven to pour out a blessing upon thee!"*

Our quest should be for wisdom and understanding according to Proverbs 4:7: **Wisdom is the principle thing; therefore get wisdom: and with all thy getting get understanding.** Cayce refers to this verse in the following advice for a successful business man in reading 520-2: *Be not ashamed of labors lowly or high. Seek not to find the favor in the eyes of the people. Rather, choose to know thou hast favor with God, for the silver and the gold is His...in the desires of thine heart thou mayest know the way to those successes that be of the worldly nature, and of the mental and spiritual nature...in* all *thine getting, get understanding...those things that make for fame, fortune, success - these are a* natural...*result; when used* [and] not *abused.*

Our labor will be rewarded! Luke 10:7 states: **In the same house remain, eating and drinking such things as they give: for the labourer is worthy of his hire.** In reading 5528-1, we find the following reference to this verse, for a 47-year-old astrologer:*...as to results...leave these in the hands of those whom the...(entity serves). Would ye serve mammon, expect those to soon turn into such secular channels as to become* [as] *Frankensteins to* [your] *endeavors...* [If these are] *kept in a purposefulness of creating* [an] *influence in the lives of those contacted* [that is] *of a creative nature, then* [you may] *expect that...desired...for the laborer is worthy of his hire...he that entereth with an understanding* of *creative forces and purposefulness...receives that...* [which] *is just* [from] *the Giver of all good and perfect gifts.*

In John 14:12 Jesus tells his followers that they shall do even greater things than He has done: *...***He that believeth on me, the works that I do shall he do also; and greater works than these shall he do; because I go unto my Father.** The following portion of 262-1 makes reference to this verse: *...he that receives shall give, he that cometh together in that name that will give, even as has been promised, "as I have given and am* [in] *the Father, so in* [me] *may* [ye] *do as I have done, and* [greater] *things than I have done shall ye do, for I go* [to] *the Father, and...as ye ask in my name, so shall it be* [done] *unto you!"*

Psalm 37:25 assures us that our needs will be met: **I have been young, and now am old; yet have I not seen the righteous forsaken, nor his seed begging bread.** In reading 853-3 a 38-year-old man was concerned about his financial affairs. Here is Cayce's advice: *Do not be impatient nor over* *anxious, for He knoweth the needs of every one, and those that are in ac-cord with those things that are His laws, His precepts, will be carried along - as has been the promise. There has never been, as has been given,* [of] *those that fear the Lord and keep His commands, even fearful - they nor their seed, or associates, among those that beg bread.*

In Matthew 10:8 we find an important principle of true prosperity; that of giving and receiving: **Heal the sick, cleanse the lepers, raise the dead, cast out devils: Freely ye have received freely give.** Cayce refers to this verse as follows in reading 262-10: *...as each will apply that given - there will come that which will be helpful to another. As ye have received, so give!* Here is a second reference about giving and receiving from 262-111: *If you say, "If I were so and so - if I had this or that - O how much I would give to charity* [and] *to the needy" and* [yet] *give not in your present es-tate, you would not give...if you had all at your command!...His com-mand was...this: If what you have is taken away, give the* all [so] *that you may be* filled! [As has been said], *"That alone* [which] *you give away, that do you possess."*

To be truly prosperous we must first recognize that only the riches of spirit are eternal. Here is Proverbs 23:5: **Wilt thou set thine eyes upon that which is not? for riches certainly make themselves wings; then fly away as an eagle toward heaven.** Reading 257-53 for a successful business man refers to this verse as follows: *...fame and fortune often take wings and fly away - but* [you are] *appreciative of the beauties in nature* [and of] *the abilities...of Him that serves in song or dance, or the piper, these also de-clare His glory...*

Perhaps the greatest prosperity we may achieve is an appreciation of the beauty and joy of life.

4

RELATIONSHIP WITH GOD

In this chapter we will be looking at twenty Bible verses and related Edgar Cayce readings which focus, at least in part, on our relationship with God. First we will review eight verses from the Old Testament. The most frequently quoted verse in this group is Leviticus 26:12: **I will walk among you, and will be your God, and ye shall be my people.** In Cayce's references to this verse, his emphasis seems to be that we must first become God's people and, then, He will become our God. Here is a portion of 262-91: *Let that thou hast held in thine heart keep thee ever. For the Glory of the Lord is nigh to those that seek Him. For He hath given, "If ye will be my children, I will be thy God." Let that seeking, then, be the Glory of thy purpose, of thy desire.*

The second most frequently quoted verse in this group is Psalm 24:1: **The earth is the Lord's and the fullness thereof; the world and they that dwell therein.** In response to a question about marriage in reading 688-4 we find the following...*the earth is the Lord's and the fullness thereof...and ye as His children* [are to] *live the life - in oneness of purpose...*[so] *that through thy hands, through thy associations, through thy love as one for another in Him, ye may be the means, the channel, through which others may know the living God. Living each YOUR life, to be sure, but in Him, in His ways.*

According to the Edgar Cayce readings our intentions are of primary importance, and, indeed, may be more significant than what we actually do or say. I Samuel 16:7 supports this view: **...man looketh at the outward appearance, but the Lord looketh on the heart.** Here's reading 262-91 which refers to this Scripture: *Let the Glory of the Father, of the Son, suffice thee. Not what man thinketh, or what man sayeth. For man looketh on the outward appearance, but God looketh on the heart. Know that* [which] *thou hast purposed in thy heart is that which comes before the Glory of God...He abides in thee and in thy fellow man...*

Our next Old Testament verse is Exodus 19:5: **...if ye will obey my voice indeed, and keep my covenant, then ye shall be a peculiar treasure unto me above all people: for all the earth is mine.** It is interesting to note that while this verse was sometimes quoted in the readings, in a greater number of instances, the individual was instructed to read Exodus 19:5. Thus, we may want to reflect on these words for a moment, knowing they are as valid today as they were over 3,000 years ago when they were first given. In reading 3538-1, for a 46-year-old lady, Cayce includes the following reference to this verse: *When ye apply the spiritual life in thy relationships to others, there will be the supply...Begin by reading Exodus 19:5, and know that it is meant for thee. Then read the whole of Deuteronomy 30, and know that the counsel is being given to thee, and that ye have to choose each day, now* [today], *and every other day. Don't say within self that these are of no avail to thee, but use them.*

Habakkuk 2:20 tells us that the Lord is in his holy temple. Of course, one might ask where is this holy temple? **The Lord is in his holy temple; let all the earth keep silence before him.** Cayce refers to this verse in the following message for a 17-year-old girl in reading 1248-1: *...each blade of grass, each blossom, each tree, each crag, each mountain, each river, each lake is as a gift from the Creative Forces in man's experience that he may know more of the love of God. And as a soul, as a developing body...sees in the creatures, in the various kingdoms, as* they *care for their young, as they are selective in their mating, as they are mindful of the influences and the environs,* [you may] *learn from these Nature's lessons or God's expression to the children of men...He indeed is in His holy temple and is* mindful *of man's estate - if* man *minds the* laws *of nature, of God. For love is law, love is God.*

Isaiah 59:1 seems to say that God's relations with us can be very personal and direct: **the Lord's hand is not shortened, that it cannot save; neither his ear heavy, that it cannot hear.** Reading 1726-1 refers to this verse as follows: *...God is not a respecter of persons; neither is He short armed, either in giving that* [which] *will mete out for the keeping of the will one with another;* [nor] *is He short sighted in that* [which] *is committed in...willful disobedience, for he that abhorreth good loveth evil, and he that buildeth contention shall suddenly be destroyed...*

In Job 21:22 we find the question, **Shall any teach God knowledge, seeing He judgeth those that are high?** This verse is referred to in the following portion of reading 262-96: *As given by the prophets...of old, "Who hath taught the Lord judgment?" With whom did He councel? Yea, as is written there... "Without Him there was nothing made that was made. The* word was *knowledge, and the Word was made flesh, and the Word dwelt among men,"* [so] *that they, too, might know that in the...humbling, in the* subduing *of self they... might know their...God. For God is knowledge...*

Haggai 2:7 tells us that the Lord will shake all the nations: **I will shake all the nations, and the desire of all nations shall come: and I will fill this**

house with glory, saith the Lord of hosts. In reading 262-64, Cayce was asked to explain this verse *...from the literal interpretation...a wayward people had forsaken their temple worship, where they had been appointed to meet with the living God. For there alone they had heard the words, and there alone they had received the instruction as of old even those that were called the heathen were shaken to the core and* granted...*again* [opportunity] *to establish the desire of their heart in rebuilding the temple.*

Now we turn our attention to twelve New Testament verses dealing with our relationship with God. One frequently quoted is Acts 10:34: **God is no respecter of persons.** This is the King James Version of this verse. Some of the more recent translations say that God does not show partiality or favoritism. Other writers say the meaning is that there are no chosen people or superior race. In reading 1650-1 Cayce told a 37-year-old man: *...He, thy Lord, is not a respecter of persons but to do good unto all men is the whole duty of man.* In 2615-1 he advised a 47-year-old man to, *deal with peoples, lands, activities, group association;* [deal with the] *study of body, mind and soul; as an instructor, director in a service that deals with groups, - not as an organized religion, but religion* [as to an] *individual. For, He is the Father of all and not a respecter of persons.*

Another verse frequently quoted in the readings is John 14:23 **...If a man love me, he will keep my words and my Father will love him, and we will come unto him and make our abode with him.** Here is a reference to this verse from reading 262-43: *For, his promises are sure; even as He gave, "I will not leave thee comfortless, but will come to you." "If ye love me,* keep *my commandments - that I may abide with you," and through* you *shed abroad the light, the Love of God, unto the sons of men!*

There are two verses in this group which say we must eventually give account to God. The one most frequently quoted is Romans 14:12: **...everyone of us shall give account of himself to God.** Reference to this verse is included in 2778-2 for a 30-year-old cashier concerning past-life association with her mother: *In the experiences in the Promised land ye held to thy faith, and thy mother wished then for thee to accede to the desires of thy persecutors. Ye would not. Hold thy attitude! For, every soul...must give an account unto Him, in the same manner as He accounted unto His God, our God, your God.*

Our second verse on this matter of an accounting is Matthew 12:36: **...every idle word that men shall speak, they shall give account thereof in the day of judgment.** This verse is discussed in the following portion of reading 262-42: *Does each individual understand that as was given, one must give account of every idle word spoken?...This is in reference to the oneness of purpose in an individual?...The mind, the body, the aptitude* *of the soul is under surveillance through such activity? And…as the body, the mind, the soul* [are] *one, so is God, in the manifestations in power, might and glory in the earth…*[This illustrates]*…why there should be joyousness* [and] *gladness in the heart* [and] *in the speech…of each individual.*

The most important aspect of our relationship with God is expressed in Matthew 22:37: **Jesus said unto him, Thou shalt love the Lord thy God with all thy heart, and with all thy soul, and with all thy mind.** Cayce discusses loving God in the following portion of reading 262-100: *…He combined it all into one, "Thou shalt love the Lord thy God with all thy heart, thy mind, thy soul"… study to show thyself approved unto thy concept of thy God. What* is *thy God? …Where is He, what is He?* [If you don't know] *Then ye may find yourselves lacking in much. How personal is He? Not as Moses painted a God of wrath; not as David painted a God that would fight thine enemies; but as the Christ* [demonstrated] *- the Father of love, of mercy, of justice. And man meets it in himself! How* can *it be then that ye do not understand God loves you…?*

We find more about the love of God in I John 5:3: **This is the love of God, that we keep his commandments; and his commandments are not grievous.** In reading 262-47 Cayce gave this message to a member of Study Group 1. *In the presenting of self's love for the ways He would have thee go, look not back upon that which would make* [you] *afraid; for they who turn their faces to the light show forth in their speech, their actions, their lives, that love…He has given, "If ye love me keep my commandments." For, they are not grievous to those that seek to know His way.*

John 10:3 is another verse which places emphasis on a personal relationship with the Master: **the sheep hear his voice; and he calleth his own sheep by name, and leadeth them out.** In reading 262-28 we find the following reference to this verse: *…He is the way, and stands at the door, and those who hear His voice are His sheep and He the good shepherd, so may* many *become His sheep through the seeking to be one with Him. This is an illustration of…how one* [may] *…apply those things given in the lessons* [and] *may now open the door* [so] *that many sheep may enter the fold, for, they hear His voice and answer by name even as He calls…*

In Ephesians 2:18 we find some instructions concerning access to the Father: **through Him we both have access by one Spirit unto the Father.** Reference to this verse is included in these words from reading 262-74: *As ye seek in the name of Him…that ye through His name might have the access to the Father, then will ye not in His name strive to be the greater channels of blessings to those that look to thee in His name for guidance, for direction, for sustainment during* [their] *periods of anxiety,* *of doubt and of fear?*

The last book of the New Testament overflows with symbology, as shown in Revelation 22:13: **I am Alpha and Omega, the beginning and the end, the first and the last.** In reading 262-55 Cayce gives us some clues as to the meaning of this verse: *"I am Alpha and Omega, beginning and the end." That God, the Father, the Spirit, the Ohm, is the influencing force of every activity is not wholly sufficient unto man's salvation, in that he is a free-will being. As intimated...Alpha* [is the] *beginning,* [and] *Omega* [is the] *ending. For, the confirmation, the segregation, the separation, the building, the adding to it, is necessary - in relation to those activities that lie between - for man's building to the beginning and* [to] *the end.*

Life is a shared experience; or at least it should be as mentioned in Romans 14:7: **none of us liveth to himself, and no man dieth to himself.** Reading 4415-1 provides some insight on this matter of shared life experience: *...First, there should be the study of self to that point where self has laid out that which it may do and that it may not do for its own better development in* [the] *mental or physical; for in the building* [it] *is seen that each has its bounds as to* [what] *it may attain, when the building is by self alone. Well that others, as well as self, be considered - for no man...lives to self, no man dieth to self; for in Him is life, and the life is eternal - for life is the gift of the Creator and is in Him...*

Matthew 10:24 tells us that the disciple is not above his master. Of course, this does not necessarily rule out moving up to the same level. **The disciple is not above his master, nor the servant above his lord.** Cayce refers to this in reading 262-46: *He, though He were the Son, learned obedience through the things which He suffered. He that climbs up any other way than accepting those things that are to be met day by day, even as He, seeks through some other channel. The servant may never be greater than the master.* [However] *He has given that we may be equal and one with Him...*

Here is another symbolic message from the last book in our Bible. Revelation 13:8: **all that dwell upon the earth shall worship him, whose names are not written in the book of life of the Lamb slain from the foundation of the world.** In reading 262-57, Cayce was asked to explain "the Lamb slain before the foundation of the world." Here is his reply: *If this is taken in conjunction with many another expression of the Master, it may be the more easily comprehended...As the Master gave, "Before Abraham was I am before the worlds were I am." Hence, when there came the necessity in the realm of the spiritual home for the coming of the Lamb into the earth for its redemption, the Truth, the light, the offering was made. Hence the expression as given. For, as has been given...the mind, is the builder.*

In this chapter we have explored certain aspects of our relationship with God. Other chapters have much to say on this subject; particularly, Chapter 8 on "God's Love," Chapter 10 on "Oneness," and Chapter 15 on "God Within."

5

RELATIONSHIP WITH OTHERS

Matthew 25:40 was quoted 418 times making it the second most frequently quoted verse in the readings: **And the King shall answer and say
unto them, Verily I say unto you, Inasmuch as ye have done it unto one
of the least of these my brethren, ye have done it unto me.** In the verses
preceding this the King had said to his servants that when he was hungry,
they had fed him; thirsty and they had given him drink; naked and they
had clothed him; a stranger and they took him in; sick and they visited
him; in prison and they came to him. The servants asked the King when
they had done these things and this set the stage for the verse quoted
above.

Conventional Bible commentary on this verse is that God is just as concerned with the prisoners, strangers, the naked, the sick and the hungry
as He is with those in better circumstances. Jesus identifies himself entirely with the needs and interests of those who are experiencing difficult
conditions.

The Cayce readings couple Matthew 25:40 with 25:45 in which the King
declares, **Inasmuch as ye did it not to one of the least of these, ye did it
not to me.** The readings seem to encourage a literal interpretation of these
verses. Other people are to be treated as we would treat Jesus Christ. Of
course, we need to keep in mind that the concern here is about the way
we treat those who appear to be of "least" importance; those who are poor,
uneducated, old, weak, sick, in jail, etc. We need to be able to behold the
Christ in all whom we meet, being particularly careful to remember to
help those who are less fortunate. Our rational mind may say that there
are far too many who need help and that we have many important things
to do. While monetary contributions are obviously important, we also
must remember to take the time to personally be helpful to those whom
we encounter in our normal activity.

Christ Consciousness is a central concept of the readings, which emphasizes that the soul of every person we encounter is a part – a spark – of
the Divine. We need to recognize and honor this in all people everywhere,
even if it does not appear to have been awakened by the will.

In Matthew 5:44 Jesus tells us to love our enemies: **...Love your enemies, bless them that curse you, do good to them that hate you, and pray for them which despitefully use you and persecute you.** In reading 1974-1, for a male 55-year-old theatrical mechanic, this question was posed: How should the entity go about getting into the right business? Cayce's reply mentions this verse: *He is in it* [the right business]*, if he will just keep on applying himself more...But learn to love thine enemies (or ye think they are.) Do unto them that hate you, as ye would have them do unto you. Do good to them that hate you...do you ever gain by being good only to those who pat you on the back for what* they *may take from you!*

Our next verse, Luke 6:28, is quite similar but not identical with Matthew 5:44: **Bless them that curse you, and pray for them which despitefully use you.** Cayce refers to this verse in the following advice for a 30-year-old man in reading 1120-3: **Live** *a thing, not profess it!* Live *and act that way and manner as ye would have others live and act toward you! And in this you will see the good even in those that would despitefully use you, that would take advantage. Remember, vengeance is the Father's - not thine.*

Our next two verses are also similar but not identical. The first is Luke 6:29: **And unto him that smiteth thee on the one cheek offer also the other; and him that taketh away thy cloak forbid not to take thy coat also.** In reading 3976-27 Edgar Cayce was asked to comment on the economic inequalities of nations. In his response he makes reference to Luke 6:29: [**The Christ Message**] *is the answer for meeting* every *problem, every question as to the economic condition of the nations. For He gave, "Let him that hath two coats give one to another. Let him that is forced to do this or that go the whole length." These are the basic principles upon which world order, world economic and social relations may be established,* [and] *manifested among men.*

Our next verse is Matthew 5:40: **If any man will sue thee at the law, and take away thy coat, let him have thy cloak also.** Here is a reference to this verse in reading 262-65: *To him who has felt antagonistic to those that have spoken unkindly, or have made accusations that would hurt the inner self...He gave, "He that would smite thee, turn the other cheek,"* [thus] *spiritualizing the desire for vengeance. "He that would sue thee and take away thy coat, give him thy cloak also."* [When] *others would use thee, or take advantage of thee, if thy desire is in the Lord, in the Creative Forces,* [this] *should not cause thee to speak harshly nor to desire that calamitous things or conditions come upon others for their unkindness. For they, as He gave, who would...destroy thy body are nothing...the* Lord *is the avenger of those that love Him.*

In Ephesians 4:26 we are warned not to sin when we get angry: **Be ye**

angry and sin not: let not the sun go down upon your wrath. In reading 262-25 Cayce was asked to comment on ***Be mad but sin not*** which he had given in a prior reading for this group. In his reply Cayce says that control of anger is the beginning of the first lesson. Even though we dislike the words, we are to love the soul of the person who spoke them. Doing this will help us to develop patience, meekness, hope, love, and pureness of heart– remembering, His promises are that the meek shall inherit the earth and the pure in heart will see God.

Romans 12:20 speaks of heaping coals of fire on the heads of our enemy, which is, of course, only a metaphor. **If thine enemy hunger, feed him; if he thirst, give him drink: for in so doing thou shall heap coals of fire on his head.** Cayce refers to heaping coals on those who are cross with us in the following portion of reading 262-72: *Ye* live *in the flesh, yet be as He - in the world yet not* of *the world; for all strength, all power, all glory, all joy is given unto Him - for* He *has overcome, and ye may in Him overcome also. Count it…a blessing…that thou art* chosen *that ye may in the name of thy Lord speak a kind word to those that are abrupt or cross with thee, and in so doing ye will heap coals of judgment upon their consciousnesses; for ye are His and He is thine, if ye will hold to that thou hast chosen.*

Before closing this chapter, I would like to add that the readings say, just as the Bible does, that we are to love others as we love ourselves. We are to love them with an equal amount of that same love that we bestow upon ourselves. As discussed in the chapter on "Love," we may encounter people or situations where *loving indifference* is the correct response.

6

AIM FOR PERFECTION

One of the most frequently quoted Bible verses in the readings is the last portion of James 1:27: **Pure religion and undefiled before God and the Father is this; To visit the fatherless and widows in their affliction and to keep himself unspotted from the world.** The usual wording in the readings from this verse is, *keep self unspotted from the world.* Some say that works of love enable people to keep themselves unspotted from the world. Others say this is an admonition to avoid the pollution of sin of any kind. These comments seem to be consistent with the Cayce readings. Trying to always do the right thing and trying always to make the proper choice in life are ways to be *unspotted.*

Here is an example, from 262-130, of Cayce's quotation of this verse where the individual was asked to be unspotted from condemnation of self or others. Many of us may have this problem: *Study to show* **thyself** *approved unto God, a workman not ashamed; rightly emphasizing the virtue, the faith, the love, the patience, in thy daily life and in thy dealings one with another; keeping self unspotted from condemnation; keeping self from condemning self or others.*

The second most frequently quoted verse in this group is Romans 14:16: **Let not then your good be evil spoken of.** In reading 281-23, for the Prayer Healing Group, Cayce makes the following reference to this scripture: *...let thy lives, thy purposes, thy desires be as one with Him in that ye do and say. And let thy words, thy counsel and thy life and thy activities be* [such] *that* [what] thou *doest may not be evil spoken of. So present thy lives, so use that which has been given thee...of love, so that they may become more and more a shinning light unto those that are along life's way...*

Our next verse on this subject of perfection concerns taking on the whole armor of God. Here is Ephesians 6:13: **Take unto you the whole armor of God, that ye may be able to withstand in the evil day, and having done all, to stand.** Some words of advice for a 37-year-old factory worker, in reading 1747-5, include reference to this verse: *Put...on...the whole armor of God, the breastplate of righteousness, the sword of the* *spirit of truth.* Know *in* whom *ye have believed, as well as in what ye be-lieve.*

Here is a second reference to this verse from reading 5749-13 for a large group of people: *...let all so examine their hearts and minds as to put away doubt and fear; putting away hate and malice, jealousy and those things that cause man to err. Replace* [them] *with the desire to help, with hope, with the willingness to divide self and self's surroundings with those who are less fortunate; putting on the whole armor of God - in righteousness.*

Philippians 2:6 tells us that Jesus thought it was not robbery to be equal with God and the Edgar Cayce readings say we, also, should aspire to this: (Jesus) **Who, being in the form of God, thought it not robbery to be equal with God.** Our first reference to this verse is from reading 262-88: *...let all be of one Mind - even as in Christ, who thought it not robbery to be equal with God, yet desiring ever that HIS followers, HIS brethren, HIS friends, be one with Him, equal to and one with the Father.* Here is a second reference, from 4083-1, for an individual who may have had some of our limitations: *...in Him, the Father-God, ye move and have thy being. Act like it! Don't act like ye think ye are a God! Ye may become such, but when ye do ye think not of thyself. For what is the pattern? He thought it not robbery to make Himself equal with God, but He acted like it in the earth. He made Himself of no estate* [so] *that you, through His grace, through His mercy, through His sacrifice might have an advocate with that First Cause, God; that first principle, spirit.*

I Thessalonians 5:22 instructs us to avoid the appearance of evil: **Abstain from all appearance of evil.** Edgar Cayce makes reference to this verse in the following comment to a study group member in reading 262-41: *...His glory is sufficient, His mercy is far-reaching...Keep thy paths straight. Avoid the appearance of evil. Find fault in no man.*

Matthew 5:48 is the verse that addresses this issue of perfection very directly: **Be ye therefore perfect, even as your Father which is in heaven is perfect.** In reading 2746-1, a 30-year-old man asked this question. How can I better prepare myself for the work I have chosen and for leadership? Here is Cayce's response: *By prayer and meditation. It is innate and natural, yet the basis of service must be as of the ideal; not merely idealistic - for that indicates unattainable, but "Be ye perfect, even as I am perfect," said He. This then is in purpose, in intent, in hope, in application. This is the manner to attain to leadership. Ask no one to do that ye would not do thyself. Ask no one to do that the Lord thy Master did not do.*

Our second reference to this verse, from the readings, is found in 262-77 and looks at some possible objections to this requirement. *He gave, "Be ye perfect, even as thy heavenly Father is perfect." Ye say, "This cannot be done in this house of clay!" Did He? Ye say, "This is too hard for me!" Did he grumble, did He falter? To be sure, He cried, "Father, if it be possible, let this cup pass." Yea, oft will ye cry aloud, even as He. Ye cannot bear the burden alone, but He has promised..."If ye put thy yoke upon me, I will guide you."*

Our third reference to this verse is found in 262-125 where this question is asked, "Was He unreasonable?" *He said, "Be ye* perfect, *even as my Father in heaven is perfect." Would we modify that? Would we say that such is only to be sought, to be tried for, to be desired in the experience, and is not attainable here or now, under the present environs...Was* He *unreasonable?*

Our next reading, 3800-1, is my favorite in this chapter: *As ye gain understanding ye may grow - not to perfection, though it is something to be striven for. For as He who is the ideal gave, "Be ye perfect, even as my Father in heaven is perfect." Not that troubles may not arise so long as ye are in the flesh.* Many of us have experiences regularly which seem to remind us that we are not perfect. What we need to keep in mind is that we are PERFECTIBLE, when we have established this as our goal and have it as our desire.

Our last Cayce reference to perfection, from 3344-1, offers some thoughts on how to comply with this verse: *In the present do look within self. Walk closer with Him in the garden. Make thine own heart and mind one with Him in purpose, in ideals. For His ideal* [is] *"Be ye perfect even as my Father in heaven is perfect." Through His promise ye may accomplish this; not of self...*[but] *Only as His spirit may work in and through thee, making ...thyself a channel...*

SOUL GROWTH

Soul growth is a major theme in the Edgar Cayce readings. Isaiah 28:10, which was quoted more than 100 times in the readings, incorporates some principles which are important to the process by which soul growth takes place: **Precept must be upon precept, precept upon precept; line upon line, line upon line; here a little and there a little.** In reading 262-24 Cayce was asked to comment on a previous message that "all great things are slow of growth." Here is his response: *...the soul grows upon that it is fed. The soul of man is the greatest...of all creation, for it may be one with the Father. Little by little, line upon line, here a little, there a little - these are the manners of growth...not only one with Him but individual in self! Not the whole, but equal* with *the whole...Ye ...are not aliens...*[but] **sons** *of the Holy One.*

Our culture seems to focus on doing things quickly. Speed is emphasized in almost all areas of life. All want to avoid the label of being a slow learner or a slow worker. But, we must be patient with ourselves and with others. Real growth at the soul level is a slow process and must take place one step at a time.

II Peter 3:18 was also quoted more than 100 times in the readings and speaks of growing in grace: **Grow in grace, and in the knowledge of our Lord and Savior Jesus Christ. To him be glory both now and forever.** In reading 281-8 a member of the Prayer Healing Group asked if she was doing all she could to cooperate with the group. Here is Cayce's reply: *Keep on keeping on as you are, but grow in grace and in the knowledge and understanding that comes with the closer walk with Him.* The very essence of the Christ life is growth which brings a deeper awareness of the favor and love of the Christ. Most Christians who believe in reincarnation view life as an opportunity for the soul to evolve. This evolution could be defined as our growth in the grace, knowledge, and understanding of the Christ.

Hebrews 5:8 tells us that even our Master learned obedience through experience and suffering: **Though he were a Son, yet learned he obedience by the things which he suffered.** In reading 281-16, on the book of

Revelation, Cayce was asked if we would be punished by fire and brimstone. Here is a portion of his reply in which he refers to obedience through suffering: *...each entity's heaven or hell must, through* some *experience, be that which it has builded for itself. Is thy hell one that is filled with fire or brimstone? But know, each and every soul is tried...as by fire; purified, purged...for He, though He were the Son, learned obedience through the things which He suffered. Ye also are known even as ye do, and have done.*

In I Corinthians 15:45 we find reference to the first man Adam and the last Adam: **It is written, The first man Adam was made a living soul; the last Adam was made a quickening spirit.** The Cayce readings say that Jesus was the first man Adam. Here is a reference to this verse in reading 262-100: *...*[ye must] *learn obedience through the things that* ye *suffer. For ye having partaken of* sin, *not* in *Adam but* as *Adam must* [now] *as the new Adam learn that God is merciful, is love, is justice, is patient, is long-suffering, is brotherly love; for these are the law, not* of *the law but* the *law. And the law is love and the law is God...that* [which] *ye give to others, that ye have; that* [which] *ye have spent ye never have; that* [which] *ye would save you have already lost.* These were the closing words in this reading. My thought would be that this reference to what we give away, spend, or save relates to all of our resources and not just our money.

In Matthew 11:30 Jesus tells the people that becoming his follower is not difficult: **My yoke is easy, and my burden is light.** In the time of Jesus, the Jewish religion was referred to as the yoke of the law. Jesus said his yoke was voluntary. It was a yoke of faith, conscience, love, meekness, and obedience. In reading 538-30, for a 51-year-old housewife, Cayce quotes this verse: *...*[have] *balance that is obtained by making* personal *application, doing that-even though it hurt-that will aid another; -* not *that self is to be crucified* [so] *that another may have* ease *in the material sense* *...*[but that] *another may have* understanding *in the mental and* spiritual *sense...for "my yoke is easy, my burden is light" is* seldom *understood. When the desire...the purpose* [and] *the application, is one...then it becomes easy...*

We find another reference by Jesus to His yoke in Matthew 11:29: **Take my yoke upon you and learn of me, for I am meek and lowly in heart, and ye shall find rest unto your souls.** In reading 262-28, for members of Study Group 1, Cayce makes reference to this verse and concludes with these words "thou wert with me in the beginning": *Take that thou hast in hand, that thou hast builded day by day, and without fear* open *the door that He may come in and abide with thee; for "He that takes my yoke upon him and learns of me, with* him *will I abide day by day, and all things will be brought to remembrance that I have given thee since the foundations* *of the world, for thou were with me in the beginning..."*

Psalm 1:2 speaks of the blessed man who has avoided sin and error: **his delight is in the law of the Lord; and in his law doth he meditate day and night.** Reading 2062-1, for a 26-year-old man, includes the following reference to this verse: *Grow in spiritual understanding, that thy mental and thy physical manifestations in thy relationships to others, and* [to] *conditions, may be tempered with that mercy, that justice, that kindness, that patience, as ye would have thy Lord, thy God, thy Savior, have with thee...Delight in the law of the Lord; meditate in same day and night; and* then *in all phases of thy experience ye will be happy, harmonious,* and *successful in every phase of thy relationships.*

In James 1:12 we are told how to receive the crown of life: **Blessed is the man that endureth temptation: for when he is tried, he shall receive the crown of life, which the Lord hath promised to them that love him.** Here are some words of advise for a member of Study Group 1 found in reading 262-37: *Keep self close to that mental and spiritual awakening that comes with the communion with Him in thine inner self, for He is able to guide through all shadows that may arise...Keep the faith, for he that endures will wear the Crown of Life.*

John 15:5 compares our relationship with Christ to a vine with branches and fruit: **I am the vine, ye are the branches: He that abideth in me, and I in him, the same bringeth forth much fruit...** Here is an interesting reference to this verse in 262-99: *...each experience in the earth is as a schooling, is as an experience for the soul. For how gave He? He is the vine and ye are the branches, or He is the source and ye are the trees.*

John 15:2 is another verse that speaks of branches and fruit: **Every branch in me that beareth not fruit he taketh away: and every branch that beareth fruit he purgeth it, that it may bring forth more fruit.** Reading 262-128 includes reference to this process of being purged as follows: *...He keepeth thee, if ye keep Him in thy purpose, in thy heart...*[Even] *when sorrow and sadness...come, these are of the Lord. For whom the Lord loveth He purgeth; that they may bear more fruit in Him.* Its just a normal part of the process of soul growth!

Acts 20:35 quotes one of the sayings of Jesus about giving and receiving: **I have shown you all things, how that so laboring ye ought to support the weak, and to remember the words of the Lord Jesus, how he said, It is more blessed to give than to receive.** The reference to this verse in 5332-1 tells us that giving out of love leads to growth within: *The entity must find in self...the ability to open the hand to give out; and in the giving out may ye receive. For that which is of the spiritual, in giving ye receive...it is...*[with] *love* [and] *friendship* [by] *those which are ever Creative* [that] *they grow within themselves by doing...*

For the past several pages we have been looking at soul *growth*. Have you ever wondered if a soul could shrink? If so, you might be interested in the following portion of reading 5089-2: *"Who would be the greatest among you? He who is the servant of all."When you find individuals too good to do this, or that, for others, something is the matter with their theories, and the soul is shrinking...* The portion of this reading in quotation marks is based on Mark 10:44: **And whosoever of you will be the chiefest, shall be servant of all.**

Now back to soul growth. John 3:8 speaks of soul growth in terms of being "born of the Spirit": **The wind bloweth where it listeth, and thou hearest the sound thereof, but canst not tell whence it cometh, and whither it goeth: so is every one that is born of the spirit.** Cayce refers to this verse in reading 262-10: *If your actions and thoughts are of God, hold them fast...The voice of the soul is seeking its creator...It is a birth of the spirit. The wind bloweth where it listeth, and thou heareth the sound thereof. Thou canst not tell whence it cometh or whither it goeth. So it is with everyone born of the spirit.*

John 14:2 states: **In my Father's house are many mansions: if it were not so, I would have told you. I go to prepare a place for you.** Cayce's reference to this verse, in reading 262-121, is followed by some insight on this matter of soul growth: *"In the Lord's house are many mansions - if it were not so I would have told you."...How...will ye furnish...that mansion? Will it be with those things that fade away, or with that which is eternal? Only that which grows by its usage is eternal. Only that which is of the fruit of the spirit of truth is eternal.* Each of us has our own distinctive, special place in the heart of our Lord, and in His house. No one else can fill our place.

Revelation 7:17 speaks of the Lamb (Jesus) feeding, leading, and comforting his followers: **The Lamb which is in the midst of the throne shall feed them, and shall lead them into living fountains of waters: and God shall wipe all tears from their eyes.** Reference to God's wiping our tears away is included in reading 262-108: *...He shall wipe away every tear, and no sickness and no sorrow shall be in that Happy land...the fundamentals are: Casting out fear first in thine own heart, and aiding others to aid themselves - in gaining an insight into* their *relationships with the Creative Forces or God. Tell them of the Happiness in the Christ Way, in the...joy and Happiness in keeping His ways...This is the mission of those who would bring Happiness into the experience of others; and as ye share, ye become Happy...*

In Mark 4:11-12 Jesus explains the purpose of teaching in parables: **He said unto them, Unto you it is given to know the mystery of the kingdom of God: but unto them that are without, all these things are done in** parables: **That seeing they may see, and not perceive; and hearing they may hear, and not understand; lest at anytime they should be converted, and their sins should be forgiven them.** In reading 262-94, Cayce summarizes the message in these two verses and explains their meaning and purpose: *"These I have spoken in parable lest they see and are converted." What meaneth this? That those individuals' times, purposes, intents, had not been completed or* [become] *sufficient* [to the point] *where they would be stable in their use or application of the* [lesson]*...So...step by step through that which has been given thee, as ye approach the Father, know the way by putting into* practical *application that thou hast* gained *day by day!* Thus, true understanding and soul growth come only from application of spiritual principles, rather than by just reading or writing a book such as this.

According to Matthew 5:8: **Blessed are the pure in heart: for they shall see God.** Reference to this verse is included in reading 262-25: [**Self control**] *is patience, and love, and hope, and meekness, and pureness of heart. The meek shall inherit the earth, said He - the pure in heart shall see God. They are promises! Believest thou Him?*

Soul growth may involve periods of testing and cleansing. Ezekiel 20:37 speaks of passing under the rod: **I will cause you to pass under the rod, and I will bring you into the bond of the covenant.** In reading 262-60 Cayce says that all of us must pass under the rod: ...all *must pass under the rod...as Moses and the children passed through the sea they were baptized in the cloud and in the sea; as an example, as an omen, as a physical activity* [that was] *spiritual, a physical separation from that which had been builded in their experience...in Egypt.* Here is another reference to this verse in reading 281-5: **All** *must pass under the rod as of that* **cleansing** *necessary for the inflowing of the Christ Consciousness, even as* **He** *passed under the rod...*

In Matthew 20:20-22 Jesus was asked to have the sons of Zebedee sit beside him in his kingdom. Here is his response in Matthew 20:23: **Ye shall drink indeed of my cup, and be baptized with the baptism that I am baptized with: but to sit on my right hand, and on my left, is not mine to give, but it shall be given to them for whom it is prepared of my Father.** Reading 262-6 for Study Group 1 makes reference to this verse as follows:...*The group...must of itself...awaken a desire, that measured or acted upon by that arising within self through its own meditation - will find what willing hands are willing to do. Each are called in their respective sphere. Each must find the answer in their own selves. Remember thou..."Lord, wilt thou grant my request when thou comest in thy kingdom, that I and my brother may sit the one on the right hand, the other on the left?"...*[He answered] *"Indeed ye shall drink, but to sit on my right or my left is not* *mine to give." He that* doeth *the will of the Father, the same is my mother, my brother, my sister.* Thus, our proximity to the Master is determined by the extent to which we *doeth the will of the Father.*

In response to a question about the payment of taxes to Caesar, in Matthew 22:21, Jesus gave the following advice: **Render therefore unto Caesar the things which are Caesar's and unto God the things that are God's.** In reading 262-83, for Study Group 1, Cayce was asked to comment on his earlier statement that anyone taking up this work would have to give up the world for a season. Here is a portion of his reply which makes reference to the payment of taxes by Jesus: *...if ye would abide in...*[Him] *ye are* not of *the world - only in the world. Hence...ye that would take up this* [work] *as a* practical *thing, or ye that would become channels of blessings to thy fellow man, give up the world. Not that there is not to be the use* of *things material. Even thy Master paid His tribute to Caesar.*

In Luke 22:32 Jesus is speaking to the disciples and addresses these words to Peter: **I have prayed for thee, that thy faith fail not: and when thou art converted, strengthen thy brethren.** The following words from reading 5259-1 discuss helping our brethren and its importance to the one giving the help: *There may be opportunities for thee, not only to help others, but to be helped by others. "For all that ye may ever keep is just what you give away, and that you give away is advice, counsel, manner of life you live yourself."...That you give away, that is all that ye may possess in those other realms of consciousness.*

Luke 3:17 speaks of separating the wheat form the chaff: **...he will thoroughly purge his floor, and will gather the wheat into his garner; but the chaff he will burn with fire unquenchable.** Cayce makes reference to this separation of the chaff from the wheat in the following portion of reading 262-32: *Glory in the Lord, not in self; not in the wisdom of the earth...*[Know] *that those things that partake of the earth are earthy, those* [things] *that partake alone of the mental may easily become stumbling stones...Let the spirit of truth separate the chaff from the wheat, and enter* [into] *the full knowledge of His presence...*

In this chapter we have touched on many important aspects of soul growth. Additional information about soul growth may be found in other chapters, particularly Chapter 10 - "Oneness," Chapter 16 - "Man's Purpose," Chapter 21 - "Prayer and Meditation," Chapter 34 - "Patience" and Chapter 37 - "Thy Will."

8

GOD'S LOVE

The Edgar Cayce readings quote from II Peter 3:9 almost 200 times. **The Lord is not slack concerning his promise, as some men count slackness; but is long suffering to us-ward, not willing that any should perish, but that all should come to repentance.** Here are two readings, 2990-2 and 2427-1 which illustrate Cayce's use of this Scripture *...God has not willed that any soul should perish. He has with every temptation prepared a way of escape.* In the second reading Cayce tells the person that understanding is the key. *...He hath not willed that any soul should perish, but hath with every temptation, every trial, given a way, a means of understanding.* The statement that *God has not willed that any should perish* has, perhaps, led some to think of this as a guarantee that no soul will, indeed, ever perish. Of course, this is not what this Scripture or the related readings actually say. A soul's free will enables it to choose not to escape or come to an understanding.

Some may question why this particular verse is the first one we look to on this subject of God's Love. Reason one is, of course, that this verse assures us that God's desire is to give us every opportunity to make the right choice, to come to a right understanding. The second reason is that this verse affirms our free will. I treasure the freedom that my Creator has given to each of us and see this freedom as the ultimate expression of love that was possible for God to give.

God's love for us takes many forms. I Corinthians 3:6-7 speaks of one form of this love in saying that God gives the increase: **I have planted, Apollos watered; but God gave the increase. So then neither is he that planteth anything, neither he that watereth; but God that giveth the increase.** The Cayce readings affirm the principle message here that God gives the increase. The readings avoid telling those that plant and water that they are not "anything." Our first reference is from 281-20: *Let those things that thou knowest be done in meekness and in truth* [so] *that the Christ Consciousness may be made more aware...*[to] *those thou would aid. For, in all things* God *gives the increase, through the power of the Christ name...*

These words are from 262-118: **Sow** *the seeds of truth, but* **do not**...*scratch them up...leave the results, the increase to Him.*

In 262-111 a study group member asked Cayce this question: "When one we love is floundering and unhappy...how can we influence such a one to become conscious or aware that He is the way?" Here is Cayce's answer: *We may only sow the seed. Remember ever it is* God *that gives the increase.* [There] *is not anything that an individual may do, except keeping in that it knows to be the right. For the knowledge...the vision...the comprehension is* [a] *GIFT of the* Father...*Only the Spirit of Truth may awaken. One can only pray and hope...You cannot force upon any soul your own estate.* There is a point, when we have done all we can do, where we need to let go and let God. The increases addressed in these particular readings are spiritual. I have no doubt that God can and does provide material increases that are consistent with His purpose. These increases, physical, mental, or spiritual are clear evidence of the activity of God's loving concern for us.

Romans 8:38 speaks of separation from the love of God: **I am persuaded that neither death nor life, nor powers, nor things present, nor things to come, nor heights nor depths, nor any other creature shall be able to separate us from the love of God which is in Christ Jesus our Lord.** In reading 3476-1 Cayce says, *...there is nothing within or without self that may separate the mind-body from the consciousness of the indwelling of the Holy Spirit excepts self.* In 262-58 he uses these words: *Keep thine heart and thine mind* singing *in the glory of the manifestations, of the beauty and of the glory of the Father in the earth, as thou hast seen manifest among men. Look not on...stumbling blocks in the lives of others, for..."there is nothing in heaven nor in earth, nor in hell, that may separate man from the love of the Father and the manifestations of that love* [except] *man's own self."* The fact that God has given each of us the option of separating ourselves from Him is further proof of His love.

God loves us and helps us to overcome our weakness and errors. This is the message of Hebrews 12:6: **Whom the Lord loveth he chasteneth and scourgeth every son whom he receiveth.** Cayce refers to this verse in the following message for a member of the Prayer Healing Group in 281-17: *Listen more often to the voice within, Kick not against those things that seem to hinder, for whom the Lord loveth He chasteneth and purgeth every one. Be thou, then, faithful in the little things of life and He will crown thine efforts with contentment, with joy, with life, with love.* We know that there are times when we need discipline. We are also aware that when we search for truth in life we are frequently driven by pain.

One of the best known verses in the entire Bible is John 3:16: **For God so loved the world that He gave his only begotten Son that whosoever** believeth in Him should not perish, but have everlasting life. Here is a reference to this verse in a message for the Prayer Healing Group in reading 281-3: *...first know what love meaneth, "for God so* loved *the world that He gave His Son, that we* through *Him might have life, and have it more abundantly..."* It is said that Martin Luther called this verse the gospel in miniature. It declares the measure of divine love for man and then gives the outcome. Few Scriptures have such irresistible appeal to so many people.

In Romans 8:26-30 Paul points out many ways that God helps those who love Him, and then, in Romans 8:31 we find these words: **...If God be for us, who can be against us.** Cayce mentioned this verse in the following message for a 46-year-old bookkeeper in 262-25: *As the trust, the hope, the faith is manifested by the patience day by day* [so] *does there become the more awareness in self's own inner consciousness that all is well with Him; knowing that if the Lord is on thy side, who may be against you?*

Jesus demonstrates his love by his promise in Matthew 11:28: **Come unto me, all ye that labor and are heavy laden, and I will give you rest.** Reading 262-119 includes reference to this verse as follows: *...when ye call* [He] *might say, "Come - I will give you rest - my yoke is easy, my burden is light"...He...passed through so much...even as thee...He knows! He understands! He hears thy call and bids thee come, drink of the water of life!* This reading says that the Master's love for us is personal rather than being some sort of universal force like the law of gravity. What do you think?

God's love for His people is present in the Old Testament as well as the New Testament. In Genesis 49:10 we find these words: **The scepter shall not depart from Judah...** In reading 262-28 Cayce was asked to explain his statement in an earlier reading that stated, *The scepter has not departed from Israel.* Here is a portion of his reply: *Israel is the chosen of the Lord, and...His promise, His care, His love, has not departed from those that seek to know His way, that seek to see His face, that would draw nigh unto Him.* This *is the meaning, this should be the understanding to all. Those that seek are Israel.*

God loves all; especially those who give of themselves, cheerfully. Here is II Corinthians 9:7: **Every man according as he purposeth in his heart, so let him give not grudgingly, or of necessity: for God loveth a cheerful giver.** The following portion of reading 281-19, to a member of the Prayer Healing Group, makes reference to this verse: *Be not as condemning of any as to their manner of approach...Know the Lord loveth the cheerful giver, not in moneys but in grace, in mercy, in peace - that* [which] *thine own activities may bring...to those in the group or* [to] *those who seek to find hope and life in the Name of the Christ.*

Each and every one of us is precious in the sight of God. In Luke 15:4 it says: **What man of you having an hundred sheep, if he lose one of them, doth not leave the ninety and nine in the wilderness, and go after that which is lost, until he find it?** Reference to this verse is included in reading 262-57: *To become aware is...to gain. For those that have lost their way, even as the Master gave with the ninety and nine, all might be left to seek the one. And the joyousness in the finding....should be expressed...*

Even if we wrestle with God's angel all night, as Jacob did, God still loves us as is referenced in Genesis 32:30: **Jacob called the name of the place Pen-i-el: for I have seen God face to face and my life is preserved.** Reading 262-28 refers to this verse as follows: *How obtained the supplanter the name Israel? For he wrestled with the angel, and he was face to face with the seeking to know His way. So it is with us that are called and seek His face; we are...Israel. Know, then, the scepter, the promise, the love, the glory of the Lord has not departed from them that seek His face!*

God's love is with us at all times and especially in periods of sadness and sorrow. Isaiah 25:8 states: **He will swallow up death in victory; and the Lord God will wipe away tears from off all faces...** Reading 262-108 includes reference to this verse as follows: *...only those who make Happiness in the lives and the experiences of others may indeed know what it is to be Happy. Have ye made anyone Happy that was discouraged, that was disturbed, that was misunderstood? Not that ye condone anything, but the love of God that taketh away sadness and sorrow. [How] is the life in the presence of the Christ depicted...That He shall wipe away every tear, and no sickness and no sorrow shall be in that Happy land.*

God's love is forever with us. We can greatly increase the flow of this love by our own living expression of love for God, for others, and for ourselves.

9

JESUS CHRIST

John 14:6 was quoted more than 200 times in the Edgar Cayce readings: **...I am the way, the truth and the life; no man cometh unto the Father, but by me.** Reading 1744-1 illustrates reference to this verse with these words: *...He is thy elder brother...He is the way, the truth, the light...*The readings refer to Jesus alternately as the Master, our Example, the Way Shower and as above, our Elder Brother. We are to follow His example, which will, indeed, bring us unto the Father.

The gospel of John is filled with symbology. John 10:1 speaks of the door of the sheepfold as well as a robber and thief: **I say unto you, He that entereth not by the door unto the sheep fold, but climbeth up some other way, the same is a thief and a robber.** In reading 364-9 Edgar Cayce was asked what part Jesus played in the development of the basic teachings of Buddhism, Brahamanism, Mohammedanism, Confucianism, Shintoism, Platonism, and Judaism. His reply follows: ...[**Jesus**] *influenced either directly or indirectly...those forms of philosophy or religious thought that taught God was One...for, as He gave, "He that climbs up any other way is a thief and a robber"...the Spirit of the Master, ...of the Son, was manifest...to each in their respective sphere...others' thought, does not change God's attitude one whit; neither does it make one above another...the whole law and gospel of every age...*[is] *"There is one God!"*

Hebrews 12:2 gives us an interesting glimpse of the Master: **Look unto Jesus the author and finisher of our faith; who for the joy that was set before him endured the cross...**Reference to this verse is included in the following message for Study Group 1 in reading 262-75: *What, then, is thy Destiny? It is made in that thou pervertest not...*[in] *that thou knowest to do in thine heart respecting thy fellow man! For ye look to Him who is the author and the finisher of faith. He is Faith, and Truth, and Light...* Jesus is the pioneer and perfecter of our faith. He is the one who led, and continues to lead, the way.

Here is another interesting glimpse of our Elder Brother in Hebrews 13:8: **Jesus Christ the same yesterday and today and forever.** Reading 1968-10 for a 33-year-old lady includes the following reference to this verse: *…keep thyself pure in mind and body. For the Lord's* [messages] *are oft spoken in dreams, in visions. For He is the same yesterday, today and forever. Be not unmindful that there is the manner of life ye live so that ye merit this or that experience.* While Christian thought about Jesus Christ has been subject to change from age to age, He has not changed.

Mark 7:37 tells us that Jesus did all things well. On the surface, this may not seem very remarkable. But, just how many people have we known who lived up to this standard entirely? **…He hath done all things well: he maketh both the deaf to hear, and the dumb to speak.** Cayce refers to this verse in the following message for a 52-year-old housewife in 538-33: *…when there arises those experiences where* fear *comes from faltering in self or another,* force *self - by* will - *"I* will *to give, live and* know *that He doeth all things* well, *in and through the expression of the Father in every soul!"* Thus, we need to remember that doing all things well is our heritage through Jesus Christ.

Acts 10:38 tells us several things about Jesus. The thing that stands out prominently to some of us is the simple phrase that He went about doing good: **God anointed Jesus of Nazareth with the Holy Ghost and with power; who went about doing good and healing all that were oppressed of the devil for God was with him.** Here is a reference to this verse in a message for a 64-year-old man in reading 281-61: *Let that mind be in thee as was in the Christ, who went about doing good, and not to the glory of self but making himself as naught that He might serve others.* Go about doing good. Perhaps I might try that for a day or so.

Jesus taught as one with authority, because he, indeed, did have authority. But, at heart, he was a humble person. Here is Philippians 2:7: **(Jesus) made himself of no reputation, and took upon him the form of a servant, and was made in the likeness of man.** In reading 2842-2 for a 38-year-old lady we find the following reference to this verse: *…take that ensample as was set in Him who made Himself of no estate that He might gain the more.*

If one is searching for true heroism, they need look no further than the pages of the New Testament. Here is I Timothy 2:6: **(Jesus Christ) who gave himself a ransom for all, to be testified in due time.** This verse is quoted in 262-119 as follows: *Know that to be absent from the body is to be present with thy conscience, thy god. What is thy god? Is it self or* [is it] *Christ?…Is it thy own desires and wishes? Or is it that* [which] *He manifested when He gave Himself as the ransom, as the way…?*

In I Corinthians 2:2 Paul tells us that his message will focus on the crucifixion. The Edgar Cayce readings tell us that the reason for the CROSS is the CROWN. Here is I Corinthians 2:2: **I am determined not to know anything among you, save Jesus Christ and him crucified.** Reading 262-34 includes reference to this verse as follows: *As given, "I am determined to know nothing among men save Jesus, the Christ, and Him crucified." So, He, with the Cross, represents something in the experience of every entity in their activities through the earth...[He] has led in all of the experiences of thought in* any *of the presented forms of truth in the earth, and comes at last to the Cross. So, this should be the central thought, the reason of the Cross [is] the Crown.* Thus, we need to be able to see that there is a reason for every personal cross that comes into our experience, and the reason is that we may receive the crown of life.

Jesus was already dedicated to His Father's business at the age of twelve, as inferred in Luke 2:49: ...**Wist ye not that I must be about my Father's business?** The following reading, 262-125, makes reference to this verse: *Draw the comparison within thyself as to those experiences indicated in...the 2nd of Luke - where we find our pattern, our lesson, and those illustrations that indicate sin versus righteousness, one willfully seeking to know the relationship to the Creator, [in] the answer, "Know ye not that I must be about my Father's business?" How different from that other, "The* woman *thou gavest me,* she *persuaded me, and I did eat.* Thus, the soul of Jesus had made great progress since its incarnation as Adam. He now accepts full responsibility for his actions and offers no excuses.

John 14:30 speaks of the prince of this world: ...**the prince of this world cometh, and hath nothing in me.** In the following reference to this verse, from reading 262-115, Cayce identifies "the prince of this world:" ...*that desire to procreate in self, or to hold to selfish interests, has grown...until it is what did He give?...the prince of this world! Know that He who came as our director, as our brother, as our savior, has said that the prince of this world has no part in Him nor with Him.* We have discovered the enemy and he is very close indeed.

Jesus asked Peter who do you say I am and he answered, You are the Christ the Son of the living God. This sets the stage for Matthew 16:17 where Jesus says: ...**Blessed art thou Simon Bar-jo-na: for flesh and blood hath not revealed it unto thee, but my Father which is in heaven.** Reading 281-37 includes the following reference to this verse: *What did Peter represent? That as had been given, "Flesh and blood hath not revealed this unto thee, but my Father in heaven." All then who have taken...that which had been given as the example, as the pattern...of the activities within self, are in that position - that they have touched...the knowledge of God...His ways, His laws, His love are...part of their...lives...and daily conversation...*

In John 14:9 Jesus affirms his oneness with the Father: ...**he that hath seen me hath seen the Father...** Reading 900-16 includes this verse: *In the life...of Jesus we find the oneness made manifest through the ability* *to overcome all of the temptations of the flesh...through making the* will one with the father... [As He gave] *"Those who have seen me have seen the Father"...In man, He, the Son of Man, became one with the Father. Man, through the same channel, may reach that perfection, even higher than the angel...* Is it true that we can also become one with the Father? Do some of us, perhaps, think this sounds just too good to be true?

Luke 2:7 tells us Jesus was born in a manger because there was no room in the inn: **She brought forth her firstborn son, and wrapped him in swaddling clothes, and laid him in a manger; because there was no room for them in the inn.** Reading 262-103, given on December 20, 1936, gives us some thoughts on the true meaning of "no room in the inn": *...His Star has appeared - and the angels' choir, and the voices of those that give the great message! Who heard these ...? Those that were seeking for the satisfying of their own desires or for the laudation of their own personality? Rather those close to* nature, *to the hours of meditation and prayer, and those that had given expression, "No room in the inn!" For no inn, no room, could contain that* [which] *was being given in a manifested form!*

Jesus had human feelings and emotions. Here is John 11:35: **Jesus wept.** Cayce refers to this verse in the following portion of reading 2995-1 for a 35-year-old secretary: *Cultivate in self humor, wit. Ye enjoy it in others, others enjoy it in thee. But too oft it becomes to thee foolishness.* Know *that thy Lord, thy God,* laughed - *even at the Cross. For He wept with those who wept, and rejoiced with those who rejoiced.*

After the crucifixion and resurrection, Jesus appears to the disciples and gives the message found in Matthew 28:18: **All power is given unto me in heaven and in earth.** This verse is quoted in reading 262-26: *He that is without those crosses has ceased to be of notice, and is no longer among the sons. In patience, then, comes the knowledge and the abilities to apply same in the relationships of men among men, for "All power is given me in heaven and in earth," and in patience may ye receive the promise...*

Here is Luke 2:11: **Unto you is born this day in the city of David a Savior, which is Christ the Lord.** Cayce refers to this Christmas verse in these concluding words of reading 262-116 which was given to members of Study Group 1 on December 19, 1937: *Let that love, that beauty as was the message to the shepherds, be thine today: "Unto* thee *is born," yea unto thee - each one here - is given a knowledge, an understanding of the* life *of the Christ that will* renew *thy life, thy purposes - if ye will but* sing *that new song, "Love one another."*

In reading 262-87 Cayce was asked "What is the Holy Church?" He refers to this verse - **...Whom do men say that the Son if man is?** - in Matthew 16:13: *That which makes for the awareness in the heart of the individual...The Church is never a body, never an assembly. An* individual *soul becomes aware that it has taken that Head, that Son, that Man...to be the intermediator.* That *is the Church; that is what is spoken of as the Holy Church...He asked, "Whom say men that I am?"...Peter answered...*[and] *He said to Peter, "* [this was revealed by] *my Father which is in heaven."* *Heaven? Where? Within the hearts, the minds; the place where Truth is made manifest! Wherever Truth is made manifest it gives place to that which is heaven* for those that seek *and love truth! but a mighty hell for those that seek gratification of their own selves!*

In this chapter we have reviewed some of the Bible verses and Edgar Cayce readings that relate to Jesus Christ, our Way Shower. Yet, there's hardly a chapter in this book that does not quote from or speak of the Master.

10

ONENESS

In this chapter on oneness we are, of course, speaking of our oneness with God. A starting point is that we are children of God, and, as such, have the capacity to grow up in God. Here is Romans 8:16 which was quoted over 100 times in the Cayce readings. **The Spirit itself beareth witness with our spirit that we are children of God.** In 1927, Cayce used the above Scripture in responding to a 40-year-old man who was seeking business advice in reading 4185-2: *...ever shall the spirit, the conscience, the soul of self, bear witness with His spirit, as to whether the entity is in the right or the wrong channel - for one may fool self for a while, yet that ever present inmost self bears that witness with self as to whether the right or wrong course is being pursued, when one keeps self in an at-oneness with the Father.*

It may be helpful to review some aspects of our oneness with God. We are co-creators with God and our Individual Higher Consciousness or Christ Consciousness is, inherently, one with All That Is or God. In this reading Cayce says that in order for *the Spirit* to bear witness with *our spirit*, we must keep ourselves "in an at-oneness with the Father." In other words, for this inherent oneness to bear fruit in our life, we must first attune our conscious mind with the Christ Mind.

The message contained in Deuteronomy 6:4 was quoted more than 100 times in the readings: **Hear, O Israel; The lord our God is one Lord.** The following words are from reading 991-1, for a 39-year-old Rabbi, Hebrew Christian: *Correlate not the differences, but where all religions meet - there is one God! "Know, O Israel, the Lord thy God is one!" Set that upon thy brow; keep it as a frontlet upon thy speech; make it such that thou may hand it on to thy brethren.* Here is some advice from reading 436-2 for a 28-year-old elevator boy: *"The Lord thy God is One!"* ...[manifest-ing] *that oneness in the little things makes the soul grow in His grace!* Oneness is, perhaps, the heart of the Cayce spiritual philosophy. The readings say that all force is one force and that everything is a manifestation of this Divine Force.

The words of Jesus in John 14:20 affirm His oneness with God and with us: *...ye shall know that I am in my Father and ye in me and I in you.* In reading 262-118 we find reference to this verse in the following message for a study group member who had some rather painful experiences: *In thy problems, in thy cares, take them all to Him in the spirit of truth and love that He expressed and manifested to those with whom He walked and talked as in the flesh; "As ye abide in me and I in you, so may the Father be glorified in me."...this [will] bring into thy consciousness...that joy, that peace which He has promised...the peace that passeth understanding; the assurance that thou art His and that He is thine...Keep the face...towards the light of the Christ, and the sorrow and care will fade.*

To achieve oneness with the Father we might start by attuning our thoughts and our mind to the thought pattern of Jesus, as inferred in Philippians 2:5: **Let this mind be in you, which was also in Christ Jesus.** Cayce's initial reading for Study Group 1 quoted this verse. In his third reading for the group, 262-3, he was asked "How may we have the mind of Christ?" Here is his reply: *As we open our hearts, our minds, our souls, that we may be a channel of blessings to others...we have the mind of the Christ, who took upon Himself the burden of the world. So may we, in our own little sphere, take upon ourselves the burdens of the world. The joy, the peace, the happiness, that may be ours is in doing for the other fellow. For, gaining an understanding of the laws [that] pertain to right living in all its phases makes the mind...attune with Creative Forces, which are of His consciousness...by putting into action that we know.* In a later reading, 262-62, for this group, Cayce makes reference to this verse as follows: *Let that mind be in each of you that was in Him, who went about doing good to those that were seeking...For, as you each make your lives a channel of blessing to some one, so may those promises, those influences of the spiritual life affect and produce that in our material world that will make for the glorifying of Him ye would name as thine ideal.*

In John 17:5 Jesus speaks of having glory with the Father before the world was: **And now, O Father, glorify thou me, with thine own self with the glory which I had with thee before the world was.** Here is a reference to this verse from reading 262-93: *...[When] the activities of self become less and less towards the Glory of self...[to] being one with the Father...then there may be that Glory, that consciousness of the oneness that thou didst occupy before thy advent or before the world was. Even as He prayed, "Now glorify thy son, that he may have the glory that was his before the worlds were."* This reading says we were one with the Father, just as Jesus was, before the *worlds* were. The Edgar Cayce readings say *planet earth is only an atom* in the universe of worlds. One might look at this bit of information as indicative of just how infinitesimally small a single soul on planet earth may be in relation to the entire cosmos. Or, knowing that we have an intrinsic oneness with All That Is, see this as an expansion of what each individual represents. It depends entirely on one's perspective.

Search the scriptures; for in them ye think ye have eternal life, and they are they which testify of me. This verse in John 5:39 raises the question of eternal life. In reading 900-147 Cayce was asked to define life eternal. Here is part of his reply which links life eternal with oneness: *Life Eternal - One with that Oneness, as is seen by the Soul becoming One with the Will, the spirit, of the Father, even as is shown in the ensample of the Man called Jesus - the Christ, the Savior of the World; through compliance* [with] *those same laws,* [that] *He complied with...For with that Force, that Spirit,* [that] *brought in* [created] *the World,* [it] *then becomes the truth...*

John 3:5 tells us that we must be born of water and spirit: **...Except a man be born of water and of the Spirit, he cannot enter into the kingdom of God.** In reading 262-80 we find reference to this verse which relates being born again to the development of oneness with the Father: *...Mind is the dividing line between that which is human, that which is man, and that which is animal...Hence the variation in that He taught as He gave to Niccdemus, "Know ye not ye must be born again?" Born of water and...spirit...be of one mind, of one purpose, of one aim, of one desire...each must approach from his or her own vision, his or her own status of development...the Mind* [eventually] *...is made* one with *Constructive Force, one with the Creator; and thus fulfill its Destiny - to become One in Him, One with the Father.* If Jesus were to give a talk today about being born again, he might speak of a new birth in consciousness.

In John 10:30 Jesus declares his oneness with the Father: **I and my Father are one.** In reading 1158-14 we find reference to this verse as follows: *...He* [God] *is...the energies in the finite moving in material manifestation. He is also the Infinite, with the awareness* [of individuals]. *And thus as ye attune thy own consciousness, thy own awareness, the unfoldment of the presence within beareth witness with the presence without...as the Son gave, "I and my Father are one,"...ye come to know that ye and thy Father are one, as ye abide in Him...until ye become as a savior, as a help to some soul that has lost hope, lost its way, ye do not fully comprehend the God within,* [or] *the God without.* Thus, until we actually do something that is Godly in its purpose, we simply cannot comprehend God, within or without.

In Ephesians 4:5-6 Paul writes that the Father is in *you all.* (Perhaps they were southern Ephesians.) **One Lord, one faith, one baptism, One God and Father of all, who is above all, and through all, and in you all.** Reference to these verses is included in reading 262-81: *...the Lord thy*

God is One. One Lord, one Christ, one faith, one hope, one baptism - in the Christ; putting on Christ.

Hebrews 9:28 promises that Christ will appear "the second time" to those who look for Him: **Christ was once offered to bear the sins of many; and unto them that look for him shall he appear the second time without sin unto salvation.** In reading 262-94 Cayce was asked to explain this verse. As you will note in his response, oneness is a key component in the proper understanding of this second appearance: *As it reads, so is it; in spirit and in truth. For, combine each promise in same to that the* Master *himself spoke. And we will find that the promises are, "He that abideth in me hath indeed then put on Christ, hath indeed become one with Christ and is no longer subject to the temptations of the earth, of the world," and hence becomes one with Him and is in that attitude, that plane of oneness. To such there is no returning to the flesh.* Graduation time at last!

And now, its time for some more symbols; this time from Revelation 21:15: **He that talked with me had a golden reed to measure the city, and the gates thereof, and the wall thereof.** This verse is explained by Cayce in reading 281-37: *...the reed to measure the city,* [represents] *the abilities of each. Not unto all is it given to be ministers, not unto all to be interpreters, not unto all to be this or that; but* [each] *measured according to that* [which] *they have purposed in their hearts. Though all are one, remember it has been given that the purpose of the heart is to know* yourself *to be* yourself *and yet one with God even as Jesus* [knew this]...

Thus, in our effort to achieve oneness with God we are to remember that we are also unique and individual.

11

CHOICES

Our first Bible verse concerning choices is Joshua 24:15 which was quoted almost 200 times in the Edgar Cayce readings: **And if it seem evil unto you to serve the Lord, choose you this day whom ye will serve; whether the gods which your fathers served that were on the other side of the flood, or the gods of the Amorites, in whose land ye dwell; but as for me and my house we will serve the Lord.** The readings usually focus on the concluding words. Cayce's advice in both 3463-1 and 2861-1, which follow, was that the individual would do well to remember these words: *Let others do as they may, but as for me, I will serve the living God* (3463-1). "*Let others do as they may, but as for me and my house, we will serve a living God* (2861-1)."

Most of us become well aware, at an early age, of the temptation to go along with the crowd. No one wants to be an outcast and miss out on the "fun" things in life. We experience peer pressure long before we become familiar with this term. There are still times when I feel some degree of peer pressure. At whatever age or stage of life we find ourselves, this Scripture is a reminder of the importance of choosing Principle or God over peer pressure or expediency.

The second most frequently quoted verse on choices, Deuteronomy 30:15, was quoted more than 100 times: **See, I have set before thee this day life and good, and death and evil.** In reading 281-31, for the Prayer Healing Group, Cayce included these words of advice: *"O today there is life and death, good and evil - Choose thou." This may be said to be symbolical...of...conflicting forces within... influences that are ever present...* This reading says, at times, there are *body elements that* [become] *conflicting one with another.* We need to make a conscious choice and cultivate peace within our mind in order to help resolve these body conflicts. In this manner, serious physical illness, frequently, can be avoided.

Each day of our life, we need to be prepared to renew prior choices, if necessary, and make new choices, as appropriate. This is a vitally important, ongoing activity of life. There may be times when standing up to be counted may not be pleasant and our choices may bring responsibilities that we would rather avoid. But, we must avoid blind neutrality. It is important to evaluate our options and to seek guidance, but we must avoid just sitting on the fence.

Choice is important in all areas of our life. The focus in Matthew 6:24 is, not surprisingly, on correct spiritual choice: **No man can serve two masters: for either he will hate the one and love the other; or else he will hold to one, and despise the other. Ye cannot serve God and mammon.** In reading 967-3 Cayce refers to this verse in the following message for a 49-year-old secretary: *...there are those abilities within the self to choose by what spirit or power ye may make manifest thy activities. Whether unto the glory of the material things or the spiritual depends upon the choice made. Ye cannot serve two masters at once, for ye will hate one and love the other.* Those who have had a job situation where you had two bosses may have some personal appreciation of this verse. For example, "They were both fallen angels, but one seemed to have fallen farther than the other. "

Some of our choices may relate to our gifts. Here is Ephesians 4:11: **And he gave some, apostles; and some, prophets; and some, evangelists; and some, pastors and teachers.** In reading 2067-6, a 53-year-old teacher asked Cayce to give a plan for her major spiritual undertakings. He refers to this verse in his response: *...this is ever to be the choice of the individual entity. For, as ye know...to some is given the gift of ministry, to some healing, to some preaching, to some teaching...choose thou - today...*how *and* Whom *ye will serve; whether self or thy Creator. He desires that each soul* glorify*...Him in the earth.*

Sometimes our choices require higher approval. This is the situation in Matthew 20:22: **But Jesus answered and said, Ye know not what ye ask. Are ye able to drink of the cup that I shall drink of, and to be baptized with the baptism that I am baptized with? They say unto him, We are able.** This Scripture poses the question of our ability to follow the path of Jesus. This question is discussed in the following portion of reading 262-107: *Be in singleness of purpose, then. Not that thy own self is to be glorified. What has been thy concept of Glory? Glory signifies that ye are able to suffer. Only those who have suffered much may ever be glorified. Do ye seek Glory? Then ye must be willing to suffer; and if ye count thy suffering, thy disappointments, thy heartaches, thy misunderstandings, as judgments upon thee, ye are unwise. For whom the Lord loveth He chasteneth and purgeth every one, that ye may bring forth fruit in due season! Would ye have thy Glory without thy purification? Would ye have thy Wisdom without thy preparation? Would ye have thy Happiness, or seek thy Happiness, without being able to comprehend, to understand? If this be so, ye* *have not gained thy lesson of Wisdom. Then how may each of you here make a practical application of Wisdom? Ye all...have been called upon to manifest that ye have chosen...Then go the whole way with thy Master.* This reading is rather long but it gives us a lot to think about. A point that stands out for me, is, that, when I'm suddenly confronted with unexpected difficulty, this reading seems to warn me not to wonder what I did that brought about the karmic necessity of having to deal with the situation. Instead, I'm to think in terms of what I can learn and how I can grow in wisdom and understanding from the experience. Just blaming it on bad karma is unwise.

Our next verse, Deuteronomy 30:19, is similar to 30:15, preceding: **I call heaven and earth to record this day against you, that I have set before you life and death, blessing and cursing: therefore choose life, that both thou and thy seed may live.** Reference to this verse is included in reading 3581-1: *There is today* [and] *every day, set before thee good and evil, life and death - choose thou...only self can separate you from the love of the Father...thou art conscious...of suffering, of sorrow, of joy, of pleasure. These...are the price one pays for having will* [and] *knowledge.*

Deuteronomy 11:9 speaks of prolonging our life on earth: **...ye may prolong your days in the land, which the Lord swore unto your fathers to give unto them and to their seed, a land that floweth with milk and honey.** In reading 694-2 a lady asked Cayce how long she had to live. He makes reference to this verse in his response: *Rather choose thou, "How long may I serve my God, my fellow man, through giving service to Him?" And stand ever in that position: "I am ready, Lord, to serve wherever, in* **whatever** *realm,* Thou *choosest that I may be of the greater service!" Many days, many years wait before thee. Do ye not know, "Honor thy father, thy mother, that thy days may be* long *in the land which the Lord thy God giveth thee"? ...It is before thee; choose thou!* The future is not set in concrete. We will live much longer if we have a purpose and proper motivation. It is up to the individual.

In the verses preceding Matthew 8:22 Jesus gave orders for the disciples to go with him to the other side of the lake. Then, one of the disciples asked permission to first go and bury his father: **But Jesus said unto him, Follow me, let the dead bury their dead.** This verse is included in reading 2112-1: *...those things that are in the past, let the dead bury their* own *dead; for* He *is God of the living,* not *of the dead! He is Life, and Light, and Immortality!* Glory *in His weakness...His might...His watchful - loving - kindness, and* all will *be right!*

Jesus tells his disciples that he must be crucified. Peter responds in a very human way saying "God forbid, Lord! This shall never happen to you." This sets the stage for Matthew 16:23: **But he turned, and said unto**

Peter, Get thee behind me Satan: thou art an offense unto me: for thou savourest not the things that be of God, but those that be of men. Choosing correctly requires that we look down the road and try to see the outcome of our choice. Reading 288-30 includes the following reference to this verse: *...when ye are beset by those forces that would unbalance* [and] *unroot thee from that thou hast believed,* [say] *even as He, "Get thee behind me, satan, for thou savorest of the things that are of the earth."* Do not dwell on negative thoughts. Put them behind you.

Matthew 22:14 calls attention to the difference in being called and in being chosen: **many are called, but few are chosen.** I remember a well-known college football coach who every August when the freshmen football recruits reported, would say that it was time to separate the prospects from the suspects. Reading 262-126 says that one is often called; they must then respond appropriately in order to be chosen: *...as may be drawn from the experiences of those who have been...or who may be called into service - if there is the sincerity towards the ideal, they as individuals will be shown, will perceive, will be awakened, will be aware of God's purposes with them. ...this should be in the mind of each one here considered and meditated upon, and applied in the daily life - let each be sincere, be direct, in that calling. For, ye each are chosen - as ye choose to serve Him in a definite manner - to be a messenger, a director - by word, by example to others - to point the way to the glorifying of the Christ Consciousness in a material world.*

One of the more important choices we make in life relates to marriage. Here is I Corinthians 7:38: **So then he that giveth her in marriage doeth well; but he that giveth her not in marriage doeth better.** In reading 866-1 a 42-year-old man asked about his prospects for marriage. Here is Cayce's reply: *He that marries doeth well; he that marries not doeth better. This is dependent...upon...the purifying of the lives of those* [involved]... Each party to a marriage must be prepared in advance to make the necessary commitments.

Luke 10:42 tells us about a good choice: **But one thing is needful: and Mary hath chosen that good part, which shall not be taken away from her.** Edgar Cayce refers to this verse in reading 254-54: *Do with thy might what thy hands* find *to do, and there will be joy, even as was said of old, "Mary hath chosen the better part."* In this incident Martha, Mary's sister, had complained that Mary's choice to sit and listen to the Master had left all the work of serving up to her, Martha. Cayce's advice to *do with thy might what thy hands find to do* suggests that Martha's choice to serve also had merit. Perhaps those who feel they have traditionally been left with the Martha role in life will appreciate this view.

Psalm 84:10 speaks of being a doorkeeper in the house of God: **For a** day in thy courts is better than a thousand. I had rather be a doorkeeper in the house of my God, than to dwell in the tents of wickedness. In reading 262-120 for Study Group 1 reference to this verse is made as follows: *...Let thy heart be lifted up; for as thou hast chosen Him, He hath chosen you to be a light unto many peoples...to be a doorkeeper in the house of the Lord is greater than he that taketh a city or ruleth a nation...Keep...the faith that has held thee to thy purpose, knowing that He standeth near to each of you.* Rely *on Him!*

Here again, in II Corinthians 6:14 is a verse pointing to the importance of choice in marriage: **Be ye not unequally yoked together with unbelievers: for what fellowship hath righteousness with unrighteousness? and what communion hath light with darkness.** Reference to this verse is included in reading 1968-10: *...there must be the choice of thy associate, thy companion, thy husband...* [who] *must be in accord...*[with] *God's purposes...which will manifest in the Christ-Jesus as their ideal...*[to] *practice...in...daily life. For, be not unequally yoked together with unbelievers...let thy choice be by Father-God showing thou the way.*

In the story of the prodigal son, the time comes when the prodigal chooses to return to his father. Here is Luke 15:18: **I will arise and go to my father, and will say unto him, Father, I have sinned against heaven and before thee.** The opening words of this verse are quoted in the following portion of reading 262-36 for Study Group 1: *...in overcoming all He set that as the Throne, or the mercy seat, that is within the temple, as the pattern...and* [is] *in the mount, "I* will *arise and go to my Father...I will, I will!"* Our choice is always correct when we have made our human will one with that of the Father.

In Matthew 27:22 Pilot asks what he shall do with Jesus: **Pilot saith unto them, What shall I do then with Jesus which is called Christ? They all say unto him, Let him be crucified.** In the following portion of reading 849-11 Cayce asks the question, what will we do with Jesus: *What will ye do with this man thy elder brother, thy Christ, who - that thy Destiny might be sure in Him - has shown thee the more excellent way.*

We might start with, What have I done with Him up to this point?

12

NATURE OF GOD

In this chapter our central focus will be the nature of God. First we will look at seven verses from the Old Testament followed by eleven verses from the New Testament. Psalm 19:7 was quoted almost 100 times in the Edgar Cayce readings: **The law of the Lord is perfect, converting the soul: the testimony of the Lord is sure making wise the simple.** This verse gives us three points about God. 1. His law is perfect. 2. He converts souls. 3. His testimony makes wise the simple. In reading 262-128 Cayce makes reference to the first two points. *The law of the Lord is perfect. It converteth the soul of those who will harken, who will make daily application of that His word and His promptings bid them to do.* Some say God's law is without a flaw. His law gives strength and fresh life to us when we encounter difficulties. It provides wise guidance to all, especially young people and those who are inexperienced.

In Exodus Moses says to God, if the people ask for your name, what shall I say to them. Here is God's answer in Exodus 3:14: **And God said unto Moses, I AM THAT I AM: and he said, This shall thou say unto the Children of Israel, I AM hath sent me unto you.** Cayce makes reference to the I AM in the following message for members of Study Group 1 in reading 262-23: [Become] *sincere in purpose, pure in mind, reasonable even to self, walking in the way that brings a* [closer] *union with Him...He seeks to find expression...in all who are called in the I AM THAT I AM, and* [He] *is an ever active force...through all ages, all peoples...* Since the name of the Lord whom I worship is I AM, then it is only through what I am that I can worship Him properly. This verse affirms our unity with God and with each other.

Psalm 11:4 tells us that our Lord is in his holy temple: **The Lord is in his holy temple, the Lord's throne is in heaven: his eyes behold, his eyelids try, the children of men.** So, just where is this holy temple? According to the Cayce readings, each of us is intended to be his holy temple, as mentioned in 262-5: *Seek as children to know His love, His law, His biddings, and as ye seek so shall ye find; for He is in His holy temples. Art thou holy? Art thou desirous of being holy? Art thou seeking rather the* *good of thy brother than thine self? Then...*be *on speaking terms with thy brother.*

In Genesis God tells Abraham that he is going to destroy the wicked city of Sodom. Abraham tries to bargain with God to spare the city. Here is Genesis 18:32: **(Abraham) said, Oh let not the Lord be angry, and I will yet but this once: Peradventure ten shall be found there. And he said, I will not destroy it for ten's sake.** In reading 281-37 Cayce was asked "the meaning of one thousand years that Satan is bound," from Revelation 20:2. In reply, he states that the prayer of ten would save a city, which is in reference to this verse from Genesis: **[Satan]** *is banished...as there are the activities of the forty and four thousand - in the same manner that the prayer of ten just should save a city, the deeds...the incarnation of those only that are in the Lord shall rule the earth, and the period is...a thousand years. Thus is Satan bound, thus is Satan banished from the earth.*

Thousands of years ago the Psalmist had an early concept of the relativity of time. Here is Psalm 90:4: **For a thousand years in thy sight are but as yesterday when it is past, and as a watch in the night.** In reading 262-57 Cayce was asked to comment on the statement in Genesis that heaven and earth were created in six days. In his reply he refers to this verse: *When it is considered...that "a thousand years is as but a day and a day as but a thousand years in the sight of the Lord," then it may be comprehended...this was colored by the writer in his desire to express to the people the power of the living God - rather than a statement of six days as man comprehends days in the present. Not that it was an impossibility - but rather that men...should be impressed by the omnipotence of that they were called on to worship as God.*

God is very concerned about human conduct both individually and collectively, as stated in Genesis 6:6: **And it repented the Lord that he had made man on the earth, and it grieved him at his heart.** In the following portion of reading 262-86 reference is made to this verse: *God Himself knows not what man will destine to do with himself, else would He have repented that He had made man? He has given man free-will.* Man *destines the body!*

Readers will be familiar with this verse: **In the beginning God created the heaven and the earth.** Here is a reference to this verse, Genesis 1:1, from reading 262-78: *In the beginning God created the heavens and the earth. How? The* mind *of God* moved, *and matter, form, came into being. Mind, then, in God, the Father, is the builder. How much more...should Mind be the builder in the experience of those that have put on Christ...[from] His coming into the earth? For as He has given, "Let that mind be in you which was in the Christ, who thought it not robbery to make Himself equal with God..."*

We will now look at eleven verses from the New Testament that relate to the nature of God. Our first verse, Acts 17:28, was quoted over 100 times in the readings: **For in him we live and move and have our being; as certain of your own poets have said, For we are also his offspring.** In reading 1468-1 for a 47-year-old secretary we find these words: *...divine love, in which each and every soul lives and moves and has its being.* The following is from, 3976-22, for the 1939 A.R.E. Congress: *For we as individuals, as we look about us, realize more and more that indeed we are live and move and have our being in Him - and we are becoming mindful also of "from whence we came."* The words, **in Him we live and move and have our being,** remind me of the statement from the readings that we are *corpuscles in the body of God.* Corpuscles obviously live and move and have their being in the body of which they are a vital component. Erythrocytes, our red corpuscles, carry oxygen to the body tissues. Leukocytes, our white corpuscles, are important in defense against infection. Thus, as corpuscles, we are vitally important to the well-being of the body of God.

John 1:3 is somewhat similar to Genesis 1:1 in that it reminds us that God is the Supreme Creator and our Source: **All things were made by him; and without him was not anything made that was made.** The gospel of John, beginning here in chapter one, equates Jesus the Christ with God to a degree that is not readily apparent in Matthew, Mark, or Luke. Reading 262-69 includes the following message which makes reference to this verse: *Come! Sing and make a joyful noise unto the Lord, thy King; for thy Elder Brother...has a mission for each of you...Fulfill that thou knowest to do... [Have] a day of joy in the earth...[and] an eternity of glory with thy brother, the Christ...For by Him all things were made...*

II Timothy 2:19 speaks of naming the name of Christ: **The foundations of God standeth sure, having his seal, the Lord knoweth them that are his. And, Let every one that nameth the name of Christ depart from iniquity.** Cayce was asked by a 54-year-old night-watchman, "What is the name of my healer. " His reply, in 281-3, makes reference to this verse: *That name above every other name! [Just as] that name, named by self, brought healing in the physical self in an experience, so may self - by holding, attaining, [and] gaining that consciousness of the indwelling and communion of that self-same Spirit - bring aid, bring help, bring hope and* faith, *to another.*

John 1:1 is another verse that is reminiscent of Genesis 1:1: **In the beginning was the Word, and the Word was with God, and the Word was God.** Cayce refers to this verse in the following message for a 29-year-old lady in reading 263-13: *...in the beginning was the word. The word was God. The word was with God. He moved... [and] as He moved, souls - portions of Himself - came into being. This entity - as a portion - may come to* *the awareness then of its relationship to that source, that glow or impulse of life.* Of course, all of us need to come to this same state of awareness of our Source.

Luke 20:38 tells us that our Lord is God of the living, not of the dead. One perspective on this verse is that God is forever Lord of our soul. But when we experience that transition called death, the body is what dies, and our Lord is no longer concerned with it: **For he is not a God of the dead, but of the living: for all live unto him.** This verse appears in 2400-1: *...God is God of the living and not of the dead. For, in Him is life, life everlasting - God of the living - as is that spirit of truth, of sincerity, of purpose, of faith, of kindness, of brotherly love, and most of all patience.*

As stated in Matthew 5:45 God blesses all of his children. This does not rule out special blessings for those who obey His word: **...he maketh his sun to rise on the evil and on the good, and sendeth rain on the just and the unjust.** Reading 262-98 makes reference to this verse as follows: **Leave** *the fruits, the increase, the change, in the hands of the Father...Do that thou* knowest *to do and find not fault with thy neighbor. For he that doeth such is not wise...For He sendeth His blessings on the just and the unjust...hoping that thou in thy Knowledge of Him will aid thy fellow man and leave the* blessings *to God.*

Jesus was brought before Pilate who said, "Do you not know that I have power to release you, and power to crucify you." In John 19:11: **Jesus answered, Thou couldest have no power at all against me, except it were given thee from above...** In reading 602-7 a 49-year-old lady asked Cayce if her good friend was in the place or position that was best for him. Cayce refers to this verse in his reply: *As He gave* [and] *consider* [this] *well... "No man is in this or that position save by the grace of God.")...*[His] *opportunities are* where *he is in the present,* using *the knowledge of the material, the mental and the spiritual life for the betterment of his fellow man where he is.* God IS present in our world in places and situations where we might least expect to find Him/Her.

God's power is unlimited, as inferred in Mark 10:27: **And Jesus looking upon them saith, With men it is impossible, but not with God; for with God all things are possible.** Reference to this verse is included in 971-1: **All** *things are possible with God...begin with the* spiritual *activity. Do not expect results in one day, nor one week...Indiscretions, and the sentiments that are based wholly upon material satisfactions, must bring the tares and the weeds in the experience of the body. Those things sown in mercy, truth,* [and] *justice, will bring their rewards in the same realm...*

If we desire to know what God is like, we need to become familiar with Jesus the Christ. Here is John 14:7: **If ye had known me, ye should have known my Father also: and from henceforth ye know him, and have seen**

him. In reading 262-44 the following reference is made to this verse: ... *"Ye that have known me knoweth my Father also, for I am in Him, and ye in me may know that love that maketh...life burn as an ember in a darkened and unregenerated world. For unto me must come all that would find the way. I AM the way. Ye are my brethren..."*

Acts 7:49 tells us that the earth is the Lord's footstool. His feet represent the understanding that is immediately available to all who seek: **Heaven is my throne, and earth is my footstool: what house will ye build me? saith the Lord: or what is the place of my rest.** Reference to this verse is included in reading 262-95: *For as the heaven is His throne, the earth is His footstool, so may we at His feet learn, know, become aware of, the knowledge of His ways. For He is not past finding out.*

If there was not an aspect of God that is a consuming fire, our life might be like living in a large city without garbage service. Here is Hebrews 12:29: **For our God is a consuming fire.** The following portion of 262-26 includes reference to this verse: *...corruption* [does] *not inherit eternal life, and must be burned up. Know that thy God is a consuming fire, and must purge every one,* [so] *that ye may enter in. In patience does one overcome.*

13

GUIDANCE

Jesus gives what many feel is an outstanding biblical message on guidance in John 8:32 which was quoted almost 100 times in the Edgar Cayce readings. The promise and the results are clear: **Ye shall know the truth and the truth shall make you free.** Cayce had the following comments about truth in reading 688-3 for a 61-year-old podiatrist: ...**[There is]** *that divine heritage within the experience of each soul, that it - too - may know the truth and that the truth may set it free. Not only in physical depressions, physical obligations, but in the mental and spiritual as well. For the spirit of truth and those forces in the Godhead itself stand ever ready to give that which is necessary for each and every soul to become more and more aware of that divine influence which works in and through each one...* Real freedom can be achieved only by real discipleship, or as the readings might say, by application of the truth that you know.

One of the promises of Jesus to his followers is guidance that will come from the Comforter or Holy Ghost. All things will be brought to our remembrance, as stated in John 14:26: **But the comforter, which is the Holy Ghost, whom the Father will send in my name, he shall teach you all things, and bring all things to your remembrance, whatsoever I have said unto you.** In reading 262-28 Cayce refers to this verse: ...**open** *the door that He may come in and abide with thee; for "He that takes my yoke upon him and learns of me, with* him *will I abide day by day, and all things will be brought to remembrance that I have given thee since the foundations of the world...thou were with me in the beginning and thou may abide with me in that day when the earth will be rolled as the scroll..."* Most of us need to be reminded from time to time of the teachings of the Christ, particularly those we have not put into practice. The Holy Spirit brings these to our remembrance. The Father, Son, and Holy Spirit are, of course, One. My preference is to seek guidance from the Son, the Christ.

In John 8:28 the Master tells us that His teaching is from the Father: **Then said Jesus unto them, When ye have lifted up the Son of man, then shall ye know, that I am he, and that I do nothing of myself; but, as my Father hath taught me, I speak these things.** In the following discourse to the Prayer Healing Group, in reading 281-27, Cayce make reference to this verse: *Those that let their mind dwell upon what others may say, upon how the world looketh upon the activity, these alone become afraid. Hence as He gave to those that saw, that understood, that comprehended that He was of the Spirit, "Of myself I can do nothing, but the spirit of the Father that worketh in and through me." So may ye as individuals not of thyselves but in allowing thy minds, thy bodies, thy purposes, thy aims* [to] *be guided in that direction,* [So may ye] *be a channel through which the Spirit of Truth, the Spirit of Life, the Spirit of Creative Influences or God through Christ work in thee! These be the manners in which ye may bring help to those that seek, to those that are afraid, to those that have been overcome, to those who have stumbled, to those who have erred.* There is a wealth of guidance here for all who desire to be a channel of blessing to others.

We need to take advantage of the better times for guidance. Early in the morning may be best for some. Just before retiring can also be a good time. Or, perhaps at two a.m. as recommended in the readings. Here is Isaiah 55:6: **Seek ye the Lord while he may be found, call ye upon him while he is near:** Edgar Cayce refers to this verse twice in this message for Study Group 1 in 262-97: ... *"First seek the Lord while He may be found, and all these things will be added unto thee in their order, in* their *place, in* their *time." Because of the worldly knowledge...many have become faint...many have fallen away...Encourage those that are weak, strengthen, the fainthearted...* [This is] *the true knowledge; in these be the perfect understanding that* His *ways, thy God's ways are not past finding out - if ye will but seek him while He may be found.* In meditation and prayer we need to genuinely turn to the Christ and bring ourselves before Him.

Fear can be one of our greatest challenges. It is said that "stage fright" or fear of public speaking is one of the worst fears that many people experience. In Matthew 10:19 Jesus assures his followers that they will receive guidance on what to say in their defense: **But when they deliver you up, take no thought how or what ye shall speak, for it shall be given you in that same hour what ye shall speak.** In reading 666-1 a chiropractor asked how he could eliminate self-consciousness and fear when addressing an audience. Cayce refers to this verse in his reply: ...[By] *entering into the silence,...not as rote, but as entering into the consciousness of that of the Creative Forces* [which] *gives to all...as was promised, "Take no thought of what ye shall say, for in the self-same hour will it be given thee." When one...*[reaches] *that consciousness of the Divine's activity within self, then* self's *consciousness, or self-consciousness, is laid aside.* In time of need God will supply both courage and words to all who trust

Him. He will speak through them.

Isaiah 13:6 says:...**the day of the Lord is at hand...**In reading 1472-12 for a 59-year-old writer and radio broadcaster we find these words: ...*as ye write, in whatever form or manner is chosen, express again and* again *that the day of the Lord is at hand! and that each soul,* everywhere, *partakes of same - in the fruits of the spirit, that are the holy gifts to every soul. For indeed, as He has given, he that gives the cup of water shall not lose his reward, Christ's reward, God's purpose.* It is interesting to note that the Scriptural context of, **the day of the Lord is at hand,** was a warning of great destruction, whereas in Cayce's use, every day and every where is an occasion for manifestation of *the fruits of the spirit, that are the holy gifts to every soul.*

I Corinthians 12:31 promises that we may be shown a more excellent way: **But covet earnestly the best gifts: and yet show I unto you a more excellent way.** Reading 1861-4 includes the following reference to this verse: *A pattern...has been made...*[by] *which each soul, each entity, may find its way....He is the way, the truth, the light. He manifested life, in a material body; taking on the desires of flesh, and yet using the mental attributes to keep body,* [and] *mind...in full accord* [with, and] *the full attunement to be,* [and] *do, that* [which] *would make for* each *soul the more perfect, the more excellent, way.*

Here is Proverbs 24:12 **If thou sayest, Behold, we know it not, doth not he that pondereth the heart consider it? and he that keepeth thy soul, doth not he know it? and shall not he render to every man according to his works.** In reading 262-96 Cayce refers to pondering things within our heart which may or may not have very much in common with this verse. You be the judge: *...there will come...to each* [who seeks, in truth]*...unusual experiences; to each according to your own attunement. To each has been given, ponder these well within thine own heart before giving expression...of same to others. Meet with thy Master as respecting same. He has promised to guide, to guard, to direct thee in thine uprisings, in thine downsittings. For to each many experiences will come.*

Psalm 111:10 tells us fear of the Lord is the beginning of wisdom: **The fear of the Lord is the beginning of wisdom: a good understanding have all they that do his commandments: his praise endureth for ever.** In reading 281-28 Cayce explains this verse as follows: *They that* [meditate] *for selfish motives do so to their own undoing. Thus has it oft been said, the fear of the Lord is the beginning of wisdom. Wisdom, then, is fear to misapply knowledge in thy dealings with thyself* [and] *thy fellow man. For as ye are honest, as ye are patient, as ye are sincere with thyself in thy meeting with thy God, thy Savior, thy Christ, in thy meditation,* [then] *ye will* [also] *be* [honest, patient and sincere] *in thy dealings with thy fellow man.*

Here is Luke 12:39: **And this know, that if the goodman of the house had known what hour the thief would come, he would have watched, and not suffered his house to be broken through.** Reference to this verse is included in reading 1467-18: *As the Master gave being forewarned ye may be forearmed. For if an individual knew beforehand he would not allow his house to be broken* [into] *by those who act as thieves in the night to the individual's purpose or...activity. Don't think that there will not be trouble, but those who put their trust wholly in the Lord will not come up missing* [anything] *but will find* [in] *conditions, circumstances* [and] *activities, someway and somehow much to be thankful for.* While there is no iron clad guarantee, being open to guidance may enable you to be forewarned and thus forearmed.

In reading 262-67 Cayce was asked to explain: "He desires truth in the inward parts," as quoted from Psalm 51:6: **Behold thou desirest truth in the inward parts: and in the hidden part thou shalt make me to know wisdom.** Here is his reply: *He that giveth his soul to the purposes of the Lord, he that loveth his enemies, he that loveth those that speak harshly to thine inner self,* desires *the Lord in the inner self. Thus the answers for all come in the love that He gave...He left His glory with the Father* [so] *that He might know the desires of the flesh as related to all those things pertaining to the waywardness of man; yet the desire that arose from the inner self* [was] *that life given by Him, life must be maintained in the* desire of *Him towards those to whom He had given the power to become the sons of God through* their *experience in the earth. So is the inner desire one with the Father-God. So is the soul made one with the soul of thy Savior.*

Appropriate words for ending this chapter on guidance.

14

HARMONY

We begin this chapter on harmony with a verse that was quoted almost 300 times in the Edgar Cayce readings, Matthew 7:12: **Therefore all things whatsoever ye would that men should do to you, do ye even so to them; for this is the law and the prophets.** The usual quotation is this: *As ye would that men should do to you, do ye even so to them.* This rule of life has been called the "Golden Rule." It is easy to understand but the fact that it was the sixth most frequently quoted verse in the readings would indicate that many people have difficulty living up to this rule in their relationships with others. Some may say this as just prudent secular wisdom in that practice of the "Golden Rule" is good for business and social relationships. However, the Master's intention was that people show the same loving kindness to others that God shows to them. Here is a reference to this verse from 281-65: *May that which has been in thine mind and heart be turned to love and grace and mercy. For as ye do unto others, others will do unto thee. Seek grace and mercy, and that peace, while it may be found.* Here is a second reference to this verse from 5502-4: *...keep that faith, that hope, in ministering to others as ye would* [desire to] *be ministered to in their own position. For as we keep the faith with others...* [then] *others will keep the faith with us...Do unto others as ye would have others do unto thee. Let there be light...* [which] *brings the life...and understanding.* There can be little doubt that the "Golden Rule" is absolutely essential to harmonious human relationships.

It is difficult to imagine harmony where love is absent. Here is John 15:12: **This is my commandment, That ye love one another, as I have loved you.** Reading 281-50 refers to this new commandment: *Let thy purposes in thy dealings with others be kept in attune, in accord, with that new commandment He gave unto those about Him, "Love one another." And as thy activities bring those trials, those doubts, those fears, place them upon the altar of service; and the joy of the Lord will fill thee with peace* [and] *contentment, that comes to those who put their trust in Him.* Here is a second reference to this verse from 5749-10: *...as He gave, "Love ye one another," thus...replace hate and jealousy...with love and hope* *and joy.* A great way to move from disharmony to harmony.

Proverbs 15:1 offers us some harmonious advice: **A soft answer turneth away wrath; but grievous words stir up anger.** In reading 274-3, for a 35-year-old man, Cayce refers to this verse as follows: ...[**Do not**] *some great deed, but rather just* [be] *kind one to another. For,* [just] *as* He *went about doing good - so may the kind word turn away wrath, so may the gentle look quicken the heart of the sad and make for the awareness that God is in His holy temple in thee...*

Our second reference to this verse is from 5098-1: *If you would have friends, be friendly, smile....Be kind and gentle. Remember, the soft word turns away wrath and it brings joy...peace* [and] *harmony...* Another reference is from 1925-1...*when the entity allows self to* think *the second time, the entity often makes for the soft word that will turn away wrath, and easily becomes the peacemaker...*

Matthew 12:25 tells us what may result when harmony is lost: **And Jesus knew their thoughts and said unto them, Every kingdom divided against itself is brought to desolation; and every city or house divided against itself shall not stand.** In reading 1541-11 Cayce gives some excellent advice for preventing a house from becoming divided against itself: *Minimize the faults. As ye would be forgiven, forgive others. Magnify the virtues, for the Lord thy God is a jealous God. So in thy own experience a soft word turneth away wrath, grievous words stirreth up anger. The sowing of the seed of the spirit bringeth peace. The sowing of the seed of strife bringeth contention.* A second reference to this verse is from 4651-1: [It is] **Never** *well that there be discord...Well that the body live alone, or in another place than with the brother, for harmony and for* [the] *best interest* [of both]. *For, a house divided can not stand.*

Being circumspect is conducive to harmony. Here is Ephesians 5:15: **See then that ye walk circumspectly, not as fools, but as wise.** Cayce refers to this verse in 262-5: *Tell not thine neighbor how he, or she, should act. Hast thou been put under the same circumstance? Rather give each that standard they may measure themselves by, and be equal -* through such measurements *to the needs of each hour, each circumstance. Walk thine self circumspect in the knowledge thou hast of thine* own *God.*

Here is another reference to walking circumspectly from 254-26: ...*Walk circumspectly before all men. Honest with self, with family* [and] *with associates...*[Honest also in] *all communications.*

Our last reference to Ephesians 5:15, from 272-7, for a young lady: ...*walk this day...circumspectly in thine own conscience...that there may come into thine experience those joys of the* right *association...of another* [and] *eventually there will come that which will bring harmony, joy and a* constructive *life...*

Isaiah 1:18 contains some good advice on harmonious relationships: **Come now, and let us reason together...** Cayce makes reference to this verse in the following portion of reading 1397-1: *First...study what ye believe* (**also**) *study what the other individual believes. Put these together. Coordinate those where cooperation can be had. Stop finding differences. Reason together. This will be to the mutual advantage of each.*

15

GOD WITHIN

The readings say that the body is closely related to the mind and the soul. Taking proper care of the body is as much a reflection of our divine stewardship as anything we do. I Corinthians 6:19, quoted more than 300 times in the Edgar Cayce readings, tells us that our body is the temple of the Holy Ghost: **Know ye not that your body is the temple of the Holy Ghost, which is in you, which ye have of God...** The usual words from the readings are, *Thy body is the temple of the living God.* In reading 3936-1 Cayce added, *and there He has promised to meet thee.* In reading 3174-1, which was a health reading, he added, *What have you dragged into this Temple.* In one reading Cayce says that it is as much of a sin to eat too much as it is to drink too much, and he was not speaking of water. Here is a reference from reading 281-56: *For, thy body* [is] *indeed the temple of the living God, where He has promised to meet thee - consecrate thyself, thy purposes, thy abilities, to that awareness of the abiding faith and hope that may be aroused within - by supping with thy Lord.*

Another reference to I Corinthians 6:19 is found in reading 262-82: *Hast thou met with Him in thine inner chamber of thine own temple? Ye* believe *that your body is the temple of the living God...Then begin to put same into practice, making practical application of that thou hast gained...*

Our final reference to I Corinthians 6:19 is from reading 281-41: *That He gave of old is as new today as it was in the beginning...call on Him* within *thine inner self! Know that thy body is the temple of the living God.* There *He has promised to meet thee!*

John 14:10 also speaks of God within: **Believest thou not that I am in the Father and the Father in me? The words that I speak unto you I speak not of myself: but the Father that dwelleth in me, he doeth the works** Reading 262-29 makes reference to this verse: *...He thought it not robbery to be equal with the Father, yet of Himself did nothing, "but the Father that worketh in me, through me." Do thou likewise, that thou may know the consciousness of the Christ Spirit, and experience the operation of that witness, that "My Spirit beareth witness with thy spirit, that the*

Father may be glorified in you, even as I am glorified in the Father through you."

Our second reference to John 14:10 is from reading 1152-4: *...as the inn could not contain His birth, neither could the grave contain His Body; because of* it being purified, *in love, in service, in harmony to God's Will. For, "Not of myself," saith He "but the Father that worketh in and through me do I bring thee health, do I bring thee hope, do I bring thee the living waters."* Our concluding reference to this verse is from 1299-1: *Know then that the force in nature that is called...electricity is that same force ye worship as Creative or God in action...spirit, mind, body...are as the trinity...the Father, the Son, the Spirit - The Body, the Mind, the Spirit - these are one. One Spirit, One God, One Activity. Then see Him, know Him...as the Son gave, "I of myself may do nothing, but as the Father worketh in me, through me."*

Psalm 82:6 seems to support the concept of God within: **I have said, Ye are gods; and all of you are children of the Most High.** Reading 262-64 makes reference to the idea that "Ye are gods": *Apply, then, that thou hast received. Know ye within yourselves as to how, in what manner and as to what fruit it will bring in thine own experience. For, as has been given, "We believed for the word of the woman, but now we believe for we have seen and heard ourselves." Apply ye that ye know, for in the application comes understanding. For, as the Master gave, "Ye* are *gods," if ye will use His force of desire and will in His kingdom, but* not *thine own.*

Our second reference to Psalm 82:6 is from reading 699-1: *In giving...a soul* [grows just] *as a tree...*[just] *as a world* grows *in its influence upon that about it. So has that force grown that we find manifested in the earth...as constructive influence of God...the All-Wise purpose...the Holy Spirit...those influences that make alive in giving, in* making *itself manifest. So* [in this same manner] *are ye gods in the making...* Growing through living, giving, and doing.

Our last reference to this verse is from reading 816-3, and seems to begin where the previous one ended: *Ye ARE indeed gods in the making! Then...*[act] *as the sons of a merciful Father; and* [just] *as ye would have mercy and find grace and have peace, so must ye show mercy, so must ye be peaceful* [in order] *that ye may become aware of the indwelling of His presence in thine inner self.*

We need to sense His presence within in order to believe He's really there.

16

MAN'S PURPOSE

A lawyer asked the Master what he should do to have eternal life. Jesus responded by asking him what is written in the law. His response is in Luke 10:27: **And he answering said; Thou shalt love the lord thy God, with all thy heart; and with all thy soul; and with all thy strength; and with all thy mind; and thy neighbor as thy self.** The essence of this verse is quoted over 100 times in the Edgar Cayce readings. Here is an example from 281-19: *Keep thine feet firm in the way the Lord may direct thee, knowing that His whole gospel is in, "Love the Lord thy God with all thine heart, and thy neighbor as thyself." In thy activities, then, make the way known that the Christ loves every soul - and wills that none should be lost.* Rules provide partial answers but love can provide exactly what is needed for any situation. Love is not as restraining as rules but demands more from us. A person that just obeys the rules is trying to save himself. Whereas, those who love are trying to serve God.

Loving our neighbor as ourselves is reasonably clear. We are to love our neighbor with the same amount of love that we have for ourselves. We are to genuinely love both our neighbor and ourselves. But, just what does loving God with all our heart mean? To start with, to me it means simply to love that which is good and to stay in touch with the God of my being through regular prayer and meditation. It also means to be productive, creative, and helpful. Each person must seek within themselves to find how loving God with all their heart is to manifest in their life. This is the first of the two great commandments and by its very nature is dynamic rather than fixed. The second great commandment to love others as we love ourselves is also dynamic but man continues to make hundreds of laws in an effort to spell this one out for us.

Here is Matthew 16:26: **For what is a man profited, if he shall gain the whole world, and lose his soul? or what shall a man give in exchange for his soul?** Cayce refers to this verse in reading 262-121 as follows: *...let thy desires be in the ways that are in keeping with those activities that...indicate to self...*[and] *others where thy heart and thy purpose lies. For, though ye gain the whole world in every way of fortune, fame or what*

not, and lose hold of that love that cometh from just being kind and pa-
tient, ye have lost that harmony, that peace which comes from being at
one with Him. The traditional interpretation of this verse has focused on
the idea that gaining everything in this life means surrendering your
chance for eternal life. As this reading reveals, if you make acquisition of
wealth and power your purpose in life you *have lost that harmony, that*
peace which comes from being at one with Him. This is the price you pay,
not in the next life, but, today, here and now, in this life.

In Genesis 1:28 God gives instructions that man is to subdue the earth:
And God blessed them and God said unto them, Be fruitful and multiply
and replenish the earth and subdue it: and have dominion over the fish
of the sea and over the fowl of the air, and over every living thing that
moveth upon the earth. In reading 262-99 Cayce mentions this verse:
...this...should be...a real turning point in your individual, *personal ex-*
perience; as you...have emptied yourselves [and] *laid the ground*
work...as was given to man, "Subdue the earth." For all therein has been
given for...man's understanding, for man's interpreting of God's relation-
ship to man. And when man makes same only a gratifying, a satisfying of
self, whether in appetite, in desire, in selfish motives for self-aggrandize-
ment, self-exaltation, these become - as from old - stumblingblocks. Cayce
seems to be saying that man needs to subdue within himself that which is
earthy. Indeed, is there anything on planet earth today that is in such need
of being subdued as those human qualities enumerated in this reading.

Here is Matthew 7:14: **Strait is the gate and narrow is the way, which**
leadeth unto life, and few there be that find it. Cayce refers to this verse in
reading 3394-2 for a 54-year-old osteopath: *...being true to self would be*
the better...and then you will not be false to any...The way to a certain
place is paved with good intentions...Be on the straight and narrow way.
Some may jump to the conclusion that the *certain place* that is referred to
in this reading is hell. However, the readings emphasize, in many places,
that intentions are more important than deeds and thus, *certain place,* as
used here, means heaven not hell, both of which are states of consciousness rather than places in the usual sense. Be that as it may, the important
thing here, in this verse, is the same as that found in the previous verse,
Genesis 1:28, which emphasizes the need for self-discipline. Many of us
have probably struggled with this in many lifetimes. A concept that has
been helpful to me is that the true source of these rules on self-discipline
is not some external God, out there, somewhere. The true source that
speaks to me regularly about my own disciplinary needs is internal. It is
also eternal. (It's either now or later and the longer I delay the more difficult it may be to change.) This Disciplinary Source is none other than my
own Higher Self. So, self-discipline is not external encroachment upon

my freedom, but an Internal Director instructing me how to use my freedom, constructively rather than destructively. The Master's pathway is filled with light and life because the negative and destructive influences have been eliminated. The Christ Consciousness is a better term than those I have used, such as, Disciplinary Source, Higher Self, and Internal Director. But these other terms help clarify some of the functions of Christ Consciousness.

Here is Psalm 19:2: **Day unto Day uttereth speech and night unto night sheweth knowledge.** Cayce refers to this verse in the following portion of reading 262-92: **Know** *that thy ability, thy service, begins first with* **cooperation** *in* being *that channel through which the Glory of the Lord may be manifested in the earth! For, "The earth* is *the Lord's, and the fullness thereof - Day unto day uttereth speech, and night unto night sheweth knowledge." If ye would, then,* [fulfill] *that whereunto thou hast been called, let thy Glory - let thy knowledge - let thy* wisdom *be in the Lord!*

I Corinthians 12:29 states: **Are all apostles? Are all prophets? Are all teachers? Are all workers of miracles? Have all the gifts of healing? Do all speak with tongues? Do all interpret?** Cayce refers to this verse in reading 281-60: *Let each individual know that it came into life with a purpose from God. Let each individual know that it is as a harp upon which the breath of God would play. While all may not be as prophets or as preachers, neither may all stand in the halls of learning as directors of men,* [but] *know that you each have your part to do.* Reflection on this verse and related reading may lead you to review your own talents and potentials to determine just what your role should be. Most of us are probably fulfilling the role for which we are best suited, but, for some, there may be need for a change.

If ye love me, keep my commandments. Cayce quotes this verse–John 14:15–in the following segment of reading 262-111: *Happiness...is of love divine; manifesting in the experiences as one gives a cup of water in His name, that may bring much greater Happiness than to he that taketh a city, or to he that ruleth even a nation. You each are endowed...with power only from one source, but to know Happiness...is to do the biddings of the Father; or as He gave, "If ye love me, keep my commandments..."*

Jesus fasted for forty days in the wilderness and then the tempter said, if you are the son of God, command there stones to become loaves of bread. Jesus gives his reply in Matthew 4:4: **But he answered and said, It is written, Man shall not live by bread alone, but by every word that proceedeth out of the mouth of God.** Bread nourishes only the body. Our more important need is for nourishment of our mind and soul. This verse is referenced in the following portion of reading 2583-1: *...He is mindful of thee. Hast thou taken thought, or dost thou take thought of what ye* *owe Him? Not that any soul* [should be] *goody-goody, but good* for *something; not merely to supply material needs. For man lives not by bread alone, not by apparel, nor by homes, nor by that which is of the earth-earthy, but rather by the spirit of truth. And do ye make the world better for living in same? Are individuals, are groups that ye meet day by day improved in any phase by thy having met with them? These questions ye alone must answer. For they refuse to be put aside. For they are a part of thy experience.*

John the Baptist is a good example of a man who knew his purpose and mission in life, which was to prepare the way for the ministry of Jesus Christ, as said in Mark 1:3: **The voice of one crying in the wilderness, Prepare ye the way of the Lord, make his paths straight.** The following reading, 2021-1, for a 23-year-old man, refers to making our path straight: *…each soul enters that it may make its paths straight. For they alone who walk the straight and narrow way may know themselves to be themselves, and yet one with the Creative Forces. Hence the purpose for each entrance is that the opportunities may be embraced by the entity for living, being, that which is creative and in keeping with the Way.* Live creatively. Be the best co-creator you can be, right now, today. This is our purpose and our destiny expressed in the broadest terms.

We need to listen carefully to determine if we hear the message of the Christ. There seem to be many voices bidding us to follow. Here is John 10:27: **My sheep hear my voice, and I know them, and they follow me.** Reference to this verse is included in the following portion of reading 262-7: *As that* [which is] *known is used, the light cometh. When will that* [known] *be put in more perfect activity? Do not become confused in waiting. Be not over-anxious* [and think] *that any source, any channel, would do. Know that He whom* thou *hast* named *has directed, for "My sheep will hear my voice, and not heed* any *other."*

Habakkuk 2:2 states: **And the Lord answered me, and said, write the vision, and make it plain upon the table, that he may run that readeth it.** The following reading, 262-99, refers to this verse: *For as given, the way the Master has shown is so simple that he who runs may read* [it]. *It is so mighty that the powers that be in the earth become subservient to same. It maketh the weak strong; it maketh the strong humble.*

One of the parables told by Jesus is known as the parable of the sower. In Matthew 13:23 He is explaining this parable to the disciples: **But he that received seed into the good ground is he that heareth the word, and understandeth it; which also beareth fruit, and bringeth forth, some an hundred fold, some sixty, some thirty.** Reading 281-9 mentions this verse: *Be sincere in self and in that sought. More and more will the aid come, as there is added to thine own self those* [qualities] *of love, and patience,* *and charity, and long-suffering.* [In doing] *So will there be awakened that* [which] *makes for the unison of strength for those that each seek to aid. Be not weary in welldoing, for* much *has been accomplished here, much has been relieved, that will bear fruits - some forty, some sixty, some an hundred-fold.*

The writer of Hebrews 11:10 speaks of Abraham, a tent dweller, and his search for heaven: **For he looked for a city which hath foundations, whose builder and maker is God.** Reference to this verse is included in reading 262-104: *...ye have not that which may be touched with hands. Ye have sought, ye have said - each of you "I seek a city without foundations, whose builder and maker is God."* That *is Wisdom!* You may have noticed that the city sought by Abraham **hath foundations**; whereas the city identified in the readings is *without foundations.*

Apparently Abraham's vision of heaven was more earth like than the heavenly vision of the members of the study group for which this reading was given. The other possibility is that the biblical account, as we have it, is not correct. In concluding this chapter on man's purpose, it may be well to point out that the title of the book used by the Edgar Cayce study groups is *A Search for God.*

17

SERVICE TO OTHERS

We may be inclined to view service to others as something that is required of us. However, the Edgar Cayce readings say we should see this as one of life's privileges. There may be times when we want to serve in one capacity, but because of circumstances beyond our control, must serve in some other way. I try to see service as a privilege, but must admit there are times when this is difficult. The One who has shown us the way believed in and practiced service to others. Here are His words from Matthew 23:11: **He that is greatest among you shall be your servant.** This message was included in more than 150 readings. Here is an example from 1799-1, for a 28-year-old male actor: *Seek to be that which is the* **greatest** *of all - the servant of all!* In reading 3420-1, for a 57-year-old female writer, Cayce said, *For who is the greatest? He that is the servant of all, he that contributes that which makes each soul glad to be alive, glad to have the opportunity to contribute something to the welfare of his brother.*

The desire or drive to excel in what we do is a primary source of motivation in our culture. There are many ways in which we can serve the needs, hopes, and desires of others. In these two readings both the actor and the writer were being told that, in order to excel, to be great, they must set as their goal, not the gratification of their ego, but their vision must be that of rendering service to others. For the writer this is identified as making other people *glad to be alive.* They are to bring joy to their readers and audience. Reading 5758-1 also makes reference to Matthew 23:11: *He that is the greatest will be the servant of all.* [Just] *as the Master signified in the bathing of the feet...in the preparation of the food* [so] *that* [those] *weary in body, in mind might be supplied...He requires of everyone, "feed my lambs, feed my sheep."*

In Genesis 4:9, after killing his brother Able, Cain is questioned by God and says, "Am I my brother's keeper?" God's response makes it clear that the answer to Cain's question is, Yes, you are: **And the Lord said unto Cain, Where is Able, thy brother? And he said, I know not. Am I my brother's keeper?** In reading 257-134 for a 41-year-old man, Cayce made the following reference to being our brother's keeper: *...all must come to the* knowledge that "*I* am *my brother's keeper.*" *And until the world, or those in authority, those in power...of...the exchange medium between individual groups...recognize that this is true, and that each group is dependent one upon another, little progress of a lasting nature* [may] *be made.* As indicated in this reading, it was Cayce's position that the economic depression of the 1930s resulted from greed, selfishness, and man's failure to recognize that he is his brother's keeper.

Here is a second reference to this verse from 5398-1: *Does mankind consider he is indeed his brother's keeper?...There will be no want in bread for mankind when mankind eventually realizes he is indeed his brother's keeper. For the earth is the Lord's...and the bounty in one land is lent to man to give his brother. Who is his brother?...each of every land, of every color, of every creed is brother of those who seek the Father, God.* Our last reference to this verse is from reading 5142-1: *God cannot think more of thee than ye think of yourself, or more than that measure in which ye treat thy brother...Thou art then thy brother's keeper, in mind, in purpose, in ideal; not to force it upon thy brother by the power of arms or by the might of circumstance. For God himself did not force it upon Cain.*

Traditional interpretation of Luke 12:48 - **...unto whomsoever much is given, of him shall be much required...** - is that the privileged groups are to clearly understand that something extra is expected from them. Cayce refers to this verse in the following advice to a male 43-year-old probation officer in reading 473-1: *Let thy going in, thine coming out, be in meekness of purpose serving the Lord. For unto him that is given much, much is required at his hand. "If ye love me," as He has given, "feed my lambs. Feed my sheep." For the service is unto thine brethren...*

I Corinthians 5:6 says: **...Know ye not that a little leaven leaveneth the whole lump.** Cayce's advice to a 34-year-old housewife which refers to this verse appears in reading 1444-1: *...each opportunity for associations or relations carries with it...the obligation...to be a channel of...constructive influences in the lives of individuals. Not as the answering to the curious...*[or] *to those that have only social or curious associations being sought, but that the spoken word, the activity, the suggestion...made by the entity - if it is constructive - becomes the leaven that may leaven the whole lump.* Cayce refers to leaven as something good that would act as a seed for more good. In I Corinthians the focus is on unleavened bread as a symbol of truth. Thus, Paul's message here is that a little leaven (sin) could contaminate the whole church and therefore it must be purged.

Our second reference to this verse, from 5395-1, seems to say, don't over do it, even with the good leaven: *This is a period when...there may be established harmonious reactions among the groups which make for the social...political...*[and] *human conditions of many lands. The application of the tenets of truth, spiritual truths - not in gobs* [but] *in small doses - remembering... "It is the little leaven that leaveneth the whole lump."...in knowledge, in understanding* [will] *bring...unified activity...*

Mark 10:45 speaks of the service Christ rendered to the world: **For even the Son of man came not to be ministered unto, but to minister, and to give his life a ransom for many.** Cayce refers to this verse in reading 993-1: *...through self a knowledge of the universe may be obtained...the acquaintance of self with universal influences and forces gives one an insight into aiding another seeking to know something of self. Keep in attunement with the all creative energy, knowing that through Him who gave Himself a ransom for many the understanding comes...He is the way, the light, the door* [and] *self may be aided by Him in that* [which] *self would gain or attain.*

Here is a second reference to Mark 10:45 from reading 5749-10: *...show joy and gladness in the lives, the experiences, the hearts, the minds of those ye meet day by day; thus becoming indeed brethren with Him* [who] *gave Himself as a ransom for all...*

Galations 6:2 tells us to lend a helping hand much as Christ did: **Bear ye one another's burdens, and so fulfill the law of Christ.** Reading 262-29 mentions this verse: *Be patient, long-suffering, bearing one another's burdens. Be joyous in the Lord. Be not tempestuous in manner, thought, act or deed; rather serving in humbleness of spirit. Enjoy the labors. Enjoy those things that make for the unison of thought in Him, knowing ye have been called...*

A second reference to Galations 6:2 from reading 262-97 follows: *THIS is knowledge, that ye love one another, that ye show forth in thy dealings with thy fellow man day by day that thou carest, thou understandest, thou art willing to take a portion of the burden of those that are so heavily burdened with the cares of life, the cares of the world, the deceitfulness of riches; that thou art willing to aid those in distress, thou art willing to feed those that are hungry - not just materially. For the world is crying* [out] *for that Knowledge.* Our third reference is from 295-9: *...His will - the Christ way - be done in thee, that others may know...as He has given, bear ye one another's burdens and thus fulfill the law of love.*

Remember, we are to see service to others as a privilege rather than a duty or obligation. A few people were told in their readings that they would not have to reincarnate again on planet earth. One lady who was given this message was asked how she felt about it. Her response was that she would be glad to come back as long as she could be of service. This may well be the attitude required for graduation!

18

FAITH

The writer of II Timothy 1:12 makes his faith in Jesus Christ very clear: **...I know whom I have believed, and am persuaded that he is able to keep that which I have committed unto him against that day.** This verse is quoted 200 times in the Edgar Cayce readings. In reading 3515-1 Cayce's words are, ***Know in Whom ye believe and in what ye believe.*** In 2408-1 the words are, ***...He is able, He is willing, He keepeth His promises to the children of men.*** In 1661-1 the individual was told, ***...He is able to keep that ye commit unto Him against any experience that may arise...***

Some may question how they can come to know Jesus better and how they can increase their faith and trust in Him. My thought is that they may wish to avail themselves of a red letter edition of the Bible and study carefully the words of Christ, with the feeling that these words are being spoken directly to them by the Master. It would be helpful to follow this period of study with a time of prayer and meditation focused upon these words. Of course, incorporating the message into our daily life is necessary for real understanding.

Job with all of his pain and loss never loses his faith, as shown in Job 19:25: **For I know that my redeemer liveth and that he shall stand at the latter day upon the earth.** In reading 1523-17 a 35-year-old female asked for Cayce's comments on "A.R.E. personnel turmoils" which were of concern to her. Here is his reply: ***Find the answers deep within self. For, as indicated, know thy Redeemer liveth. He may live in and with thee. Open the door. Coordinate purposes with hopes, with desires. Then act that way; expecting thyself to do thy share and thy Lord, thy Christ, to do His - and He will!***

Revelation 2:10 was addressed to the church at Smyrna. There was great persecution and many of the early members were faithful unto death, dying as martyrs: **...Be thou faithful unto death, and I will give thee a crown of life.** In reading 281-17 Cayce makes reference to this verse in the following message for a 58-year-old doctor: ***Be patient, be kind. Be gentle in thy ministering day by day; for though there may come those periods when the burden seems heavy, and the light fades in the life, yet he that is*** *faithful unto the end shall wear the crown.*

Here is one of the promises of the Master in Matthew 21:22: **And all things, whatsoever ye shall ask in prayer believing, ye shall receive.** Cayce cites this verse in the following comment to a 56-year-old choral director in reading 556-1: *... "serve a living God."...not one of position or power, but...that which lives in the hearts and souls of those that come and seek as He gave, "As ye ask in my name, believing, it will be done unto thee..." So let the inner self direct thee...Do not lift others to an exalted position but rather, as He, stoop down where they are, that they may...become aware that the Father...[speaks] to them today.*

In I Corinthians 16:13 Paul encourages the followers to hang in there: **Watch ye, stand fast in the faith, quit you like men, be strong.** In current translations, be courageous, is used in place of, **quit you like men.** Reading 281-26, for the Prayer Healing Group makes reference to this verse as follows: *...in thy undertakings be...that ye are - the sons and daughters of a merciful, heavenly Father. Do ye quit yourselves like men; do ye act in a way and manner...that one not knowing* [what you have] *claimed, would know that* [you have] *chosen to be a channel for the manifestation of that love in the earth?*

The writer of Hebrews 11:1 gives us a frequently quoted definition of faith: **Now faith is the substance of things hoped for, the evidence of things not seen.** In reading 262-12 Cayce was asked, "How may I increase my faith?" Here is his reply: *Use that thou hast in hand, has been the command from the beginning, will be unto the end, as to how to increase faith. Faith, the substance of things hoped for, evidences of things unseen. Using that known brings those attunements, those emoluments in every form, that makes for creative Forces in themselves - which is, must be, the basis of faith.* There is no substitute for the personal application of spiritual principles for those who wish to grow spiritually.

In Matthew 9.29 two blind men came to be healed. Jesus asked them if they believed he could heal them and they replied that they did. **Then touched he their eyes, saying, According to your faith be it unto you.** Cayce refers to this verse in reading 281-5 for the Prayer Healing Group: *The concerted effort on the part of a group merely accentuates that...force, or power, that may manifest in or through an individual...Hence, the activity must be as much on the part of* [the] *one seeking aid through such a channel. Remember, there was given through that same channel as these would ask: "Thy healing be according to thy faith."...To another, with the laying on of hands, was said, "According to thy faith, so be it unto you."...consider* [these things] *in thy meditation, in thy prayer.* Thus, according to this reading, for prayer healing to be effective for another person, that person must also be praying for their own healing. A ten fold accentuation of zero would be zero. This reading applies to prayers for physical healing. Sending love and light to all for whom we have concern is always good.

The writer of II Timothy 4:7 feels he has reached the end of the road: **I have fought a good fight, I have finished my course, I have kept the faith.** Reference to this verse is included in reading 5330-1: *...keep the faith. Ye know in whom ye have believed. Trust others, yes,* [but] *not to thine own undoing...if ye would have friends, be friendly. If ye would have others, to have faith in thee, have faith in them. Keep the faith!* Trust others, particularly, those that have proven themselves trustworthy.

God promised Abram he would have an heir and in Genesis 15:6 we find these words: **And he believed in the Lord; and He counted it to him for righteousness.** Reading 262-53 quotes this verse: *In those periods when there are the doubts and the fears that arise, these are as the testing times in each soul's experience. He that endureth, he that looketh to the promises - and believes and acts in that manner, to him it is counted as righteousness.*

When the disciples were unable to heal an epileptic son, the father brought the boy to Jesus and the boy was healed. The disciples then asked the Master why they had failed. Here is Matthew 17:20: **And Jesus said unto them, Because of your unbelief: For verily I say unto you, If ye have faith as a grain of mustard seed, ye shall say unto this mountain, Remove hence to yonder place, and it shall remove; and nothing shall be impossible unto you.** Thus, our effectiveness in prayer healing for others is related to their prayers and *faith* as well as our prayers and *faith.* Cayce makes reference to this verse in the following portion of 262-14: *...as has been said, ye with faith, as much as a mustard seed may say unto the mountain be thou removed and cast into the sea.* Most *say they believe, and yet begin at once to explain...how this means in the mental rather than in the material source. Hence we find faith not of the senses, else it becomes confidence in personalities...within themselves or others. Then, when troubles and doubts arise, they immediately begin to sink, even as Peter in the presence of Life itself.*

Here is Mark 9:23: **And Jesus said unto him, If thou canst believe, all things are possible to him that believeth.** In reading 5749-4 Cayce was asked, "How may I raise my vibrations so as to contact the Christ?" He refers to this verse, as well as Matthew 9:29, in his reply: [By] *Making the will, the desire of the heart, one with His; believing in faith, in practice, all becomes possible in Him,* [and] *through Him to the Father; for, He gave it as it is. Believest thou? Then, according to thy faith be it done in thee.*

Our concluding verse deals principally with belief, which is not the same thing as faith. Here is James 2:19: **Thou believest that there is one**

God; thou doest well: the devils also believe, and tremble. In reading 262-119, Cayce was asked to comment on "The devil and Satan, which deceiveth the whole world; he was sent out into the earth." This statement had been included in a prior reading. Reference to this verse is included in his reply: *Did He not - the Christ, the Maker - say this over and over again? that so long as spite, selfishness, evil desires, evil communications were manifested, they would give the channels through which* that *spirit called satan, devil, Lucifer, Evil One, might work? Also He has said over and over again that even the devil believes, but trembles - and that is as far as he has gone except to try to deceive others. Then he that denies in his life, in his dealings with his fellow man, that the Spirit of Truth maketh free, denies his Lord!*

The point I wish to leave with you is this: Belief is a human quality. Faith is a spiritual quality. Faith transcends belief just as Christ love transcends romantic love.

19

FORGIVENESS

Forgiveness is one of the most important spiritual principles that we must embrace. Luke 6:37 which was quoted more than 100 times in the Edgar Cayce readings states: **Forgive, and ye shall be forgiven.** Reading 1968-1, for a 28-year-old lady, includes the following reference to this verse: *Be not puritanic, for as ye would be forgiven, so forgive those who disappoint and disturb thee oft in their shortcomings.* Here is a second reference from 262-21: *"Forgive me, Father, even as I forgive my brother" should be that lesson...that...position each would take, would they know the face of Him who seeks fellowship with His creatures...may the Father gather those close that would seek fellowship with Him.* Know *that as ye forgive will ye be forgiven.* There are a number of key ideas contained in the Lord's Prayer. One of these is a request that we be forgiven as we forgive others. In order to stress the importance of this, immediately following the text of this prayer in Matthew 6:14-15 Jesus tells us that the heavenly Father will forgive us only if we forgive others. I do not feel that the importance of forgiveness can be overemphasized. Most of the people who have come to me for spiritual counseling have difficulty forgiving others and/or themselves. Forgiveness is a key to avoiding criticism and condemnation. God's forgiveness is always available to us. But, as long as we insist on our right to hold on to our resentments and grievances, feeling they are more than justified by past events, we thereby block ourselves from receiving God's unlimited love and forgiveness. We must leave judgment to God and in the meantime be hopeful, patient, loving, and forgiving.

It is just as important to forgive ourselves as it is to forgive others. I John 2:1 seems to recognize this need: **My little children these things write I unto you, that ye sin not. And if any man sin, we have an advocate with the Father, Jesus Christ the righteous.** In the following reading, 1440-1, for a female high school teacher, Cayce makes reference to our "advocate with the father." *Only* [in] *the promises, the faith, the activity...for whom and from...there has been obtained an advocate with the Father may mercies be shown* [to thee]...*only as ye show patience, longsuffering,* *brotherly kindness, may these be shown to thee. For thou art indeed a god in its making, for He would have thee as one with Him; yet the choices must be made by thee, or else ye become only as an automaton...Be not...merely good, but...good for something - in His name!*

In Luke 23:34 Jesus asks God to forgive those who have crucified him, giving us an example of the level of forgiveness that we must strive to achieve: **Then said Jesus, Father forgive them; for they know not what they do...** This verse is referred to in reading 262-109: *Happiness then is knowing, being in touch with, manifesting in the daily life, divine love. Being glad when you are persecuted for His name's sake, being in that attitude of forgiving those who speak unkindly, being in that mind that was in Him when He gave, "Father, forgive them, they know not what they do", and not saying under your breath, "Poor saps! I'm the one persecuted but they are the ones that must receive the damnation," for you have turned it then on self.* Our prayers must always be totally honest, sincere, and truthful, otherwise, as the readings might say, we are only fooling ourselves.

Revelation 7:14 speaks of forgiveness symbolically in terms of washing our robes and making them white in the blood of the Lamb: **And I said unto him, Sir, thou knowest. And he said to me, These are they which come out in great tribulation, and have washed their robes, and made them white in the blood of the Lamb.** This verse, as well as James 5:20, are referenced in 262-58: *Let the love of the Father in the Son guide thee. Be not impatient, nor be thou longing for those things that are other than the love of the Father in the Son... they, as He has promised, that have saved a soul from sin...have covered a multitude of* [their own] *sins, and their robes are washed in the blood of the Lamb...*

In Hebrews 9:22 and the related Cayce reading, there is further discussion of forgiveness as related to the blood of Christ: **And almost all things are by the law purged with blood; and without shedding of blood is no remission.** In reading 262-45 Cayce was asked to explain his previous statement that "the blood of Jesus Christ cleanses from all sin." He replied: *As given, without the shedding of blood there was no remission of sin...the error that man makes is the more oft against himself...love is law...law is love, in its essence...the shedding of the blood in the* man *Jesus made for the atoning of* all *men, through making Himself in at-onement with the law and with love...*[In] *the ...shedding of the blood comes the redemption to man, through that which may make for...man's...at-onement with Him.* His atonement plus His AT ONE MENT makes possible our attunement and AT ONE MENT with Him.

Isaiah 1:18 likens God's forgiveness of sin to changing colors from scarlet or crimson to white: **Come now, and let us reason together, saith the**

Lord; though your sins be as scarlet, they shall be as white as snow, though they be red like crimson, they shall be as wool. In reading 262-28, which mentions this verse, Cayce was asked "Can lost opportunities be redeemed." His reply includes this verse: *Nothing is lost; we have used or abused our opportunities and there abide by them. In Him,* [and] *through Him may they be blotted out, for "Though your sins be as scarlet, in Him they shall be as wool. He that heareth my voice and abideth in me shall* know *no lost opportunity!"* For those on the path, opportunities are continuous. Even those not on the path continue to have ample opportunities for finding the Way.

As long as we live there is opportunity for forgiveness. A thief on a cross next to Jesus said, "Lord remember me when thou comest into thy kingdom." Jesus responds in Luke 23:43: **And Jesus said unto him, Verily I say unto thee, Today shalt thou be with me in paradise.** In reading 262-92 Cayce was asked the meaning of paradise as used in this verse. His reply follows: *The inter-between; the awareness of being in that state of transition between the material and the spiritual phases of consciousness of the Soul. The awareness that there is the companionship of entities or souls, or separate forces in those stages of the development.*

Here is Luke 19:8: **And Zacchaeus stood, and said unto the Lord; Behold, Lord, the half of my goods I give to the poor; and if I have taken any thing from any man by false accusation, I restore him four fold.** Reading 5195-1 was given to an elderly man who was approaching that transition called death. Cayce makes reference to this verse in this reading: *...the time cometh, as it must to this body, when no work is to be done but ye must stand before the judgment bar of thine own conscience, as must each soul, and determine as to whether in the light of the knowledge, in the light of thine opportunity, ye can as thy friend, thy God say, "I have dishonored no man, I have taken naught from my brother, but what I restore fourfold".*

This should serve as a reminder that we need to seek forgiveness, as needed, from others and to make appropriate restitution for our past mistakes.

20

SEEK WITHIN

To seek within is not a new concept and is recommended in Deuteronomy 30:11-14 which may have been originally recorded over 3,000 years ago: **It is not in heaven, that you shouldest say, Who shall go up for us to heaven and bring it unto us, that we may hear it and do it. Neither is it beyond the sea, that thou shouldest say, Who shall go over the sea for us, and bring it unto us, that we may hear it, and do it. But the word is very nigh unto thee in thy mouth, and in thy heart, that thou mayest do it.** Cayce quoted the basic idea from these verses in somewhat abbreviated form to many people. The purpose was clearly to encourage them to seek guidance from within. Reading 5000-1 illustrates Cayce's approach: *...think not who will descend from heaven that ye may hear or know; think not who will come from over the sea that a message may be brought; for lo, it is within thine own self...there is to come within the entity's own consciousness the awareness of how the application is to be made.*

Here is another reference to these verses from reading 5752-5: *The spirit of truth is nigh unto thee; not who will ascend to bring him down or to bring him over the sea, but seek him in thine own heart; for thy soul is the image of thy Father - and as ye seek in truth...in sincerity...so will it be opened unto thee. Today - if ye will hear His voice.*

Our concluding reference to this verse is from reading 5696-1: **[Keep]** *...in accord with that as speaks oft from within. Think not as to who will ascend to make known His will, or who would go that we may hear...making one's will in accord with that as speaks from within gives the sure knowledge and understanding of what He would have us do.*

Revelation 3:20 assures us that He is ever at our door: **Behold, I stand at the door, and knock, if any man hear my voice, and open the door, I will come into him, and will sup with him and he with me.** Cayce includes reference to this verse in the following reading, 987-4, for a 49-year-old housewife: *"...I stand at the door and knock." If ye will but open thy tabernacle of consciousness to allow the holy to come in and sup with thee, yea,* **all** *the beauties of peace and harmony* are *thine; for they are the birthright of each soul.*

A second reference to this verse is found in reading 5246-1: *...ye need those companionships that are in accord with thine own ideas and ye will find them if ye seek...as has been given: "Behold I stand at the door and knock, if ye will open I will enter."...thy mind seeks a Savior, but most of all companionship of the Master* [attracts] *that which* [brings]*...understanding, peace and harmony.*

Our last reference to Revelation 3:20 is from reading 3376-2: *...He can and does say to thee, "Behold I stand at the door and knock. Open!" Ye must open, ye must wish, ye must hope, ye must act in such a manner that He may enter.* [Once this door is opened] *and realized in thy heart, in thy mind, in thy soul, no one may surpass thee in thy accomplishments.* This is a remarkable promise for attunement to inner guidance. The immediate benefit may differ from one person to the next. But, it seems to me that each of us should make the effort.

I Kings 19:12 tells us about the still small voice: **And after the earthquake a fire; but the Lord was not in the fire; and after the fire, a still small voice.** For many years my conception was that this still small inner voice was heard following an external earthquake and fire. While this may be the experience of some, it now seems to me that the earthquake and fire are symbolic of inner experiences, perhaps more emotional than physical. Be that as it may, Cayce makes reference to the still small voice in these words to a member of the Prayer Healing Group in reading 281-22: *...meet thy Lord within. Let Him, in the still, small voice from within guide thee. For, He is not far from thee. Thou only needest to open the door of thy consciousness, that He may enter in.*

Here is a second reference to this verse from 3976-5: *Remember that it was the still small voice, and not the wind nor the lighting, that was the voice of the Creative Energy that rules the world. Remember* [also] *that action - with the correct purpose - builds in the hearts and minds of individuals who are co-workers and ambassadors of that living force we call God.*

Our concluding reference to this verse is from reading 3188-1: *Seek not to justify thyself but rather to glorify God in the earth. Be a channel of blessing to others daily...it is...the still small voice within that convicts, that convinces, that leads the way to truth and light.*

The three Bible references we have looked at thus far in this chapter, Deuteronomy 30:11-14, Revelation 3:20 & I Kings 19:12, were quoted a combined total of 250 times in the Edgar Cayce readings.

Here is a reference to Deuteronomy 30:14 –**But the word is very night unto thee, in thy mouth, and in thy heart, that thou mayest do it**–from reading 262-58: *So simple...is it to know the Father* [but] *all stumble in that they* think *of themselves more highly than they ought to think. Be* *rather as a channel through which the Father may make His love, His glory, manifest in the earth.* Listen *to the voice from within. For, He is very nigh unto each of you, if ye will but look* within...*the desire that thy self be nothing,* [so] *that the Father, the Christ, may be glorified in the earth, brings to the experience of all the consciousness of being a manifestation of the love of the Father to the sons of man.*

Here is a second reference to this verse from 1933-1: *Spiritually, look within. Know, as was pronounced by the lawgiver of old - Lo, it is within thine own heart, thine own bosom that ye may find contentment and happiness.*

21

PRAYER AND MEDITATION

The Edgar Cayce readings frequently recommend regular prayer and meditation. These are defined in reading 281-13: *Prayer is the concerted effort of the physical consciousness to become attuned to the consciousness of the Creator, either collectively or individually!* Meditation *is* emptying *self of all that hinders the creative forces from rising along the natural channels of the physical man to be disseminated through those centers and sources that create the activities of the physical, the mental, the spiritual man; properly done* [this makes] *one* stronger *mentally* [and] *physically...*

John 15:16 makes reference to prayer: **Ye have not chosen me, but I have chosen you, and ordained you, that ye should go and bring forth fruit, and that your fruit should remain; that whatsoever ye shall ask of the Father in my name, he may give it you.** This verse is mentioned in the following message for a member of the Prayer Healing Group in reading 281-1: *That...to be stressed...is raising the Christ Consciousness in self and visualizing its activity upon that one, or those, to whom the aid is to be brought... "As ye ask in* my *name,* believing, *so* shall *it be in the self-same hour..."*

Here is Psalm 19:14: **Let the words of my mouth and the meditations of my heart, be acceptable in thy sight, O Lord, my strength and my redeemer.** If our words are acceptable in God's sight, we have succeeded as teachers. If our meditations are acceptable, it is as though Jesus were at our elbow. In reading 262-58 Cayce had these words of counsel for a 27-year-old man: *Let the words of thy mouth and the meditations of thine heart be acceptable in the sight of Him...What greater manifestations could there be in the inner soul of anyone...than...that those that hear* [you] *may know that thou hast indwelling in thine inmost soul the knowledge of the Father, in the Son, and the* love *of the Father to the sons of men!*

The evening before Jesus is to be crucified He prays this prayer in Luke 22:42: **Father, if thou be willing, remove this cup from me: nevertheless not my will, but thine, be done.** A 40-year-old female writer asked Cayce for some thoughts or a meditation that would help her to overcome the crisis in her life. Here is his reply in reading 954-5: **"O God! Not my will, not my purpose but thine!"** *Remember the prayer...He gave.* **"If possible let this cup pass from me...not my·will [but] thine, O God be done in and through me! Here am I, Lord - use me..."** We should never try to hide from God our heart's desire. And, we need to remember that Jesus' attitude was not one of resignation but rather one of glad surrender.

The Bible comes to life for people in times of trouble and in Psalm 102:2 one finds times of trouble: **Hide not thy face from me in the day when I am in trouble; incline thine ear unto me: in the day when I call answer me speedily.** It will be noted that the author of this verse is asking God to answer speedily when he calls. Cayce's reference to this verse gives assurance that God will answer promptly. In reading 262-69 Cayce refers to this verse in the following comment to a 38-year-old housewife: *...as the heavens open before thee...thine prayers have been heard, thine supplications have come before the Throne. Be not weary in thy turmoil or thy strife, for He has heard and will answer speedily.*

In Hosea 6:6 God gives his people some instructions: **For I desire mercy, and not sacrifice; and the knowledge of God more than burnt offerings.** This idea of mercy instead of sacrifice is discussed in reading 262-71 as follows: *...ever may thy prayer be, "Mercy, Lord - not sacrifice," and it will break a light in thine heart and mind that will bring peace, harmony and joy...* The law of mercy is discussed in reading 262-72: *...the law of mercy...is demonstrated in the life of...Jesus...who offered Himself as the sacrifice...for all...as many as have named the Name - come under the law of mercy,* not *of sacrifice...not...that no man offers sacrifice, for the life of every soul that seeks in the material world to demonstrate the spiritual life is a life of sacrifice* from *the material angle...*

The Master includes some words of advice on prayer in Matthew 6:6: **But thou when thou prayest enter into thy closet, and when thou hast shut thy door, pray to the Father which is in secret and thy Father which seeth in secret shall reward thee openly.** In reading 2842-2 a 38-year-old lady wanted to know how best to draw people of the right vibration to her. I've met many people who would like to do this! Cayce cites this verse in his reply: *By the correct vibration in self. Like begets like...when thou prayest enter into thine closet, or into thine self, and thine Father that see-eth in secret shall reward thee openly.* Our prayer must be sincere. We need to be free of all distractions when we pray and to be completely open with our Creator. Also, we should begin by expressing gratitude for all the blessings we now enjoy.

Jesus tells his followers not to use empty phrases as do the Gentiles, and in Matthew 6:8 gives the following advice: **Be not ye therefore like** unto them; for your Father knoweth what things ye have need of, before you ask him. The following reading, 262-64, makes reference to this verse: *Thou hast been given that thine heavenly Father knoweth what ye have need of before ye ask. Then the weak or the pessimist may say, "Why do I have need to ask, if it is known?" The very act* [of asking] *shows what the desire is. The very expression shows...what is the motivative force in the experience of...*[the] *soul. But seek ye For he that seeketh findeth. To him that knocketh it shall be opened.*

Here is John 14:4: **And whither I go ye know, and the way ye know.** The following portion of reading 281-3, for the Prayer Healing Group, makes reference to this verse *... seek through meditation, singleness of purpose, to be guided* [to] *that...in which each may* be *a channel of blessing to those who seek. In this manner may ye know the way; for, as has been given, "I go - and the* way *ye know." The manner in which each may know they are* in *attune, is the ability to feel that consciousness of the sincere desire* within *to* be *a blessing, A channel, to someone.*

Matthew 5:15 says: **Neither do men light a candle, and put it under a bushel, but on a candlestick. and it giveth light unto all that are in the house.** Reading 341-31 for a 23-year-old man refers to this verse: *When thou prayest, enter into thine closet - that is, within self - not shutting oneself away from the world, but closing self* [into] *God's* presence, *and pray in secret and the reward will be in the open; for, as was given, "Men do not light a candle and put it under a bushel, but it is set...on a hill, that it may give* life [and] *light, unto all."*

Psalm 51:10 is a prayer request that is just as important today as it was thousands of years ago. **Create in me a clean heart, O God, and renew a right spirit within me.** Cayce mentions this verse in the following words of a prayer, he gave, for use by a member of Study Group 1 in reading 262-118: *"Father, keep Thou my mind, my heart open to thy calls! May I choose ever the spirit of the Christ to be the author of my activities day by day. May I be patient and longsuffering. May I be gentle - yea, may I be humble. For without these, the very activity may become a stumblingblock. Then, keep my heart pure. Renew the righteous spirit within me, O God! day by day! May I hear again, as in the days of yore, the voice of the Christ as He calls to men to renew their faith and manifest their love of God in their dealings with their fellow man. "May I fill that purpose whereunto Thou hast called me into service in the vineyard of the Christ..."*

Here is a promise by the Master in Matthew 18:19: **Again I say unto you, That if two of you shall agree on earth as touching any thing that they shall ask, it shall be done for them of my Father which is in heaven.** Cayce refers to this verse in reading 5346-1 for a 53-year-old man: *...the judgment of two is better than one, and where two agree and they ask, believ-*

ing it may come to pass. Do not ask for, then, selfish things lest they turn upon thee and destroy thy good purposes. Ask only as the Lord wills.

The disciples were not able to heal a boy who had had convulsions since early childhood. After this youth was healed by Jesus, the disciples asked why they could not cast out the unclean spirit. Here is the Master's reply in Mark 9:29: **And he said unto them, This kind can come forth by nothing, but by prayer and fasting.** In reading 254-46 the question was asked, "Should a program be started for developing assistants to Edgar Cayce?" The response, which makes reference to this verse, was a conditional yes: *...this must be approached with prayer and fasting, for such can only be accomplished through prayer and fasting. Not as man counts fasting - doing without* food; *but one that would abase himself* [so] *that the creative force* might *be made manifest...* As used here, "abase himself" probably meant to "humble himself" and thus not be looking for glory and recognition.

Jesus tells a parable which speaks of the prayer of a publican in Luke 18:13: **And the publican, standing afar off, would not lift up so much as his eyes unto heaven, but smote upon his breast, saying, God be merciful to me a sinner.** In reading 262-17 Cayce was asked the best position for meditation. He refers to this verse in his reply: *If* **form** [**position**] *becomes...the guiding element, then the hope or the faith is lost in form. He that made long prayer, or he that not even raised his eyes but smote his breast and said, "God be merciful to me, a sinner!" Who was justified? He that in humbleness of self, humbleness of mind, humbleness of the whole* **individuality** (losing *personality in Him) comes; and in* whatsoever **manner...whether prone, whether standing, whether walking, or whether sleeping...**[he succeeds.] In prayer and meditation, position is not so important, but our attitude is all important.

In reading 281-20, for the Prayer Healing Group, Cayce was asked if the Lord's Prayer, as recorded in the Bible, is correct. He replied that while there may be misinterpretations and poor translations, we should use what we have. This reading was given on April 27, 1934. Less than a month later, on May 21, 1934 in reading 378-44 Cayce gave, spontaneously, the following modified version of the Lord's Prayer: **Our Father who art in Heaven, hallowed by Thy name, Thy kingdom come. Thy will be done; as in heaven, so in earth. Give us for tomorrow the needs of the body. Forget those trespasses as we forgive those that have trespassed and do trespass against us. Be Thou the guide in the time of trouble, turmoil and temptation. Lead us in paths of righteousness for Thy name's sake.**

22

DO IT NOW

The Edgar Cayce readings encourage us to be active, as is emphasized in Ecclesiastes 9:10 which was quoted over 50 times: **Whatsoever thy hand findeth to do, do it with thy might...** Here are some words of advice for members of the Prayer Healing Group in reading 281-27: *Pray ye that the Lord of the harvest find ye not idle but up and doing, with a might, that* [which] *thy mind, thy heart, thy hands find to do...Are ye ready for His coming? Hath ye fulfilled that as has been purposed in self to do? Why tarry ye in the waitings - tomorrow - tomorrow - tomorrow?* Don't delay. Do it now.

To the weak became I as weak, that I might gain the weak; I am made of all things to all men, that I might by all means save some. There are some who say this verse, I Corinthians 9:22, relates to Paul's decision to decline remuneration for his work as an apostle, adding that Paul followed in the Master's footsteps, who was accused of being a friend of sinners and publicans.

In reading 1158-15 a 47-year-old housewife told Cayce of a friend who had a good understanding of spiritual law and then asked why the friend smoked and drank cocktails occasionally. In the following response, Cayce reminded the lady that some had found similar fault with Jesus: *"...the son of man comes eating, drinking with his fellow man and ye say, 'Behold a glutton and a winebibber!'"...All good, all force is in* doing - *in applying, in* being! *As another has put it, "I will be all things unto all men that I may thereby save the more." If such* offends *thee, have no part then with same. But* do not *find* fault... Do as the Master, take time for prayer and meditation and then do something!

Here is Hebrews 11:6: **...he that cometh to God must believe that he is and that he is a rewarder of them that diligently seek him.** We do not really trust God unless we believe that he rewards those who seek him and do his bidding. Expectancy is a companion of true faith. Cayce includes reference to this verse in the following comments to Study Group 1 in reading 262-42: *How sincere* is *the* desire *on the part of each* to *know The Lord Thy God is One? Sufficient to be active rather than just* *passive...For, he that would gain the concept must believe that He is; and that He rewards those who seek to do His biddings. Then, let each be active; up and doing, with a heart that is singing...*

Get up and do something, or as stated in I Chronicles 22:16: **...Arise, therefore and be doing, and the Lord be with thee.** Cayce refers to this verse in the following counsel for a 27-year-old writer in reading 849-11: *What* will *ye do with this man thy elder brother, thy Christ, who...has shown thee the more excellent way...Then, be up and doing; knowing that as thou hast met in Him those things that would exalt thy personal self...these ye must lose in gentleness, in patience.*

Today, right now, is the accepted time according to II Corinthians 6:2: **For he saith, I have heard thee in a time accepted and in the day of salvation have I succored thee, behold now is the accepted time, behold now is the day of salvation.** Cayce refers to this Scripture in reading 909-1 for a 62-year-old man as follows: *Think never that the opportunities have passed; for ever is there set before thee a choice to make..."Today is the acceptable...day...of the Lord!" It is never too late to begin...an experience; for Life...is a ...continuous effort...whereby man may justify himself before the throne of grace...* It is never too late!

Matthew 9:37 speaks of a labor shortage: **Then saith he unto his disciples, The harvest truly is plenteous, but the laborers are few.** Reference to this verse is included in reading 262-13: *...many are called but few have answered. The harvest indeed is ripe, the laborers are few! The lords have called, do call, for laborers in His vineyard. Who will work today? He that has seen a vision of the love of Him that has been set as thine example, as thine ideal* [will work today].

Here is John 14:11: **Believe me that I am in the Father, and the Father in me, or else believe me for the very works sake.** Cayce refers to this verse in reading 262-12: *Study that thou sayest, that thou doest, and reserve nothing...of body or mind - in your service to others,* [This] is *a reflection of that He would have thee do, as* [best] *thou knowest how. As was given by Him, let thine works, thine efforts, be even as was said by Him - "If ye will not believe me, ye* will *believe for the very works sake - for the things I do bespeak* that [which] *I believe* [and that which] *I* am!

James 1:22 tells us to be doers: **Be ye doers of the word, and not hearers only, deceiving your own selves.** This verse is referenced in reading 262-29: *"...I will serve a* living *God," who has shown in man -* [in] all *men, everywhere - that* [the] *image of the Creator...the soul may grow in grace, in knowledge, in peace, in harmony, in understanding. Be ye doers of the word; not hearers only. Thus ye become the door* [so] *that the* way, *the Christ, the Savior, may enter in; for* He is *the way, the truth, and the light.*

Isaiah 6:8 encourages us to volunteer for God's work: **I heard the voice** of the Lord, saying, Whom shall I send, and who will go for us? Then said I, Here am I; send me. Cayce mentions this verse in reading 262-3 for Study Group 1: *Let thy prayer be continually:* **Not my will but Thine, O Lord, be done in and through me. Let me ever be a channel of blessings, today, now, to those that I contact, in every way. Let my going in, mine coming out, be in accord with that Thou would have me do, and as the call comes, "Here am I, send me, use me!"** Don't wait to be drafted; volunteer today.

When Jesus came to Jerusalem and the people shouted their blessings to Him, the Pharisees tell Jesus to rebuke his followers. Here is Jesus' reply in Luke 19:40: **And he answered and said unto them, I tell you that if these should hold their peace, the stones would immediately cry out.** Cayce makes reference to this verse in reading 262-45 for Study Group 1: *If the life is so lived that it makes manifest His love, the very rocks and stones will cry out in praise should man keep his mouth* [shut].

In Mark 1:17 it states: **Jesus said unto them, come ye after me and I will make you to become fishers of men.** Cayce cites this verse in reading 262-6 for Study Group 1: *...find what willing hands are willing to do. Each are called in their respective sphere. Each must find the answer in their own selves. Remember..."Come ye with me, and I will make you fishers of men?"*

Each day is a new opportunity for us to be about our Father's business, as referenced in John 9:4: **I must work the works of him that sent me, while it is day: the night cometh, when no man can work.** Reading 262-70 includes the following reference to this verse: *Each soul has been called* [into] *this group for a service unto the Lord. Hence the day draweth nigh, for the night cometh when no man labors...So, keep the paths straight...Be joyous in thy service in that thou hast to meet day by day, for the day of the Lord draweth nigh when ye who have been called must give an account unto the keeper of thy Lord's vineyard. Each soul is writing His* [own] *gospel day by day...What is the gospel of thy Lord, according to you?*

Each day the record of what we do, or attempt to do, reflects what we believe, as well as who and what we are.

23

SOME DO NOTS

In this chapter we will be looking at some Bible verses and related Edgar Cayce readings which identify some specific things we should avoid. These are, of course, in addition to the things covered in the Ten Commandments and other Scripture.

In Romans 12:3 Paul tells us not to rate ourselves higher than we should: **For I say, through the grace given unto me, to every man that is among you, not to think of himself more highly than he ought to think; but think soberly, according as God hath dealt to every man the measure of faith.** Cayce refers to this verse in the following words of advice for a 45-year-old advertising executive in reading 262-121: *Think not more highly of thyself than ye ought to think. For He humbled Himself and became as one with the lowest of men* [so] *that love might be made manifest. So may ye, in the humbleness of heart, come to know the greater glory by and through the greater service ye may render to thy fellow man.* Avoidance of pride is essential. We must cultivate humility. A false estimate of our worth is the greatest threat to true self understanding.

Matthew 7:6, **Give not that which is holy unto dogs, neither cast ye your pearls before swine, lest they trample them under their feet, and turn again and rend you.** While we should always be glad to share our pearls of wisdom with those who are seeking truth, there are some who would react negatively, and thus we need to exercise prudence in our sharing. In the initial reading for Study Group 1, 262-1, Cayce includes the following reference to this verse: *...first learn cooperation! Learn what that means in a waiting, in a watchful...world seeking to know, to see, a sign. There...will only be the sign given to those that have drunk of the cup...of enlightening a seeking desiring world. Cast not pearls before swine, neither be thou over-anxious for the moment.* Help those who are seeking and, thus, are open and receptive to help.

Getting even with others is God's job, as is mentioned in Romans 12:19: **Dearly beloved, avenge not yourselves, but rather give place unto wrath; for it is written, vengeance is mine, I will repay saith the Lord.** Cayce mentions this verse in reading 815-3 for a 35-year-old business man:

...use *not others for stepping upon their hearts or minds - because others may have used thee. Bear ye up under same, knowing* [that] *The Lord is the avenger of those that misuse His love in their relationship with their fellow man. And He, the Lord - the* life *that is* within *thee; that is thinking* [and] *moving; the* being *within self -* is *the avenger;* not *self:* Glory *in the Lord!* We should not consider reprisals as one of our alternatives. The tendency to judge others springs from pride in which love of self drives out love for others.

Luke 17:32 encourages us to forget the past: **Remember Lot's wife.** For those who may not recall, she looked back at the city of Sodom and turned into a pillar of salt. A male 33-year-old radio announcer, who had relationships with two women, asked Cayce in reading 3674-1 if he had had past-life association with either of them. Cayce quotes this verse in his reply: *...forget the past. Forget-forgive, and begin where you are. Look not back - remember Lot's wife.* Here is a second reference to this verse from reading 262-23 for Study Group 1: *...When an experience of self is in question, then ask self in the mental being, so that the answer may be yes or no...Then in meditation and prayer* ask *the Spirit whether* that *answer* received *in the mental is yes or no, and...the Spirit answers! Doubt not! For he that looks back, or doubts, is worse than the infidel. Remember Lot's wife!* This reading offers some excellent advice on how to make difficult decisions. Once the decision is made DO NOT LOOK BACK.

In Luke 9:62 a man told Jesus that he would be a follower but that he must first say goodbye to those at home. **And Jesus said unto him, No man having put his hand to the plough, and looking back, is fit for the Kingdom of God.** Edgar Cayce refers to this verse in the following comments from reading 3976-4: *...before each there is set a way, and in that way is set a light. Veer not from same! Let him that is weak of mind or heart not take the handle, for he that ploweth and looketh back is worse than the infidel.* Any who have tried to plow a straight furrow will understand this verse. It requires one's undivided attention. The central message here is the same as that found in Luke 17:32 preceding, DON'T LOOK BACK.

Matthew 6:19 asks us to consider what we treasure most: **Lay not up for yourselves treasures upon earth, where thieves break through and steal.** In reading 262-111 we find the following reference to this verse: *What you desire and seek after mentally and spiritually, and what you desire and seek for in the material things are not* always *from the same promptings...know in* whom *you believe as well as in* what *you believe; so that you* [may] *know whether or not thy treasure is laid in that where moth and rust doth not corrupt, and where thieves do not break through nor steal...*

Here is Romans 12:16: **Be of the same mind one toward another. Mind not high things, but condescend to men of low estate. Be not wise in your own conceits.** The problem of being wise in our own conceit is discussed in the following portion of reading 262-93: *If we as individuals will but look about us, as to the ways of man and his knowledge of those things that go to make up the elemental influences in the earth, we can see and experience that as the Master gave; that the children of this world are wise in their own conceit; again, that the children of this world are wise even unto those that are the children of light. Hence as He gave to those lacking in worldly wisdom and in the wiles of those that would make for deceitfulness in any of its phases or experiences of man's activity, the Glory of the Father may manifest through the prayer, the activity, the seeking of those though they may be to the worldly wise as but babes in understanding.* Many who have gained academic and professional recognition in our society may have but limited understanding of spiritual truth.

They measuring themselves by themselves, and comparing themselves among themselves are not wise. Reference to this verse, II Corinthians 10:12, is included in reading 1264-1: *Ye cannot hide thine self in numbers, in running away to distant places or anywhere! Self is ever in the presence of the godly conditions of thy making. If thine ideal is set in the material things, [then] only material things can be the reaping or the harvest. If thine ideal is set in higher things, and thine acts day by day are in keeping with those, then the harvest may be expected to be in that proportion commensurate with that given. Measure self not by self, for [he] who does such is unwise. Condemn self not because self has condemned another. Condemn another not because self has condemned self; for this is judging self by self. Know in* WHOM *there is hope, for it comes only from the answering of a pure conscience from within.*

Here is I Timothy 6:17 which states: **Charge them that are rich in this world, that they be not high-minded, nor trust in uncertain riches, but in the living God, who giveth us richly all things to enjoy.** Reading 1234-1 mentions this verse: *...be not high minded, but condescend rather to those of low estate; not [so] that [these] may be lorded over; rather that in...service to others there may be builded that which will enable self to enjoy...peace [and] quietude...*

As stated at the opening of this chapter, the issues of conduct we have looked at in these nine verses are not represented as being the worst errors that people make. But, they are important and merit our prayerful attention.

24

BALANCE

To have balance in our life we must observe the principle of putting first things first. In Matthew 6:33 Jesus gives us some words of advice on this: **Seek ye first the kingdom of God and his righteousness; and all these things shall be added unto you.** Here are some comments to a young man, in reading 4406-1, which make reference to this verse: *Do not allow the* material *things to outweigh the mental or the spiritual life - for to become lopsided in* any *direction is to make for* discontent, *and discouraging conditions...so attune the mental* [and] *the physical, that when the needs be for the responses of the spiritual from within their reaction will be as the bulwarks of life...Live not for self alone...seek first to* [establish] *thine relations with thine Maker and all those things needed, all those necessary forces in life will be added in* their *proper order.* We must establish proper priorities.

Here is Proverbs 23:7: **For as he thinketh in his heart, so is he...** In a health reading, 257-136, for a 41-year-old man, Cayce makes reference to this verse as follows: *Keep an even, normal balance in diet of body, diet of mind...for as a man thinketh in his heart (not as he speaks, but as he thinketh in his heart) so is he. So, keep the body fit, keep the mind fit. Do not allow little antagonisms of body* or *mind to undo that thou hast builded in thine experience.*

II Corinthians 3:6 says: **Who also hath made us able ministers of the new testament; not of the letter, but of the spirit: for the letter killeth, but the spirit giveth life.** In connection with operation of the Association hospital at Virginia Beach many years ago, Cayce was asked, in reading 900-450, if they should insist "that patients await their discharge from here before permitting them to depart." Here is his reply: *This should be one of the rules, that patients would not depart until so ordered...This* made *when entering. If not subscribed to, don't let them enter! Of course, conditions may arise wherein such may be not adhered to, to the letter - for, as has been given, the letter killeth, but the law maketh alive, or the* truth *maketh alive.* In a properly balanced life there is a place for some degree of flexibility.

I Corinthians 14:40 so states: **Let all things be done in decency and order.** In November of 1934, during the Great Depression, a 31-year-old man was threatened with unjust dismissal from his job and wrote to Edgar Cayce for advice. In reading 1932-3 Cayce informed the man that while the situation may have seemed alarming when it arose, that now drastic changes seem unlikely. The man had asked if it would be advisable for him to write to the headquarters of the company in another city about his situation. Here is the answer to this question: *...if there are the abilities of the body to adjust the conditions* without *appealing to those...in higher authority, then we would settle same. But...should it seem...necessary* [to appeal] *then* [it would] *be well for this to be done in decency and in order; not railing; not in a manner...detrimental...*[to] *anyone, but rather that which would be consistent with good judgments...*Decency, order, and good judgment would seem to be aspects of a balanced life.

Here is Psalm 1:3: **And he shall be like a tree planted by the rivers of water, that bringeth forth his fruit in his season; his leaf also shall not wither; and whatsoever he doeth shall prosper.** This verse is referenced in reading 1727-1: *Build not a one-sided life...*[Know] *that he that is well-grounded is* [like] *a tree planted by the waters of life...that given out is...for the healings of many - whether in...the mental forces or...*[the] *material gains of life...*

Remember the Sabbath day to keep it holy. Reading 349-6 for a 25-year-old lady makes reference to this verse, Exodus 20:8, as follows: *"Remember the Sabbath to keep it holy."...One day must be kept in that way that will feed the mental and* spiritual *life of a body. All work and no play will destroy the best of abilities...life must be a well-balanced life, not lopsided in any manner, to bring contentment - not necessarily be satisfied, for that is to become stagnant...*

Luke 12:27 states: **Consider the lilies how they grow: they toil not, they spin not; and yet I say unto you, that Solomon in all his glory was not arrayed like one of these.** Cayce cites this verse in reading 3352-1 for a 46-year-old man: *...not enough in the sun, not enough of hard work. Plenty of brain work, but the body is supposed to coordinate the spiritual, mental and physical. He who does not give recreation a place in his life, and the proper tone to each phase, - well, he just fools self and will some day - as in this body in the present - be paying the price...There must be certain amounts of rest. These are physical, mental and spiritual necessities. Didn't God make man to sleep at least a third of his life? Then consider! This is what the Master meant when He said, "Consider the lilies of the field, how they grow." Do they grow all the while, bloom all the while, or look mighty messy and dirty at times? It is well for people, individuals, as this entity, to get their hands dirty in the dirt at times, and not be the* *white-collared man all the while! These are natural sources. From whence was man made? Don't be afraid to get a little dirt on you once in a while. You know you must eat a certain amount of dirt, else you'll never get well balanced.*

So, now that we've revealed the secret of being well-balanced we can move on to our next subject.

25

PROTECTION

In our journey on the spiritual path one of the recurring dangers for many of us is that of temptation. For example, the temptation to take a chance and then find ourselves at risk physically, mentally, or spiritually. I Corinthians 10:13 assures us of God's availability to guide us safely through these experiences. There are more than 150 references to this verse in the Edgar Cayce readings: **There hath no temptation taken you but such as is common to man: but God is faithful, who will not suffer you to be tempted above that Ye are able; but will with the temptation also make a way to escape, that ye may be able to bear it.** This verse may be particularly useful to those who are dealing with a problem of addiction. Temptation must be met in order to achieve true maturity. Graduation from the school of life can not be reached without temptation. Even the Master was severely tempted. But, the presence of the Christ is near and thus divine power is available to us. This verse is cited in reading 262-116: *...though the days at times* [are] *hard, and the way seems to be* [not] *of the direction sought, yet know He is mindful of thee, and will not allow thee to be tempted...persecuted* [or] *disappointed, beyond thy capacity to serve. Then, let that love* [that is] *manifested at this Season in the Christmass spirit be the light to thy feet and the guiding way to thy desires - in the Lord.*

Here is a second reference to this verse from 262-104: *...He is Strength, He is Love, He is Patience, He is Knowledge, He is Wisdom. Claim* all *of these, then,* in him! *For He is in thee, and the Father hath not desired that any soul should perish but hath prepared a way of escape; a way of love, of peace, of harmony for every soul - if ye will but claim same, live same, in Him.*

Our third reference to this verse is directed to members of Study Group 1 who are troubled, in reading 262-85: *Ye that worry and are troubled, ye that are doubtful and fearful, who hath brought this upon you? God? God hath not at any time tempted man, but if ye will but accept it He hath prepared with every temptation, with every fault in man, a way of escape...the will of man is* just *combative.* Yes, and some of us may be inclined to be more combative than others. Our last reference to this verse is from 5030-1: ...[Come] *to that consciousness which is a part of the universal consciousness...[Then] ye abide - in body, mind and purpose - as one with the Creative Forces [and] ye are at peace with the world and have nothing to fear. For God will not allow any soul to be tempted beyond that it is able to bear - if the soul puts its whole trust in the Creative Forces manifested in the Christ-Consciousness.*

Psalm 46:1 has inspired people for thousands of years: **God is our refuge and strength, a very present help in trouble.** Reference to this verse is included in the following portion of reading 1222-1: ...*hold fast to that faith in Him. For as He is, was, holy; so may ye be holy in Him...He hath promised to be thy counsel, thy guard, thy stay, and a very present help in trouble. Remember Him also then, in thy joys as well...*

Here is another reference from reading 2403-1: ...*each soul enters with a purpose - and it is not by mere chance that this or that experience comes in the activities of the individual...He hath...with every temptation given a way [out], if the soul will rely upon Him. For He is the strength, the power, and a very present help in trouble.*

Our last Bible verse on protection relates to angelic assistance–Psalm 91:11: **For he shall give his angels charge over thee, to keep thee in all thy ways.** There is an army of invisible angels which are heavenly beings that do God's work among men. Cayce includes reference to this verse in the following message for a member of Study Group 1 in reading 262-31: ...*in thine own experiences...there is a way opened before thee. With fear and...trembling hast thou put forth efforts...at times; hence the injunction "Be not dismayed;"* [Remember] *that He hath given His angels charge concerning thee,* [Thus] *thine guide, thine guard, is ever in His presence...*

Our second reference is from reading 5754-3 where this question was asked: "How may one be constantly guided by the accompanying entity on guard at the Throne?" Here is Cayce's response: ...*the subconscious...or the unconscious conscious, is the mind of the soul* [and]...*is on guard ever with the Throne itself...*[For] *"He has given his angels charge concerning thee..."* [When you heed this message]...*Then He is near...That self that has been builded...that* [which] *is as the companion...is before the Throne itself!* Consciousness [physical] *consciousness...man seeks...for his* own *diversion. In the sleep* [the soul] *seeks...the* real *activity of self.* This is why it is important for us to study our dreams.

Our third reference to Psalm 91:11 is from reading 5749-6: ... *"I have given my angels charge concerning thee..." This He demonstrated in the experience of thy Brother, thy Savior, thy Jesus, thy Christ;* [who] *would come and dwell in the hearts and lives of you all - if you will but let Him, if you will but invite Him...open thy own heart...*[so] *that He may enter and abide with you.*

After Cayce had used the phrase *enlisting the aid of angels* in a reading, the individual, in his next reading, 2533-7, asked how to do this. Here is Cayce's reply: *...the face of the angels ever stands before the throne of God;* [heed] *the awareness in self* [so] *that* [these] *may be one with, equal with, the Father-God, as His child, as the brother of the Christ, thy Savior, thy Brother. And as the awareness comes, it is as the angel of hope, the angel of announcing, the angel of declaiming, the angel that would warn, the angel that would protect. For, these are ever as awareness, as consciousness of the abiding presence of that "He hath given his angels charge concerning thee..."*

Additional material on angels may be found in Chapter 44 - "Angels/ Holy Ghost/ Spirits. "

26

PERSISTENCE

Most agree that Paul's missionary work was largely responsible for the rapid spread of Christianity during the first century. Paul exhibited many fine qualities, one of which was persistence. Many credit him as being the author of the four Bible verses used in this chapter. Our first verse is Galatians 6:9: **Let us not be weary in well doing: for in due season we shall reap, if we faint not.** The Edgar Cayce readings usually quote only the first part of this verse. Our first example is from reading 262-109 for a member of Study Group 1: *The light and love draws near to thee, and thy ways are close to His ways. Keep faithful in the little things. Be not unmindful that persistence is a whole sister of patience, and if ye would know the greater joy, the greater love of the Christ Consciousness, these ye must keep in thy daily life. Grow not weary, then, in well-doing, but let the love divine, the beauty sublime, the joy as of the Lord, keep thee.*

Our next quotation of this verse is from reading 281-19 for a member of the Prayer Healing Group: *Be not impatient with thyself nor with thy neighbors. Be not unmindful that He, the Pattern, suffered long - and still was kind; that He endured unto the end and is seeking ever to aid thee in every condition that confronts thee in thine daily experience. And be not weary, then, in well- doing, but keep the heart singing - and [keep] the expectancy for great things to be accomplished in His name.*

Here is some good advice from reading 5049-1: *Be not weary in well-doing, for it is those who endure to the end who find...peace within themselves...doing good to others, for others...is well pleasing in His sight...just [be] good for something...bring cheer to others, and never [belittle] thine own self, nor thy ideals.*

Our last quotation from Galatians 6:9 is found in reading 281-40: *Be ye not weary, then, in well-doing; nor become negligent or unmindful of the little things that may bring to thy consciousness the spreading of the awareness of the Christ's love for each of you.*

Our next Bible verse is I Thessalonians 5:21: **Prove all things; hold fast that which is good.** In reading 683-1 for a 43-year-old lady, Cayce includes the following comment pertaining to this verse: *...if the entity will hold* *fast to that which is good...the days must come in the earth...when many will call it blessed and count it a privilege to have known...the entity...* The Cayce readings frequently reminded people of the importance of keeping on, keeping on, of being persistent and consistent.

Our second reference is from reading 262-7: *Hold fast to that thou hast, pressing on to the mark of the higher calling as is set in Him; keeping thine own garments white, and seeing less and less fault in the other fellow.*

Our third verse is Philippians 3:14: **I press toward the mark for the prize of the high calling of God in Christ Jesus.** In the following remarks to a member of the Prayer Healing Group, from reading 281-22, Cayce makes this statement: *Be patient; be kind; be gentle; be forgiving, even to those who in their ignorance speak unkind. For, remember, how they buffeted thy Lord! Let thy watchword be: "Through the power of the Christ in me, I can - and will - do that He would have me do! Trusting only in Him I will press on - on - to the mark of the calling whereunto He has called, and does call me."*

Here is a reference to this verse from reading 5717-2: *Only by assistance to our* [fellow-man] *do we raise ourselves toward that mark of the higher calling, which is set in Him.*

Our last example is from reading 4835-1: *The body must learn that the will of self must be exercised, if it would attain to the mark of the higher calling, as set in Him. Be ready, up and doing, with the efforts necessary to overcome those that so easily beset the body through its own physical and mental appetites.* Whenever we fail to control our appetites, then, they control us. Keep on, keeping on.

In reading 281-19 a member of the Prayer Healing Group asked if she should resign from the group. Cayce makes reference to I Timothy 5:8, **But if any provide not for his own and specially for those of his own house, he hath denied the faith, and is worse than an infidel.** He said in his response: *Withdraw not, for he that looketh back is worse than the infidel. Keep ye all in the Way. Be happy. Be joyous. And may love and mercy and peace, that cometh from the Father to those who use themselves in His service, be with thee.*

Here are some words of advice from 5295-1: *Don't make promises to self, or to Him, lest ye mean to keep them under any circumstances which may arise. For they who make promises to their God within themselves and don't keep them are worse than the infidel.*

Be persistent, true to yourself and to others.

27

DOUBT—CONFUSION—CONFLICT

There are times in our life when each of us experiences doubt, confusion, or conflict, or, perhaps all three at the same time. Luke 17:33 says: **Whosoever shall seek to save his life shall lose it: and whosoever shall lose his life shall preserve it.** Do you feel somewhat confused when you read Scripture such as this? Cayce helps to clarify the meaning of this verse in reading 2080-1 for a 35-year-old male pharmacist: *...He gave, "He that would have life must lose it," - he that would have friends must show himself friendly, and not merely to be wellspokenof, but that the law of the Lord may be made perfect in the daily life, and* lived *in such...manners as to be real in the experiences of the entity!" And not merely in...outward appearance...*

Proverbs 14:12 is equally confusing: **There is a way which seemeth right unto man but the end thereof are the ways of death.** Reference to this verse is included in reading 1222-1 for a 34-year-old housewife: *...we find that emotions...spiritual emotions rather than the body emotions - make for ruling influences in* [your] *life...keep* these *coordinate...know that there* is *a way at times that seemeth right yet the end is confusion - unless* [you are] *directed by those forces, those influences:....of the spirit of truth; as in patience, longsuffering, charity, fellowship, grace and mercy.* We must look up and see where we are headed.

John 16:33 speaks of tribulation: **These things I have spoken unto you, that in me ye might have peace. In the world ye shall have tribulation: but be of good cheer; I have overcome the world.** Edgar Cayce cites this verse in reading 3976-29 as follows: *There are...two principles, two conflicting forces in the earth today: the prince of this world, and that principle that says to every soul, "Fear not, I have overcome the world and the prince of this world hath nothing in me." Can ye say that? Ye must! That is thy hope...* Peace comes by union with Christ and results from belief in Him. Peace requires effort because there must be a personal victory over the prince of this world. Courage and faith, as exemplified by Jesus, are required for this.

Have you ever experienced rejection? Here is an example in John 1:11:

He came unto his own, and his own received him not. Cayce refers to this verse in reading 2524-3: *Minimize the faults, in others - as ye would have them minimized in thee. Forgive, if ye would be forgiven. Show mercy if ye would have mercy shown. These are simple in speech, yet so hard oft in application - because we judge one another...He came to His own, His own received Him not...He is the way, the truth, the light...Analyze thy life's experiences, - see thy shortcomings, see thy virtues...*

Do you kick against the pricks of life? Acts 9:5 speaks of this: **And he said, who art thou Lord? And the Lord said, I am Jesus whom thou persecutest; it is hard for thee to kick against the pricks.** In a number of readings Cayce advised, "Do not kick against the pricks," in reference to this verse. In reading 295-3, for a 27-year-old female, Cayce was asked the meaning of "Do not kick against the pricks." Here is his reply: *Where there are trials or tribulations, indecisions, make thine self one with the spiritual forces.* Information on how to do this may be found in Chapter 10 on "Oneness."

An unclean spirit can cause major problems, as shown in Matthew 12:45: **Then goeth he, and taketh with himself seven other spirits more wicked than himself. And they enter in and dwell there: and the last state of that man is worse than the first...** Have you ever tried to eliminate one problem and have things go from bad to worse? Cayce refers to this verse in a health reading, 3512-1, for a 35-year-old man: *Do the first things first. Do not begin to apply the material applications suggested, until the body comes to the physical and mental realization, through the study of divine manifestations in the earth, of the entity's relationship to that divinity; else the last estate will be worse than the first.* Just remember, the key is to do first things first, and, I might add, do them correctly.

Have you ever felt betrayed? Matthew 27:46 addresses this: **And about the ninth hour Jesus cried with a loud voice, saying, Eli, Eli, la-ma sa-bach-tho-ni? that is to say, My God, my God, why hast thou forsaken me?** In reading 281-3 a member of the Prayer Healing Group asked why there are times when their meditations seem unsatisfactory. The reply refers to this verse: *For ye are still in the flesh. Why did He [say], "Father, why hast thou forsaken me?" Even when the world was being overcome, the flesh continued to rebel; for, "When I would do good, evil is present with me - but, Though I take the wings and fly to the utmost parts of the heavens, Thou art there; Though I make my bed in hell, Thou art there." So, when doubt and fear comes, close thine senses to the material things and lose thineself in Him. Not that ye shall not be joyous in the things that partake of the pleasures...of life; for so did He - but keep thine consciousness ever alert, ready and willing to be the channel that will make known His love, and HE will speak with thee!*

Trouble is usually close at hand for most. Here are some words from Paul in Romans 7:21 that speaks to this: **I find then a law, that when I would do right, evil is present with me.** In the second reading for the Prayer Healing Group, 281-2, Cayce was asked if the healing energy should be channeled through a specified member of the group. In his reply, reference is made to this verse: *Come together in one mind, as one purpose, one designated as one, cleansing themselves in mind, in body, to be the messenger, or the channel for that individual. Each seeking for aid may then be aided according to the faith in those that seek to aid in His name. These bring the strength of union [to the] group, rather than individuals - who may in self find turmoil, [such as] "when I would do good, evil is present;" [the one] who in being designated as a channel for an individual...may - with the consecrated effort on the part of [the group] - bring...manifold strength to others. Come in singleness of heart, in oneness of purpose...knowing [that] peace, mercy and grace, is granted as the faith, and the hope, is in Him.*

We also must be prepared to deal with deception. Luke 21:8 states: **And he said, Take heed that ye be not deceived: for many shall come in my name, saying, I am the Christ and the time draweth near: go ye not therefore after them.** Cayce was asked to explain this verse in reading 262-30. Here is a portion of his response: *As has been given, many have arisen; for as He gave in the same connection, there were many false prophets, even those that would lead the very elect away. There be those who, finding something of the power that is in the material activities of those that would walk in the light, turn same into their own selfish purposes; [and] hence become false prophets, false Christs, and lead many astray. Let's remember, there has been given the manner, the way to determine as to whether such a prophet is of the Spirit of God or not. They that deny the call of the prophets of old, or the burdens of the world upon the Son or His death [and] resurrection, are not of the spirit; for "As ye have seen Him go, so shall He come."*

In Luke 16:31 it says: **And he said unto him, If they hear not Moses and the prophets, neither will they be persuaded, though one rose from the dead.** This verse is quoted in the following portion of reading 262-89: ... *turn to thine temple where He has promised to meet thee ever. It is not who will ascend to bring Him down, nor who will come from over the way...For how said He? If they hear not Moses and the prophets, they would not heed though one rose from the dead! Think how gracious has been the gift to man, that only those who have crossed the border through being glorified...have vision. For they that are on the borderland are only in that state of transition. If they were to speak to all, how terrible would be the confusion!* God knows what He/She is doing in making it difficult for communication to occur with those in the borderland!

Peter tells us that some of Paul's letters were confusing. Here is II Peter 3:16: **As also in all his epistles, speaking in them to these things; in which are some things hard to be understood, which they that are unlearned and unstable wrest, as they do also the other scriptures, unto their own destruction.** In reading 262-87 reference to this verse is made as follows: *...what is the stumblingblock to us today? If we do a good deed we want God to repay us tomorrow! So did Paul! Did he not groan continually that the mark, that scar in him, was not removed? Did he not bring* [up] *those things as said by Peter concerning same? That, "He speaketh many things hard to be understood, that many wrest with to their own destruction." To what did he refer? That their idea (of many who spoke) of time and space was limited; for they had even less conception of same than the weakest among you here!*

Perhaps one of the verses Peter had reference to in II Peter 3:16 was I Corinthians 1:27: **But God hath chosen the foolish things of the world to confound the wise; and God hath chosen the weak things of the world to confound the things which are mighty.** This verse is mentioned in reading 257-53: *Keeping the body in...attunement* [with beauty] *aids physically* [and] *mentally, and the growth to the soul becomes, as one that has made peace with the Creator. These are but little things in the eyes of many. These, by their very foolishness to many, confound the wise. These* [provide] *contentment that makes one seek and seek for knowledge of Him that gives the gifts in life; for, He* [is] *the God of the living...and material things are but...dead* weight *when one has not attuned self to the beauties in every field...Even the toad is as beautiful in the sight of the Creator as the lily, and he that heedeth not the little things may not be master of the great things...*

The Bible tells us that Job never lost his faith, but he did have some questions, as in Job 14:14: **If a man die, shall he live again? All the days of my appointed time will I wait, till my change come.** In reading 262-54 the following reference is made: *does Day and Night present that experience sought in every soul that is given expression to as in days of yore, when it was said, "If a man die, shall he live again?" From whence came man into the consciousness of Day and Night? What makes for the awareness, in the experience of each soul, of a change? Are such questions merely answered in the heart of each, as "the sun goes up, the sun goes down," and "there will be a big night tonight?" These are questions. These are basic truths. What thinkest thou?*

Perhaps the purpose for our doubts, our conflicts, and our confusion is to stimulate us to think. *What thinkest thou?*

28

INNER PEACE

After thirteen verses of doubt, confusion, and conflict, perhaps you are ready for five verses of inner peace. But, don't overdo it, because we have some questions for you at the end of the chapter. Here is John 14:27: **Peace I leave with you, my peace I give unto you; not as the world giveth, give I unto you. Let not your heart be troubled, neither let it be afraid.** In reading 281-35, for the Prayer Healing Group, Cayce delivers these words about peace: *...each may become...more...attuned to that spiritual awakening which brings that peace as He promised. Not as the world knoweth peace, but that connection within the heart...Though the experiences of the physical are oft as torments in our material experience, there is the advocate with the Father and He will comfort, He will bring peace, harmony and understanding to those who seek to know His face - and who have the courage to dare to do the right in the face of all oppositions of every nature.*

Some teachers say the gift of peace Jesus left with his disciples is also His joy and is related to His gift of eternal life in Him. This kind of peace can be found by trusting wholeheartedly in God. Surrender your self entirely to Him, without reservation and you too can have peace that passes understanding. Here is a reference to this verse from reading 262-116: *...ye will find grace and mercy shown thee; and His presence...His voice coming...closer...to thee... "Peace I leave with you, my peace I give unto you" saith He that is the Lord, the Master, the keeper of those that would know Him.*

Our third reference to John 14:27 comes from reading 262-75: *... "let not your heart be troubled, and be not afraid...Keep the faith. Look only upon that which brings peace, harmony [and] joy, in the lives of those that thou may serve from day to day...Listen to the voice within; for He is nearer even than thine own body!*

Our last mention of this verse is from reading 2879-1: *Seek ye...to walk with Him. That peace He giveth thee. Not as the world knoweth peace, but as His peace that openeth the door of understanding, of comprehension, of how God maketh peace with man through the law of love. For He is law. He is love.* These words are very reassuring.

In Philippians 4:7 Paul tells us of the peace that passes all understanding: **And the peace of God, which passeth all understanding, shall keep your hearts and minds through Christ Jesus.** This is a comforting verse. Cayce refers to it in the following comments to a member of Study Group 1 in reading 262-98: *The cares of the world, the bickerings of those that are fearful, cause thee to wonder. But let these not shake thy* faith...*He hath shown the way, and He will keep thee and sustain thee...the ministering of those things...that He hath given thee...will bring to thee, to thy house, to thy hands, to thy mind, to thy heart, peace and harmony that passeth understanding.* The peace of God results from a deliverance from our self. This peace passes all understanding because it comes as a reward of self-surrender. The characteristics include humility, singleness of mind, and forgiveness.

Our second reference to this verse is from reading 5758-1: *Let grace keep thee. Let mercy and justice direct thee,* [so] *that the peace which passeth all understanding may be thine in the consciousness of the Christ-Presence.*

Our last reference to Philippians 4:7 is from reading 262-118: *...bring into thy consciousness...*[that] *awareness, that joy, that peace which He has promised...that is a part of thy inheritance in Him - the peace that passeth understanding; the assurance that thou art His and that He is thine!* This becomes true for us as it becomes our heart's desire.

In John 14:18 Jesus tells us that He will come to us to bring us comfort: **I will not leave you comfortless: I will come to you.** In the following remarks to Study Group 1, in reading 262-24, Cayce starts with a reference to the Comforter: *...know there is that Comforter present that will speak for thee under* every *condition; for, as He gave, "I will not leave thee comfortless. Be* not *afraid." Be mad, but sin not! In thine* understanding *gain the presence of Him ever as thy companion, in every act, in every word; for every thought must be accounted for, and in grace...will there be that constant, prayerful attitude for a purposeful life...Lose self in Him.* These *will answer. Not as an outward, but an* inward *growth - that makes for the beauty of the soul that has patience* shining *through.*

The second reference to this verse is from reading 262-69 for a member of Study Group 1: *Open the door of thy heart to Him. In thy prayer, in thy meditation, call on Him; for He is near. Hath He not chosen thy body for one of His companions in the earth? Then know that He will not leave thee comfortless, but will come to thee.*

Our last reference to John 14:18 is from reading 281-5 for members of the Prayer Healing Group: [Hold to the thought] *that the mental and physical body is surrounded by, is protected by, that consciousness of the*

Master that gave, "I will not leave thee comfortless"...the greater the physical can be submerged, the greater will be the activity of the spiritual forces in...such bodies. Some of us may feel that we are now submerged entirely in the physical. This is just a concept which we can replace by the concept, as expressed in this reading, that we are submerging the physical to control by the spiritual. Make a deal with your body: "I'll take care of you and you take care of me, but just remember, I'm the boss." This may sound juvenile to some, but it's helped me!

In the silence we may come to know God, as stated in Psalm 46.10: **Be still and know that I am God**...Cayce makes reference to this verse in reading 281-60 for the Prayer Healing Group during World War II on February 3, 1942: *Then, at that period when ye each are first aware, as ye awake, be* still *a moment and know that the Lord is God. Ask that ye be guided,* this *day, to so live that ye may stand between the living and the dead. In the evening as ye sit at meat, be* still *a moment. For there is greater power in being still before thy God than in much speaking. Again give thanks for the day and its opportunities. And so may ye, as seekers for divine guidance, be uplifted; and thus may ye hasten the day when war will be no more.*

Our other reference to Psalm 46:10 is from reading 281-59: *Keep that awareness of His presence. For, as He hath given, "Lo, I am with you always, even unto the end of the world."...be still within thine own heart, thine own consciousness, and know that He IS with thee.* He is, indeed, with us. But, as expressed in this verse, we must first become still, become quiet, become silent in order to sense an awareness of His presence.

Numbers 6:24-26 assures us of the blessing and peace which are gifts from the Father: **The Lord bless thee, and keep thee: The Lord make his face shine upon thee, and be gracious unto thee: The Lord lift up his countenance upon thee, and give thee peace.** Cayce quotes from these verses in the following words of encouragement for members of Study Group 1 in reading 262-86: *In the way of the Lord the earth seems afar off. In the way of the earth the Lord seemeth far off. Keep, thou, close to the ways of the Lord. [His] ways are not past finding out, if ye will seek them...Let* Him *have His way with thee. The Lord keep thee; the Lord bless thee, and cause His face to shine upon thee and bring thee peace!*

Our next reference to this verse is from reading 938-1: *Let the light of His countenance rest upon thee and bring thee peace. Let His ways be thy ways. Let joy and happiness be ever in thy word, in thy song. Let* hopefulness [and] *helpfulness, ever be thy guide. The Lord is thy shepherd; let Him keep thy ways.*

Our last reference to Numbers 6:24-26 is from reading 1626-1: *Hold to Him as thy light, thy standard; and ye will find peace such as He alone gives...The Lord bless thee, the Lord keep thee - cause His face to shine upon thee, and bring thee peace!*

Some of you may remember my promise to provide some questions at the end of this chapter. Those that are not interested should proceed to the next chapter. For those who like a challenge here are the questions:

1. When you listen to the voice within, just how near is He to thee?

2. What characteristics come to us as a reward for self-surrender?

3. When we lose self in Him there is inner growth. What effect does this have on the soul?

4. What guidance were members of the Prayer Healing Group instructed to ask for "as ye awake?"

29

SOME DOS

In this chapter we will be looking at some of the things we need to remember to do. We may not be giving these items the attention that is
merited. For example, the admonition in our first verse is to be truthful.
Am I always truthful? Here is James 5:12 which was quoted 100 times in
the Edgar Cayce readings: **Let your yeas be yea and your nays be nay.** At
the time James wrote these words many people did not consider it necessary to be truthful unless they were under oath to God. The meaning of
this verse then and now is to always speak the truth. In reading 3394-2
Cayce said, *let thy yeas be yea and thy nays be nay in the Lord.* This would
mean to speak not just the truth, but to say that which would be in accor-
dance with what God would have you say. In reading 5469-1 we find: *Re-
proach not self nor others...Let thy yea's be yea's and thy no's be no's.
Learn when to say yea, and when to say nay.* Here the individual needs to
be not only careful to be truthful, but also to be careful in their choices.

Paul gives us some winning advice in Romans 12:21 **Be not overcome
of evil, but overcome evil with good.** Cayce refers to this verse in the following message for a member of Study Group 1 in reading 262-58: *Keep in
the glory of that thou hast purposed in thine heart. For, in the gentleness
of the speech, in the kindness of the activity, thou showest forth the love of
the Father. Be not overcome of those things that would hinder, but overcome the evil with the good, and give the glory - always - to the Father.*
Some say that evil tends to overcome goodness when we permit the forces
of darkness to take control and dictate the terms under which we conduct
our relationships with others. We must see to it that good maintains the
initiative in our life.

Share life, sincerely, with others, as inferred in Romans 12:15: **Rejoice
with them that do rejoice and weep with them that weep.** This verse is
mentioned in reading 3179-1 for a 53-year-old lady: *Practice all you
preach. Never ask anyone to do that you don't do yourself...Thus may the
light of the Christ-Consciousness shine through...He mourned with those
who wept and rejoiced with those who rejoiced. Do thou likewise...*

In Matthew 6:3 the Master instructs us to give in such a way that we do not seek or call attention to our giving: **But when thou doest alms, let not thy left hand know what thy right hand doeth.** Reference to this verse is made in reading 792-1 for members of Study Group 1: *Do all things for conscience' sake, that ye may never find cause to condemn thine own self. Put thine trust, thine understanding, thine self, into the hands of the* merciful *Father. And as ye would have* mercy *from Him,* show *mercy to those thou dost contact day by day. Let not thy right hand know what thy left hand doeth, when thou givest honor to thy fellow man; but rather in humbleness of heart... "ye may grow in grace, in knowledge* [and] *understanding..."*

Exodus 20:12 gives us one of the Ten Commandments: **Honor thy father and thy mother: that thy days may be long upon the land which the Lord thy God giveth thee.** Reading 262-79 quotes this verse and explains its application: *...be one in Him with the Father, and thus fulfill in each experience that which is the fulfillment of that destined for thee. Hast thou then aught to do with thy days in the earth? How readest thou? "Honor thy Father and thy mother, that thy days may be long in the earth which the Lord, thy God, giveth thee." Honor, then,* [all] *to whom honor is due destines that greater opportunities for an individual soul...will be the result of such activity. How doth honor come? First by the* thinking, *the meditating upon; so that in the acts, in the words, these...bring that which is honor to such in a material manifestation.*

In Mark 13:33 our Way Shower instructs us to watch and pray: **Take ye heed, watch and pray: for ye know not when thy time is.** Reading 262-26 for Study Group 1 includes the following reference to this verse: *Watch, that ye be not overcome. Watch and pray, for as the Father giveth so does the understanding come as to what may be accomplished in...relationships to others...ye are the lightbearers for Him.*

The Master says the kingdom of heaven is like a merchant looking for fine pearls. Then we have Matthew 13:46: **Who, when he had found one pearl of great price, went and sold all that he had, and bought it.** This verse is included in reading 1789-7: *...have friends, be friendly...find that which is love, beauty, joy...* [and provide] *these in the experiences of others...*[These] *are as the pearl of great price - a smile, a loving touch, a tender word...*[These] *are worth much more than all those...*material *things.* I think this reading is very clear. The kingdom of heaven is a heavenly state of consciousness available to us here and now.

In Matthew 5:17 Jesus assures his followers that He came to fulfill the law: **Think not that I am come to destroy the law, or the prophets: I am not come to destroy but to fulfill.** Reference to this verse is included in reading 2441-2: ... [Teach] *the purifying needed; in body* [and] *mind, for...attunement to the Creative Forces...attune all such to Him, the law* *giver...*[and] *interpreter, who came not to do away with the law but to fulfill;* [just] *as ye must do in thy daily life and daily application.*

Mark 16:15 tells us to preach the gospel: **And he said unto them, Go ye into all the world, and preach the gospel to every creature.** Reading 262-100 helps to clarify just what the gospel is: *"Go ye into all the world and preach the gospel." What was that gospel? Not much that is being given so oft over and over. For He combined it all into one, "Thou shalt love the Lord thy God with all thy heart, thy mind, thy soul;* [and love] *thy neighbor as thyself." For this is the ...whole law.*

In Ecclesiastes 9:8 it states: **Let thy garments be always white; and let thy head lack no ointment.** Reference to this verse is included in reading 262-7: *In transformation comes a light for those that look for same...Hold fast to that thou hast, pressing on to the mark of the higher calling as is set in Him; keeping thine own garments white, and seeing less and less fault in the other fellow.*

The people are directed to be circumspect in Exodus 23:13: **And in all things that I have said unto you be circumspect...**This admonition to be circumspect is discussed in reading 281-16: *...seek, then, as known, to present self spotless before that throne; even as* all *are commanded to be circumspect, in thought, in act, to that which is held by self as that necessary for the closer walk with Him. In that manner only may each atom (as man is an atom, or corpuscle, in the body of the Father) become a helpmeet with Him...*

Some of you scholars may remember that in Chapter 14 on "Harmony" we looked at Ephesians 5:15 where Paul instructs the followers to "walk circumspectly." (The meaning is to be careful to consider all related circumstances before deciding or acting .)

30

FEAR AND WORRY

The Cayce readings say that fear is the basic cause of most negative thoughts and actions. Here is I John 4:18: **There is no fear in love; but perfect love casteth out fear: because fear hath torment. He that feareth is not made for perfect love.** In reading 5459-3 Cayce refers to this verse in reply to a question from a 54-year-old man concerning how to overcome fear: *Fear is the root of most of the ills of mankind, whether of self, or of what others think of self...To overcome fear is to fill the mental, spiritual being, with that which wholly casts out fear; that is, as the love that is manifest in the world through Him who gave Himself as the ransom for many. Such love, such faith, such understanding, casts out fear.* True Christian brotherly love comes from God and moves toward perfect expression in our activity, thus eliminating fear from our life.

In John 14:1 the Master tells us not to worry: **Let not your heart be troubled, ye believe in God, believe also in me.** Jesus sensed that the disciples were disturbed and fearful about His leaving them. To overcome their fears, He reminds them of their faith in God and asks them to believe in Him also. Edgar Cayce had these words of counsel for a 47-year-old secretary in reading 2615-1: *Do not allow failures (so-called, by man) to deter thee. For, man's weakness is God's strength - if man puts the faults far behind and magnifies the virtues in his dealings with his fellow men...Let not thy heart be troubled; ye believe in God, believe in Him...who is able to keep thee in the way...[ye] should go.*

In Matthew 6:34 our Elder Brother tells us not to worry so about the future: **Take therefore no thought for the morrow; for the morrow shall take thought for the things of itself. Sufficient unto the day is the evil thereof.** We are to live one day at a time and not borrow trouble from the future. This verse is not intended as a veto against wise planning. Cayce was asked to comment on the work plans of a 37-year-old sales manager. His reply in reading 5502-3 makes reference to this verse: *Let him prepare himself as God has planned. Be a channel of blessing, [Do] not tell the forces nor God, how to do His work...Rather be that channel through which individuals may...approach the throne itself...Let the day be suf-*

ficient unto the evils thereof. Hang loose. Be open to guidance on a daily or hourly basis.

Thinking is important but it is not a panacea, as stated in Matthew 6:27: **Which of you by taking thought can add one cubit unto his stature.** Edgar Cayce mentions this verse in reading 3976-24 on world affairs: *...if there is the turning of every man and woman to the thought of God, then we may solve every problem. For it is not by mere thought, not by any activity other than the moving force within each entity, each body; and when more of patience, more tolerance, more thought of others is advanced and kept in the heart of the individual, this lends that power, that influence, that force for good.*

Do worry and fear serve as a lightening rod in attracting negative experience to manifest in our life? Job 3:25 says: **For the thing which I greatly feared is come upon me, and that which I was afraid of is come unto me.** Reference to this verse is included in reading 3175-1: *Anger, to the entity is a fearful state. Do not let that which ye fear come upon thee. Replace same rather with patience...and - most of all - consistency...in conversation with others.* This reading suggests how anger and fear can have negative consequences in our life. Apparently this individual's anger and fear caused him/her to be impatient with others and to be inconsistent in conversation, which may well be just a kind way to remind this individual to always tell the truth. He/She needs to replace anger and fear with patience, consistency, and truthfulness. Not bad advice for any of us.

And fear not them which kill the body, but are not able to kill the soul: but rather fear him which is able to destroy both soul and body in hell. This verse, Matthew 10:28, is cited in reading 281-59: *...though the world, the earth may pass away, though it may...bring destruction to the material things, we look to Him, we know there is safety in Him.* Fear *not he that may destroy the body, but rather fear him that may destroy the soul in torment. Then, in love, in obedience, in prayer, follow Him.*

Here is Micah 4:4: **But they shall sit every man under his vine and under his fig tree, and none shall make them afraid.** Edgar Cayce makes reference to this verse in reading 262-13: *...the morrow has its evils and its goods, sufficient unto self. Today is! Use that thou hast in hand. So does the awakening come. Even as called by God to lead a peoples, as was Moses, a shepherd...Use that thou hast in hand, for the ground whereon thou standest is holy! Do thou likewise! [just] as Ram...Phares or Tama, each under their own vine and fig tree, learned first that opening self to be a channel of the living forces, not the dead past - nor that that makes afraid, but Thy will, O God, be done in me - use me as Thou seest fit!*

Isaiah 43:5 reminds us not to fear for He is near: **Fear not: for I am with thee: I will bring thy seed from the east, and gather thee from the west.**

Cayce refers to this verse in a health reading, 1089-2: *"Fear not, I am with thee." This should be upon the mind* [and] *the heart* [so] *that there may be the renewing of the life-flow in the* blood *of the body,* [so] *that the organs thereof may be attuned to the* spirituality...

The Master is able to bring a great calm, whenever and wherever, fear may occur in our life, as referenced in Matthew 8:26: **And he saith unto them, Why are ye fearful, O ye of little faith? Then he arose, and rebuked the winds and the sea; and there was a great calm.** Reading 262-104, for members of Study Group 1, makes reference to those of little faith: *Ye are chosen, ye are sufficient - if ye will but apply that ye know. For as ye apply day by day that ye know, then is the next step, the next act, the next experience shown thee. Because thou hast...failed here or there, do not say, "Oh I cannot - I am weak." To be sure thou art weak in self, but O ye of little faith! For He is thy* strength! That *is Wisdom! Let no* one...*ever say "I cannot." It's...*[as if] *saying "I* will *not - I want* my *way." This is foolishness; and ye know the Way. For He is Strength, He is Love, He is Patience, He is Knowledge, He is Wisdom. Claim* ALL *of these, then,* in Him! *For He is in thee...*

And, thus, He can be the answer to all of our worries and fears.

31

BLESSINGS

When I think of the many blessings that come into and enrich my life, I am grateful and give thanks. So, join me now in giving thanks for our many blessings.

<u>Thanks, God.</u>

Our first Bible verse does not include the word blessing but the Master tells us how to receive His blessings. Here is John 14:13: **And whatsoever ye shall ask in my name, that will I do, that the Father may be glorified in the Son.** Of course, this is not an unconditional promise. For our prayer to be "in my name" that for which we pray must be something that is in the nature of the spirit of the Christ. Thus, the blessings that come to us from the Son will be those things that will meet our needs and be truly beneficial to us.

Edgar Cayce includes reference to this verse in the following message for a 53-year-old female in reading 262-58: *...be thou the channel through which some blessings may come day by day. For in so doing may thou come to know more and more how great is the glory of the Father, through the Son. For, as He has given, "What ye ask in my name, believing, that I will give unto thee, that the Father may be glorified in me and in thee."*

As with all spiritual principles, that of blessings is a two-way street - giving and receiving. **For whosoever shall give you a cup of water in my name, because ye belong to Christ, verily I say unto you he shall not lose his reward.** In this verse, Mark 9:41, Jesus stresses the divine importance of little acts of kindness and service to others, being a source of blessings. Many of us need to be reminded of this truth regularly. Cayce refers to this verse in the following message for a member of the Prayer Healing Group in reading 281-8: *Be, and dare to do,* [what] *He would have you do...in each act, in each condition, that arises in the experience, and press on to the mark that is set in Him; for, as was given thee by Him, "Thou shalt not lose thy reward."*

One of the many qualities I admire in Paul is his eternal optimism, as expressed in Romans 8:28: **And we know that all things work together for good to them that love God, to them who are called according to his pur-**

pose. Many times it may be a real challenge to find the good in our experiences, but it's there for those who seek with an open mind. Cayce makes reference to this verse in reading 262-36 for members of Study Group 1: *Remember the pattern in the mount, in self, in the physical body, in the mental body, in the spiritual body. That is the mount! So long as there is perfect coordination in the mount, all things work together for the good of the mount.* The term mount, as used here, refers to our own indwelling Christ Consciousness. This verse promises blessings that may come later, at some unexpected time, to "make our day."

Our next verse, John 14:14, is essentially the same as John 14:13, but is worded differently: **If ye shall ask any thing in my name, I will do it.** The following portion of reading 853-9 for a 43-year-old man cites this verse: *...if* [**your request**] *is for self-gain, for self-exaltation, for the making of the way easy,* [then] *ye seek that which may turn upon thee and destroy thy very activity. But if it is that He may be glorified in thy fellow man, then ye may know. For as He hath given, "...as ye abide in me, ask and it shall be given thee the desire of thy heart!" If that desire is in accord, in attune, in at-onement with the constructive forces of thyself, thy experiences and thy relations.* Thus, for our own protection and well-being the promises of both John 14:3 and 14 are conditional.

An instinctive response to Mark 4:25 may be to question the fairness of God: **For he that hath, to him shall be given: and he that hath not, from him shall be taken that which he hath.** Cayce makes reference to this verse in the following words of encouragement for a member of Study Group 1 in reading 262-72: *As others look to thee for strength, for guidance in Him, in thine home, in thine life, in thine meetings day by day, so be ye strong in Him. For to him whom much is given, from him is much required; yet him that hath, to him it shall be given...thou hast known His ways. Keep thine way perfect, then, in thine walks, in thine talks with those that trust in thee. For as thou dost represent the home, the way, the light to many, so will He give His strength, His power, His grace...*

This verse is concerned with principles of spiritual law. A very logical question is, how can <u>anything</u> be taken from one who has nothing? - "he that hath not, from him shall be taken even that which he hath." In order for the message to be clear we need to insert one of Cayce's words - apply - so that we have, "he that hath not (applied), from him shall be taken even that which he hath." And thus the meaning is clear: Use it or lose it!

As I said before, one of the things I love about Paul is his optimism. Here is I Corinthians 2:9: **But as it is written, Eye hath not seen, nor ear heard, neither have entered into the heart of man, the things which God hath prepared for them that love him.** This verse is mentioned in reading

281-37 for members of the Prayer Healing Group: *...as the desires, the purposes, the aims are to bring about the whole change physically, So does it create in the experience of each soul a new vision, a new comprehension. For as has been given, it hath not entered the heart of man to know the glories that have been prepared, that are a part of the experiences of those that love* only *the Lord and His ways.* God truly rewards and blesses those who love Him. However, our love for him should not be motivated by a desire for the rewards and blessings. We should love Him simply because He is lovable; it's His nature.

Most of us cherish freedom. In John 8:36 it states: **If the Son, therefore shall make you free, ye shall be free indeed.** Reference to being made free, by Him who is the pattern or the Son, is included in reading 1167-1: *Know then the influences that are about thee, that are good, that are constructive, that are creative in their nature,* [these] *can have* only one source *of emanation* - good, *which is God!...those disturbing forces that, as we find, are existent in the body in the present, most of these arise from suppression of emotions...know, too, that as ...given by Him who is a pattern...by which an individual soul may be free; if ye know the truth, the truth* shall *make you free indeed.*

Matthew 5:3 says: **Blessed are the poor in spirit: for theirs is the kingdom of heaven.** In reading 262-111, Cayce was asked who are the poor in spirit. He replied: *They that have not allowed and do not allow themselves to be directed by other influences than that of Godly-Force itself. They that are not acquainted with the familiar spirits but with the Divine. They that are meek yet proud in their meekness and their humbleness. These are they that are poor in spirit.* As we can see, Cayce's interpretation of the verse is unique.

The promise of Jesus in John 15:7 is not essentially different from that found earlier in John 14:13 and 14: **If ye abide in me, and my words abide in you, ye shall ask what ye will, and it shall be done unto you.** Reading 1089-2 includes the following reference to this verse: *Then - in preparation of self-fear not. Let thy mind, thy body, be consecrated, set aside,* [and] determined *that "As the Lord wills, so may it be done," and that the Lord will have His way with thee;* [so] *that the words of thy mouth, the meditations of the heart, may be acceptable in His sight; taking only Him as thy guide who hath given, "If ye will abide in me, I will abide in thee."*

Here Psalm 103:2 adds: **Bless the Lord, O my soul, and forget not all his benefits.** Edgar Cayce refers to this verse in reading 2834-1: *...forget not the Lord and all His benefits. In thy interpretation of the spirituality of thy successes, forget not the source from whence life, consciousness* [and] *awareness, comes.*

The seventy sent out by the Master returned and reported that "in your name, even the demons submit to us." He responds to this report in Luke 10:20: **Notwithstanding, in this rejoice not, that the spirits are subject unto you; but rather rejoice, because your names are written in heaven.** This verse is included in reading 2753-2: *...the entity will always be one to whom many will go with their troubles. These* [opportunities] *ye may use to the glory of Him by whom ye were blessed! And count thyself as blessed for thy name is written in Him.*

Here is Matthew 5:4: **Blessed are they that mourn: for they shall be comforted.** In reading 262-111 Cayce was asked to explain, "Happy are they that mourn," as given in an earlier reading. Here is his reply: *Happy are they that have known sorrow, for their joy will be filled if they trust in the Lord. For He is the force, the power, the might that comforts those that mourn for those things even as He wept over Jerusalem...*

Here is Genesis 18:18: **Abraham shall surely become a great and mighty nation, and all the nations of the earth shall be blessed in him.** This verse is referenced in reading 281-10 for members of the Prayer Healing Group: *...be not fearful of results - and because they do not arise or come as quickly as some feel they should, don't become impatient. Leave it with Him. How long was the promise in coming to the faithful one, as He looked out upon the lands and* [it was] *said to him, "In thee shall all nations of the earth be blessed?"*

The joy of life and joy in Christ may be our greatest blessings as stated in John 15:11: **These things I have spoken unto you, that my joy might remain in you, and that your joy might be full.** Reading 281-25 refers to this verse as follows: *So attune thyselves that ye may...live and be the experience in the hearts of those that are seeking to find their way...Be the experience to someone to light their lives, their bodies, their minds to thy living Lord, thy brother, the Christ! For He has promised... "Ye finding me may know the joy of the Lord."*

Here is Psalm 1:1: **Blessed is the man that walketh not in the counsel of the ungodly, nor standeth in the way of sinners, nor sitteth in the seat of the scornful.** Cayce refers to this verse in the following portion of reading 281-12: *Each should be patient first with self, in honor preferring one another. Sit not in the seat of the scornful. Stand not in the place of the cynic. Be mindful not of things of high estate; rather give place to that* [which] *makes for sweetening in the lives of all; for he that wishes his brother well, yet makes no move to aid or supply, or to comfort, or to cheer, is only fooling self. He that would know the way must be oft in prayer, joyous prayer,* knowing *He giveth life to as many as seek in sincerity to be the channel of blessing to someone; for "Inasmuch as ye did a kindness, a holy word, a clothing in act* [for] *one of these the least of my little ones, ye have done it unto me."*

This reading reminds us once again that blessings are not only gifts that we receive from God, but encompass those things which we, as aspiring co-creators, give to others.

32

CONTACT WITH THE DIVINE

Our first verse on contact with the Divine is Matthew 28:20 where the Master assures us that He is with us always: **Teaching them to observe all things whatsoever I have commanded you; and lo I am with you always, even unto the end of the world.** One of the distinctive things about Christians is our belief that, as promised, Christ is alive as our friend. Preparation is necessary, of course, for contact with the Christ of our being. Edgar Cayce makes use of this verse in reading 1152-9 for a writer who asked for guidance in meditation: *...prepare thy mind and body as if ye would meet thy Lord and Master! Then sit as in readiness, at designated periods. Talk with Him from thine inner self, as though He were physically present...For, He has given, "Lo, I am with thee always..." This is not merely a saying, not merely a mental condition, but it may be made a reality...*

Here is Revelation 22:17: **...Let him that is athirst come. And whosoever will, let him take the water of life freely.** All people thirst for that which only God can supply. The supply is always available; the fountain of life stands there like a waiting friend. In reading 1598-1 a 67-year-old male missionary and writer asked if he should study and try to develop psychic ability, and write a book about this. Cayce references this verse in his reply: *...it is well to write about these. For the book of Books is the greater source of psychic experiences of individuals, and...what they did about such!..."Whosoever will let him come and take of the water of life freely." Study in that manner...*[Study by] *those that seek for self-effacement* [is] *well; but* [study by] *those that seek self-glory, never!*

In Matthew 18:20 the Master encourages group prayer and meditation: **Where two or three are gathered together in my name, there am I in the midst of them.** Cayce makes reference to this verse in the following message for the Prayer Healing Group in reading 281-20: *...let each enter into its own inner self and ask for direction...believing His presence will be with thee. For, He has promised, "Where two or three are gathered together in* my *name,* there *I will be in the midst of them."* The Christ presence attends and empowers group prayer and meditation. Of course, this in no way limits the need for private prayer and meditation.

In Psalm 27:14 we are instructed to wait on the Lord. Patience is conducive to contact with the Divine: **Wait on the Lord: be of good courage, and he shall strengthen thine heart: Wait, I say, on the Lord.** In reading 262-9 this verse is quoted to members of Study Group 1 as follows: *In seeking, ye shall find. Know that there are the openings ever for those that seek to know His face, for those who will wait upon the Lord. Be not overanxious. Wait ye on the Lord. In seeking, do not seek something afar, nor...something new; rather* [seek]*...the proper ideals.*

In John 4:21 the Master tells us that the physical location of our worship experience is not important: **Jesus saith unto her, Woman, believe me, the hour cometh, when ye shall neither in this mountain, nor yet at Jerusalem, worship the Father.** Reference to this verse is made in reading 262-64 for members of Study Group 1: *As ye have received from Him, "The day cometh when neither in Jerusalem nor in this mountain shall ye seek or desire to know the Lord, for ye will find Him in thine own heart, in thine own conscience;" and if the desire of thy heart will be that the temple of thy soul (the image of thy Maker...) shall be renewed in Him, thou shalt be able in self to know that - and the* way *that thou shouldst go.*

In John 4:24 the Master tells us how to have an experience of worship: **God is Spirit: and they that worship him must worship him in spirit and in truth.** Reading 816-10, for a 54-year-old man, makes reference to this verse as follows: *...Spirit is the natural, the normal condition of an entity. For hath it not been given, God is Spirit and seeketh such to worship Him, in spirit and in truth? ...That there is spirit, mind and matter is self-evident in the expressions in which one finds oneself by the very awareness or consciousness of existence...Other individuals are individual manifestations of their individual portion of that Creative Force.*

In Exodus 3:5 God tells Moses that he is standing on holy ground: **And he said, Draw not nigh hither: put off thy shoes from off thy feet, for the place whereon thou standest is holy ground.** In reading 262-13 a member of Study Group 1 asked in what way he could best attain his ideal. In his reply Cayce says: *Use that thou hast in hand, for the ground whereon thou standest is holy!* A few weeks later in reading 262-15 this member asked for an explanation of the statement just quoted. Here is the reply: *As each individual uses that knowledge and understanding* [which] *pertains to the attributes of the spirit of truth, life, light and understanding, so does there come that growth...* [Just[*as* [that which] *brought the worlds into being...and* [the] *places, things* [and] *spots, that are brought into being through such activity of an entity,* [this]*...is indeed holy. There is that, then, in the...entity,* [which is] *seeking that* [which it] *may find, and may come to know* [specifically] *the closer relationships with the holy* *activating forces in a material world.*

Here is Psalm 139:8: **If I ascend up into heaven, thou art there: if I make my bed in hell, behold, thou art there.** Edgar Cayce refers to this verse in reading 262-33 for members of Study Group 1: *...not only is He the resurrection, not only is He to come in the hour of trial, but He supped also in the hours of joy with those in Cana, He enjoyed even the feast with Zaccheus, laughed and joked. "Yea, though I walk through the valley of the shadow of death - thou art with me; though I fly to the utmost parts of the heavens thou art with me." Will we, as individuals, then, know His presence? How? "If ye love me, keep my commandments."* Wherever we may be the presence of the Christ is with us. This reading does not include comment on the presence of God in hell, unless, of course, *the utmost parts of the heavens,* include whatever hell there is.

For contact with the Divine, we need to use initiative and open the door, or as stated in James 4:8, draw nigh to God: **Draw nigh to God, and he will draw nigh to you...** Cayce quotes from this verse in reading 262-58 for members of Study Group 1: *Keep in the way thou hast set before thee, in the love of the consciousness of the Christ in thine activities day by day. Doubt not. Faint not in thine activities, for - as He has given - "If ye will draw nigh unto me, I will draw nigh unto thee." And through* thee *may there be the manifestations of God's love in the earth, through the Father, through the hope, through the activity of the fruits of the spirit in the earth.*

The author of Proverbs 7:15 tells us how he contacted the Divine: **Therefore came I forth to meet thee, diligently to seek thy face, and I have found thee.** Reading 262-47 speaks of those that seek His face: *Glory in the Lord...the ways that He would guide are the ways in which the soul may know Him better. In the love of the Father, He gave the Son. In the love that self would show...*[keep] *His ways day by day. For, His ways are not grievous; nor are they hid from any that would seek to know His face.*

In Revelation 1:10 John tells us about his contact with the Divine: **I was in the Spirit on the Lord's day, and heard behind me a great voice, as of a trumpet.** Cayce refers to this verse in reading 281-16: [**John**] *was banished to the isle, and was in meditation, in prayer, in communion with those saints who were in that position to see, to comprehend the greater needs of those that would carry on. And, as given in the beginning, "I was in the Spirit on the Lord's day, and beheld, and heard, and saw, and was told to write."*

The writer of Deuteronomy 4:29 gives us some tips on how to contact the Divine: **If from thence thou shall seek the Lord thy God, thou shalt find him, if thou seek him with all thy heart and with all thy soul.** Reference to this verse is mentioned in reading 262-3: *Know in self that He is* faithful *to fulfill that...promised,* [to the extent that] we *are faithful in caring for those to whom, for whom, the promise is made. They that seek* God *may find Him! Would ye have mercy shown* [to thee], *then be merciful* unto *those* ye *contact. Would ye be forgiven, forgive them that know not what they say* [or] *what they do; for "As ye lift Me* in *thine life, so shall* ye *be lifted* in *the life here, now, and hereafter."*

Here is Psalm 91:1: **He that dwelleth in the secret place of the most High shall abide under the shadow of the Almighty.** In reading 262-30 Cayce was asked to explain "the secret place of the Most High." Here is his reply: *In understanding the secret place of the Most High, let's determine what in the seeker is being sought...* [Is it] *the knowledge of the interpretation of the Most High's manifestations to men, or that* [which] *determines the relationship of that manifested* to *the Most High; for...in the secret chambers of one's own heart are stored that* [which] *makes for the real activities of...soul-consciousness* [and] *is the Holy of Holies where one meets with that* [which] *they worship as their God.*

Thus, true contact with the Divine occurs within our own being; it's an innerconnection, an inside job.

33

HUMAN WEAKNESS

In Matthew 26:41 our Elder Brother speaks of our weakness, and, in fact, gives us a means of identifying weakness: **Watch and pray, that ye enter not into temptation: the spirit indeed is willing, but the flesh is weak.** We find it easy to avoid most of the things we need to avoid. However, there are some things that tempt us, and these are our weaknesses.

Edgar Cayce discusses the weakness of the flesh in the following comments for a 40-year-old lady in reading 1301-1: *...in thine experiences through the earth ye...have seen the light and* [then] *lost thy way... He put on flesh that He, too, might know the ways of the flesh...the desires...the urges that have* [brought]*...that...blindness of self-glory, self-indulgence or self-aggrandizement that has led many astray, even with the forces of* [the] *Divine at times working through them. For, the Spirit is willing, the flesh is weak. And the strength, the influence, the force and power, is by that trust, that faith in Him.* Trust and faith in Him can be the key to overcoming temptation. Also, our will may need to be strengthened through regular prayer as advised in the opening words of the verse.

In Luke 6:39 Jesus identifies two weaknesses: **And He made a parable unto them, can the blind lead the blind? Shall they not both fall into the ditch?** Some may have the weakness of attempting to lead others when they themselves do not see the way. While others, at times, may not know who to follow. A serious weakness, indeed. Cayce makes reference to this verse in comments to a member of Study Group 1 in reading 262-121: *Boast not thyself because of those experiences that have brought thee to be in that position of power over others. For with thy purposes ye may become the blind leading the blind, and both may fall in the ditch. Let rather the love, that has been shown in the Father through the gentleness and patience with the children of men, be manifested in thy own life. Then may peace rest with thee indeed.*

Yielding to the temptation to criticize others is a weakness. Here is Matthew 7:3: **And why beholdest thou the mote that is in thy brother's eye, but considerest not the beam that is thine own eye?** Reference to this verse is included in reading 262-29: *When one has set the ideal, and knows what the ideal represents, and then knows self measured by the ideal, one sees, is aware of that lacking or that overdone in self, and plucks it out, and beholds* not *the mote that is in his brother's eye but considers rather the beam that is in his own eye.* Working with our ideals is probably the best possible way to overcome our weaknesses.

In Luke 13:34 our Way Shower shares a few thoughts about human weakness in Jerusalem: **O Jerusalem, Jerusalem, which killest the prophets and stonest them that are sent to thee; how often would I have gathered thy children together, as a hen doth gather her brood under her wings, and ye would not.** Reading 845-4 for a 37-year-old lady makes reference to this verse as follows: ...*each soul, each entity,* constantly *meets self. And if each soul would but understand, those hardships which are accredited much to others are caused most by self. Know that in those you are meeting* thyself! *All of these things then, in associations, in relationships that come about - let it be even as He gave, "How oft would I...have gathered thy children, even as a hen gathereth her chickens, and ye* would not!" When it comes to making changes in our life most of us are rather stubborn.

God didn't give Adam and Eve very many rules but they quickly broke one rule they had received. Here is Genesis 2:17: **But of the tree of the knowledge of good and evil, thou shall not eat of it: for in the day that thou eatest thereof thou shall surely die.** In reading 3188-1, for a 23-year-old man, Cayce mentions this verse: ...*He has said... "In the day ye eat thereof ye shall surely die." Yet the tempter said, "Not surely die," for it may be put off; and it was* [for] *six hundred years - and* [then] *death came,* [and] *the pangs of the loss of self. Yet in that day when the voice was raised on the Cross, He said, "Father, why - why the way of the Cross?"* The readings say that the soul of Adam grew and became the soul of Jesus.

As we know so well, change can be difficult, as referenced in Proverbs 26:11: **As a dog returneth to his vomit, so a fool returneth to his folly.** The Cayce readings, in 275-22, include the following reference to this verse: *Then* [came] *the entrance into the world of the* Prince *of Peace, that they who found in Him that way, that light, that water, that brother* [who] *gave them the access to the throne of grace itself, might have those errors forgiven - and* remembered *no more,* [except] *as has been given,* [for] *those things that so easily beset and* [then] *the dog returns to the vomit and the hog to his wallow!*

Speaking of weakness and temptation here is Matthew 5:28: **But I say unto you, That whosoever looketh on a woman to lust after her hath committed adultery with her already in his heart.** Reading 262-119 makes reference to Matthew 5:28: ...*the sons of God looked upon the*

Daughters of Men and saw that they were fair, and lusted! *What did the Christ say? "Ye say in the law that ye shall not commit adultery. I say unto you, he that looketh on a woman to* lust *after her hath committed adultery already!" Understandest thou...two influences...are ever before thee; good and evil, life and death; choose thou!*

In Matthew 26:40 we find an entirely different kind of weakness: **And he cometh unto the disciples, and findeth them asleep, and saith unto Peter, could ye not watch with me one hour?** The following reference to this verse is from reading 281-7: *Be not fainthearted because failure seems to be in thy way, or that self falters - but "how many times shall I forgive, or ask forgiveness - seven times?" "Yea, seventy* times *seven!" or, "not how I faltered, but did I seek his face again?"* [or] *"Could ye not watch with me one hour?" ...Seek to be one with Him, in body, in mind, in soul!* When past mistakes come to mind I try to remember, *not how I faltered, but did I seek His face again.* It's never too late.

Rebellion is a common problem, as mentioned in Numbers 20:24: **Aaron shall be gathered unto his people: for he (Moses) shall not enter into the land which I have given unto the children of Israel, because ye (Moses) rebelled against my word at the water of Meribah.** Reference to this verse is included in reading 281-29: *...there* must *be the* disseminating *or the giving away of the egotism of self. Consider as an example in thy study of same, the servant Moses. For these become, as may be found...from that record as ye have, the stumblingblock at Meribah.*

From Moses' weakness we go back in time and look at another one of Adam's problems in Genesis 3:10: **And he (Adam) said, I heard thy voice in the garden, and I was afraid, because I was naked; and I hid myself.** Cayce refers to this verse in reading 1759-1 for a 41-year-old man: *...unless the ideal as set...is of a creative force or nature, and takes hold upon that which is constructive and creative, what* must *the experience be when the soul has shed material consciousness, and...stands before its own conscience, its God,* [it is] **bare**. *There is in the material experience that which is ever as a manifestation of that excuse of old, "I was aware that I was naked and hence I covered myself with leaves."* Many of us probably try to hide our shortcomings from others and perhaps even from ourselves. We may have the weakness of not facing the facts until we are compelled to do so.

In II Corinthians 12:7 Paul tells us of his "thorn in the flesh" which he accepts as necessary to keep him humble: **And lest I should be exalted above measure through the abundance of the revelations, there was given to me a thorn in the flesh, the messenger of Satan to buffet me, lest I should be exalted above measure.** This verse is referenced in reading 281-18: *Oft is a thorn left in the flesh to tempt, yea, to keep one aright.*

When one acquires the development to meet [it]*...then self is healed also.*
Our thorns are not to punish but to teach.

Daniel 1:8 tells us about some common human weaknesses: **Daniel purposed in his heart that he would not defile himself with the portion of the king's meat nor with the wine which he drank...** In reading 341-31 for a 23-year-old man there is reference to this verse as follows: *As has been given of old, when the children of Israel stood with the sons of the heathen and all ate from the king's table, that which was taken...exercised the imagination of the body in physical desires - as strong drink, strong meats* (and) *condiments that magnify desires* within *the body - this builded as Daniel well understood, not for* God's *service -* [So] *he chose rather that the* everyday, *the common things...be given,* [so] *that the bodies, the minds, might be a more perfect channel for the manifestations of* God; *for the forces of the Creator are in* every *force that is made manifest* in *the earth.*

I saved this one in order that we might end with a man who had conquered many human weaknesses. If Daniel can do it, there's hope for all.

34

PATIENCE

Some may think that patience means passive submission. However, the Edgar Cayce readings insist that true patience is an active force which grows as we employ it to meet each new trial in our life. It is the cornerstone of the development of our soul. Our patience or impatience is a measure of our overall spiritual development and reflects other spiritual qualities such as cooperation, faith, virtue, understanding, and love. It is the key to being a helpful influence in the lives of others. To grow in patience, rule one is to *use* what you have. Would you like a beautiful soul? Practice patience and that's what you will become, more and more.

Luke 21:19 was quoted more than 100 times in the readings: **In your patience possess ye your souls.** Here is a reference to this verse from reading 922-1: *Be patient, even with thine own self; not as some men count patience, but as an activative principle, as an activative experience in thine own self. For as the Master of Masters has said:* in patience *possess ye...ye become aware of, thine own soul!*

Our second reference is from reading 3459-1: *That lesson the entity in the present is to attain is that of patience; which...is that to be attained by most individuals. For in patience, as He gave, ye become aware of thy soul...we are body...mind...soul. The soul is in the image of God, thus eternal, everlasting. Life in its expression, then, in a mental and... material world, is only a mental and material manifestation of the soul-entity; that which was brought into being as a part of Creative Forces. Thus it is eternal.*

Our third reference to Luke 21:19 is from reading 3902-2: *...in thy dealings with thine own body, thine own mind, thine own soul, act as though it were a consciousness. As ye act and as ye speak, and as ye apply, ye will become more and more aware. For as He has given, in patience, in perseverance, ye become aware of thy soul. Are ye in attune, then, with that consciousness? It is up to thee.*

Hebrews 12:1 tells us we are encompassed by a great cloud of witnesses and should run with patience, trotting perhaps: **Wherefore seeing we are compassed about so great a cloud of witnesses, let us lay aside every**

weight, and sin which doth so easily beset us, and let us run with patience the race that is set before us. The advice here, to "run with patience," reminds me of Cayce's occasional comment to "make haste slowly." The readings include an interesting reference to this verse in the following portion of 262-24: *...as one loses their hold on self in the lack of patience, so does that give the opportunity for the entering in of those things that would make afraid. Not that one should remain...inactive, but in patience run the race that is set before thee, looking to Him, the author, the giver of light, truth and immortality. That should be the central theme in every individual. Not in submissiveness alone, but* [also] *in righteous wrath serve ye the Living God.*

Reading 262-26 is our second reference to this verse: *In knowledge and power comes responsibility, that in patience may be tested in self. Be not overcome by...trials or by those joys that may make* [for] *forgetfulness of the source from which the power comes. In patience is the race of life run, that the joys may be the greater in Him.*

Our last reference to Hebrews 12:1 is from reading 967-3: *So live...in that awareness, that ye put away those things which might so easily beset; running the race that is set before thee day by day unto the glory of the Father in Him, and unto the honor of thine own self.*

Following the resurrection of the Master, he meets with the eleven and tells them to remain where they are until they receive power from on high, as stated in Luke 24:49: **And, behold, I send the promise of my Father upon you: but tarry ye in the city of Jerusalem, until ye be endued with power from on high.** The word patience is not used in this verse or the related readings. However, it appears that the act of waiting to be **endued with power from on high** requires considerable patience. Reference to obtaining "power from on high" is included in the initial reading for Study Group 1, 262-1: **Wait** *ye on the Lord; for, as has been promised, he that* **seeks** *shall find, and ye* **will** *receive - each of you - powers from on high.* Use *that in a constructive* [manner], *in a manner as befits that desire of the group...Think not of thine* own *desire, but let that mind be in you as was in Him...*

A second reading, 2533-8, concerns the appearance by Jesus to the disciples following the resurrection: *...the body-physical entered the Upper Room with the doors closed, not by being a part of the wood through which the body passed but by forming from the ether waves that were within the room, because of a meeting prepared by faith. For as had been given, "Tarry ye in Jerusalem - in the upper chamber - until ye be endued with power from on high"...The body (flesh) that* [had] *formed* [before] *that seen by the normal or carnal eye of Mary was such that it could not be handled until there had been the conscious union with the sources of* *all power, of all force.*

In Romans 5:3 Paul says tribulation produces patience: **We glory in tribulation also; knowing that tribulation worketh patience.** Christian faith rewards one who is steady under tribulation: they grow patient. When we have weathered a storm, it gives us a profound conviction. In reading 262-26 Cayce was asked, "How does tribulation work patience?" Here is his reply: *As has been indicated...* "Whom the Lord loveth He *chasteneth," and purgeth every one; for corruption may* not *inherit eternal life, and must be burned up. Know that thy God is a consuming fire, and must purge every one* [so] *that ye may enter in. In patience does one overcome.*

In James 5:8 the earthly brother of the Master tells us to be patient: **Be ye also patient; stablish your hearts: for the coming of the Lord draweth nigh.** In reading 262-25 Cayce was asked, "What time is referred to" in this verse. Here is his reply: *...this is the time - today - when the time draweth nigh for each soul to become more aware of the necessity of magnifying* His *presence through the patience borne one...with...another, that He may be glorified in us, through the promise of the Father that such will be to those that love His coming. Let each live, then, as though they expected their concept of the Master Christ to* dine *with them today. What would ye have to offer as the fruits of thine own life, thine thoughts, thine acts, thine deeds?*

Peter asked how often shall I forgive someone - seven times? His answer comes in Matthew 18:22: **Jesus saith unto him, I say not unto thee, Until seven times: but, Until seventy times seven.** It would seem that forgiving someone seventy times seven would require an abundance of patience. In reading 696-3 a 38-year-old female writer asked, "What is my specific work with the Association for Research and Enlightenment?" Here is Cayce's response:*...*[**Just**] *as thou hast presented* [**spiritual truths**] *to thy self-centered, wayward brethren here and there, then present them again and again. How oft shall I forgive my brother? Seven times? Yea, seventy times seven!...that His way may be had among men!* Much patience will be required.

In reading 262-114 Cayce tells us that: *...time and space...*[are] *portions of this three-dimensional plane. And what is the other?* [patience -] *Time, Space, Patience!...in patience we become aware of our souls, of our identity, of our being each a corpuscle...in the great body, in the heart of, our God...what is the Spirit of God?* patience, time *and* space *in the material understanding.*

We will end this chapter with one last reference to Luke 21:19 from reading 5755-2: *...realms of systems* [**star systems**] *came into being* [**galaxies**]; *as vast as the power of thought in attempting to understand infinity, or* *to comprehend...Yet time* and *space, in patience, you may comprehend.* At this point Mr. 5755 asked if the soul, after working out its entanglement in earth, would be immune to the attraction of other star systems. The answer was no, since all star systems are unique and different. In reading 5749-3 Cayce tells us that the planet earth is only an atom in the universe of worlds. In 5749-14 Cayce says, *Arcturus is that which may be called the center of this universe* [galaxy], *through which individuals pass and at which period there comes the choice of the individual as to whether it is to return to complete there...in this planetary system...the earth sun and its planetary system - or to pass on to others.*

This might be an interesting possibility to consider before we reach that day of decision. If we can "complete" during the next millennium, it might be best to return to planet earth, otherwise, passing "on to others" could well be the better choice, assuming, of course, that we have earned the right of choice.

There is an abundance of time, space, and realms. The question is when will we develop enough patience for a proper understanding?

35

PROPHECY

In this chapter we will look at thirteen Bible verses containing an element of prophecy which was quoted or discussed in the Edgar Cayce readings. 12 of these verses are from the New Testament. The prophecy verse most frequently quoted is Mark 13:31: **Heaven and earth shall pass away but my words shall not pass away.** The Master's words are timeless. During the past 2,000 years a great many things have been a part of man's activity in the earth. These have had their day and passed away. But Jesus' words are as alive today as they were when he spoke them originally. In reading 262-59 a member of Study Group 1 expressed a desire for greater understanding. Cayce refers to this verse in his response: *...if ye will follow in not only His precepts but His example thy life will become as joyous as He has promised in the service for Him and His activities in the earth. For, though the heavens may pass away, though the earth may fail, His promises shall not fail. For, all that was made, all that is active in the influences in the earth, are His.*

In John 14:3 Jesus promises that where he is going, he will prepare a place for us. Perhaps he's now working on or has completed a new heaven: **And if I go and prepare a place for you, I will come again, and receive you unto myself; that where I am, there ye may be also.** In reading 262-58 Cayce was asked by members of Study Group 1 to discuss "the kingdom and His coming." Here is a portion of his reply: *How long has been the cry of those that have manifested in the earth the glory of the Father through the Son, "Hasten, O Lord, the day of thy kingdom in the earth." How have the promises read that the Son has given? "I go to prepare a place that where I am there ye may be also. I will come again and receive you unto myself." Then...the individual heart attunes its mind and its body-activity into that consciousness of the desire for the hastening of that day. Yet the merciful kindness of the Father has...delayed the coming...know that, as thine mind, thine activities, long more and more for the glorifying of the Son in the earth, for the coming of the day of the Lord, He draws very nigh unto thee.*

Here is our prophecy from the Old Testament, Isaiah 11:1, which foretells the coming of the Master: **And there shall come forth a rod out of the stem of Jesse, and a Branch shall grow out of his roots.** Reference to this verse is included in reading 853-9 for a 43-year-old man: *Then the premise from which judgments may be drawn, and that from which the entity may know that there is soul development, there is the attunement of self with that consciousness...that is the bright and morning star, that is that rod of Jesse that still cannot be lost in the experiences of men...the love as was shown, as was manifested by Him, is* alone *the way, the manner in and through which the soul may become aware of its activity...For just being kind, just being gentle, is the means and the manner, the way. Not in a passive way, but...as He - who went about doing good each day.*

Acts tells of the Master's resurrection, his appearance to the eleven and his ascension in these words, "he was taken up; and a cloud received him out of their sight." Here we have Acts 1:11: **Which also said, Ye men of Galilee, why stand ye gazing up into heaven? this same Jesus, which is taken up from you into heaven, shall so come in like manner as ye have seen him go into heaven.** In reading 262-49 Cayce was asked about his statement in an earlier reading that "the day of the Lord is near at hand." In his reply he refers to this verse: *That as has been promised through the prophets and the sages of old, the time - and half time - has been and is being fulfilled in this day and generation, and that soon there will again appear in the earth that one through whom many will be called to meet those that are preparing the way for His day in the earth. The Lord, then, will come, "even as ye have seen him go."*

In Acts 2:17 we find a restatement of an Old Testament prophecy which appears in Joel 3:28-32: **And it shall come to pass in the last days, saith God, I will pour out my Spirit upon all flesh: and your sons and daughters shall prophecy, and your young men shall see visions, and your old men shall dream dreams.** In reading 281-58, for the Prayer Healing Group, Cayce was asked to comment on the function of the pituitary gland. He refers to this verse as follows: *It* [the pituitary] *is the door...through which physically all of the reflex actions respond through the various forces of the nerve system...in the mental it is that which gives judgement ...understanding...tolerance...Hence we find some grow old gracefully, some tolerantly, some fussily and some very meanly...This is the influence also, or the activities spoken of, as the door upon and through which the old men may dream dreams* [and] *the young men may see visions.*

Paul tells us that all shall be made alive in Christ in I Corinthians 15:22: **For as in Adam all die, even so in Christ shall all be made alive.** Reading 262-83, for Study Group 1, makes reference to this verse: *...each* [are to] *make the lessons living truths, make personal application of same. For* *the body being of the earth earthy, true indeed is the destiny as is set; that as in Adam ye all die, so in Christ are all made alive.*

In I Corinthians 15:51 Paul speaks of a mystery involving sleep (physical death?) and change: **Behold, I shew you a mystery; We shall not all sleep, but we shall all be changed.** In reading 262-87 Cayce was asked to explain this verse. Here is his reply: [**He was**] *Referring to the body; though the individual here speaking* (Paul) *looked for this to happen in his own day...Did he not bring* [up] *those things as said by Peter...That, "He speaketh many things hard to be understood, that many wrest with to their own destruction." To what did he refer? That their idea* [then]...*of time and space was limited; for they had even less conception of same than the weakest among you here!*

Revelation 21:1 speaks of a new heaven and a new earth: **And I saw a new heaven and a new earth: for the first heaven and the first earth were passed away; and there was no more sea.** In reading 281-16 Cayce was asked the meaning of "a new heaven and a new earth." He says: [**It means**] *Former things have passed away, when there is beheld within self...the whole will of the Creator, the Father,* [then]...*the forces within and without* [create] *the new heaven* [and] *the new earth.*

In our next verse, Revelation 21:2 John sees a new Jerusalem: **And I John saw the holy city, new Jerusalem, coming down from God out of heaven, prefaced as a bride adorned for her husband.** Cayce explains the meaning of this verse in reading 281-37: [**For**] *Those...that are come into the new life, the new understanding, the new regeneration, there is...the new Jerusalem. For as has been given, the place is not as a place alone but as a condition, as an experience of the soul. Jerusalem has...symbolically, meant the holy place, the holy city - for there the ark of the covenant in the minds, the hearts...the comprehensions of those who have put away earthly desires...become...the new purposes in their experience, become the new Jerusalem, the new undertakings, the new desires.*

In Revelation 21:4 John tells us that all pain, sorrow, and death have passed away: **And God shall wipe away all tears from their eyes; and there shall be no more death, neither sorrow, nor crying, neither shall there be any more pain: for the former things are passed away.** Reference to this reading is included in the following beautiful portion of reading 262-108 for members of Study Group 1: ...*only those who make Happiness in the lives and the experiences of others may indeed know what it is to be Happy. Have ye made anyone Happy that was discouraged, that was disturbed, that was misunderstood? Not that ye condone anything, but the love of God that taketh away sadness and sorrow. What is...life in the presence of the Christ depicted as? That He shall wipe away every tear, and no sickness and no sorrow shall be in that Happy land...the fundamentals* are: *Casting out fear first in thine own heart, and aiding others to aid themselves...gaining an insight into their relationships with the Creative Forces or God. Tell them of the Happiness in the Christ Way, in the manner that Jesus showed Himself to be the Christ; and the joy and Happiness in keeping His ways, His promises, His joys, His life before thee and before them always. This is the mission...and as ye share, ye become Happy...*

In Matthew 16:21 Jesus tells his disciples that he will be crucified: **From that time forth began Jesus to shew unto his disciples, how that he must go unto Jerusalem, and suffer many things of the elders and chief priests and scribes, and be killed and be raised again the third day.** Reference to this verse is contained in reading 262-119: *"Know ye not that the Son must go up to Jerusalem, there be tried, condemned, and die - even the death on the cross?"Why? That there might be indeed an advocate, a way to the Father - from the lowest depths of man's desire...*

Chapter 24 of Matthew is filled with prophecies, including the return of, "the Son of man coming in the clouds of heaven with power and great glory." Then we have Matthew 24:36: **But of that day and hour knoweth no man, no, not the angels of heaven, but my Father only.** Reading 262-58, for Study Group 1, mentions this verse: *...He has given, in patience, in listening, in being still, may ye know that the Lord doeth all things well. Be not weary that He apparently prolongs His time, for - as the Master has given, "As to the day, no man knoweth, not even the son, but the Father and they to whom the Father may reveal the Son prepareth the way that all men may know the love of the Father." And as ye would be the channel to hasten that glorious day of the coming of the Lord, then do with might that thy hands find to do to make for the greater manifestations of the love of the Father in the earth.*

In Matthew 24:34 Jesus says his prophecies will occur before this generation passes away: **Verily I say unto you, This generation shall not pass, till all these things be fulfilled.** In reading 262-60 Cayce was asked to explain this verse. Here is his reply: *Those individuals that were in hearing and in keeping of those things presented by the Master in that experience would be in...manifested form in the earth during the periods of fulfillments in the earth of the prophecies spoken of. Not in what is termed [a] generation of four score and ten years, but the experiences of those souls in the earth during those periods when there must shortly come the completing or fulfilling of those things spoken of.*

It may be any day now!

36

LOVE

Love is an emotion, a feeling. Love is also action and is reflected in what we do. The Bible verses and related Edgar Cayce readings in this chapter are primarily concerned with love as it is expressed in our activity and words.

Paul speaks of the need for brotherly love in Romans 12:10: **Be kindly affectioned one to another with brotherly love, in honor preferring one another.** We should be prepared to enter sympathetically into the experiences of our friends. Cayce makes reference to this verse in the following message for members of the Prayer Healing Group in reading 281-12: *Keep in that way, in patience, in persistence, in sincerity, in truth. Faint not that there are periods when apparently little is seen to be accomplished externally. Know that thou hast set in motion that leaven that worketh all unseen, yet will bring the consciousness of His love, His hope, His presence, into the lives of all. Each should be patient first with self, in honor preferring one another.*

Our next verse is I Corinthians 13:1 where we encounter the word charity. In the more recent Bible translations, love is used in place of charity throughout this chapter of the Bible: **Though I speak with the tongues of men and angels, and have not charity, I am become as sounding brass, or a tinkling cymbal.** Cayce refers to this verse in reading 3795-1: *...let thine heart, thine mind, thine being, be opened as with the love that passeth all understanding; remembering, as it was said of old, "Though I have faith that removes mountains, though I speak with the tongues of angels, though I may conquer even the world and have not that love, it is nothing..."*

In I Corinthians 13:4 it says: **Charity suffereth long and is kind; charity envieth not; charity vaunteth not itself, is not puffed up.** Reference to this verse is included in reading 1404-1 for a female doctor: *...love thinketh no evil; ...it is not puffed up, it is kind, it is gentle, it is patient...do not stand too oft upon thy privileges but rather humble thyself.*

Our fourth and final Bible verse by Paul on love is I Corinthians 13:7: (Love) **beareth all things, believeth all things, hopeth all things.** Reading

349-1 for a 22-year-old secretary cites this verse as follows: *...Love is the key of earth and Heaven; for though there be many lands, many joys, many blessings, without love these are as nothing, for "Love suffereth long, is kind; believeth all things, endureth all things; vaunteth not itself, is not puffed up,"* [Love] *endureth through the entire life in earth and maketh the soul One with Him.*

In John 13:34 the Master gives us a new commandment: **A new commandment I give unto you, that ye love one another; as I have loved you, that ye also love one another.** We are to be unselfish and helpful to those about us and to be kind and generous as demonstrated in the life of our Elder Brother. Cayce makes reference to this verse in the following message for Study Group 1 in reading 262-112: *...He will* hold *thee and sustain thee if ye will but put your trust in Him...what is His commandment? "That ye love one another, even as I have loved you, that the Father may be glorified in you."* Earlier in his ministry the Master had said that we are to love our neighbor as we love our self. Perhaps he had observed that this rule may not work very well where people have a very low regard for themselves, and, thus, some clarification was needed.

Here is John 15:13: **Greater love hath no man than this, that a man lay down his life for his friends.** Since this is just what He did, it sets a very high standard for us to follow in meeting His new commandment. Reading 262-29 cites John 15:13: *Be joyous in the labor that is before thee! Be the* best *of whatever position thou doth occupy; as a wife, the best* wife *in the whole community; as a friend, the* best *friend; and there is the friend that sticketh closer than the brother; yea, the friend that gives...his life for a friend. Ever gave ye the truths* [so] *that thine brother might enjoy...a moment's rest in the Lord?*

In Mark 12:31 we find the second of the two great commandments: **And the second is like, namely this, Thou shalt love thy neighbour as thyself. There is none other commandment greater than these.** Cayce makes reference to loving our neighbour as ourselves in reading 262-58 for members of Study Group 1: *Love God. Eschew evil. Love thy neighbour as thyself. For, as He gave, "A new commandment I give unto you, that ye love one another," even as the* Father *hath loved you in giving His Son that ye through faith...through the love that He has shown, may know the love of the Father and thus be the greater channel of blessings to those ye meet day by day. For ye have been called into a purpose, as into the service of the Son of man. Make known to Him thy desire, in His will...* [that] *thy will* [be] *one with His - there will come to thee many blessings, physically, mentally, spiritually.* As you will note Cayce merges the second great commandment with the Master's new commandment and then clarifies its application.

A rich young man came to the Master and asked what he must do to inherit eternal life. Jesus cites the Ten Commandments, and the young man replies that he has kept these since he was a boy. This brings us to Mark 10:21: **Then Jesus beholding him, loved him and said unto him, One thing thou lackest: go thy way, sell whatsoever thou hast and give to the poor, and thou shalt have treasure in heaven: and come, take up the cross, and follow me.** In the following reading, 281-35, Cayce refers to the very first part of this verse: *Let each of the members of the prayer group, the Glad Helpers, realize that your personality must be lost in the love of service to others...*[and] *that personal consideration as may be given any on the...prayer list becomes personal, even as it is said of Him, "and he looked on him and loved him." So you each will find a helpfulness in yourselves, and a service to those on the list, by there occasionally being...*[sent] *a cheery word to those who have asked to be remembered by the Glad Helpers in their prayer. Hence though it only be a word remember - take time to be holy; this means to find time to speak a kind word.* It's good to feel love for others and even better to demonstrate our love.

The Bible says that the rich young man became sad and went away and grieved. This is the only account we have of him in the Bible. But, the Edgar Cayce readings say this young man eventually accepted the Master's instructions and became a follower of the Christ.

In Matthew 5:46 the Master tells us to love others even if they do not love us: **For if ye love them which love you, what reward have ye? do not even the publicans the same?** Reference to this verse is made in reading 262-98 as follows: *The beauty of service is the understanding of the Knowledge of God. And as God is Knowledge, let that service, let that love that hath been shown thee be given in love, in mercy, in justice, even to those that are doubters, that are fearful, that even say unkind things. For to love those only that love thee, what profit hath thou in the Knowledge of the law of love in the Christ? For He loved those that hated Him. He died for those that would take His life - in the earth.*

Our last verse in this chapter, Matthew 12:30, does not seem to relate to love, at first glance. However, the Cayce readings cite this verse as the basis for what is termed "loving indifference": **...He that gathereth not with me scattereth abroad.** This verse is quoted in reading 1152-2: *...how can there be* loving indifference?*...How gave He, thy pattern...*[When] *they said, "See, these in thy name heal the sick, cast out demons, yet they gather not with us. Rebuke them." But what was His answer? "Nay; nay, not so - for they that gather not with us scatter abroad the praises."*

For those not familiar with the term "loving indifference," the Cayce readings include thirty-one occurrences of this term. In 603-2 Cayce was asked how to practice loving indifference. Here is his answer, *Where there may be aid given, give it. But* busy *thyself rather in other fields of activity...*In 2709-2 he says: *...not ordinary indifference, but loving indifference - that of knowing the heart, the mind, the purpose in self, is correct, and in keeping with that* [which] *is progressive in every sense.* In 352-1 we find, "How should she be treated by her family?" Here is Cayce's answer: *In that manner which may be called as loving indifference to the temperamental outbursts; not condemnation, but in that of quiet, peaceful contemplation.* In 1125-1 Cayce says, *Do not* withdraw, *but rather let thy associations be as a* loving *indifference. Not mindful of the slights and slurs...*In 1273-1 Cayce advised, *...showing a loving indifference to that which is an aversion to the entity will bring constructive experiences...*

Indifference is not loving. But, loving indifference reflects mature love and understanding. There may be some relationship between loving indifference and what has been termed "tough love."

37

THY WILL

While Jesus was speaking to a large group of people his mother and brothers came and asked to speak with Him. They remained outside and their request was relayed to the Master. Jesus identifies his disciples as his mother and brothers. This brings us to Matthew 12:50: **For whosoever shall do the will of my Father which is in heaven, the same is my brother, and sister and mother.** Reference to this verse is included in reading 262-119 for members of Study Group 1: *"Who is my mother, who is my brother, my sister? He that doeth the will of the father, the same is my mother, my brother, my sister?" These words ye know, but have ye comprehended, have ye understood? For, when there has come the slight here, the harsh word there, or the disappointment, have ye smiled and with a song upon thy heart said, "Thy will, O God, not mine, be done?" Until ye do, ye cannot comprehend the purpose for which the souls of men came into materiality; for periods of lessons* [and] *examinations.*

Here is a second reference to this verse in reading 587-6: *...who is his mother, his brother, his sister? They that do the will of the Father. What is the will? The law, the love, as expressed in... "Love the Lord thy God with all thine heart, thine body, thy soul;* [and love] *thy brother as thyself."*

Our third reference to Matthew 12:50 is from reading 866-1: *Who is thy father? Who is thy mother? They that do the will of thy Father in heaven; they that do that which makes for the glorifying, the purifying, of* [their] *lives* [and] *associations of one with another.*

This verse is also mentioned in reading 824-1: *...who is thy mother - and who is thy brother? They that do those things that make for the greater advancement of themselves and their fellow man in all their walks of life.*

In reading 5749-4, a 52-year-old housewife wanted to know how she could contact Jesus the Christ. Cayce's reply refers to Matthew 14:27: *...*Be of good cheer; it is I; be not afraid. *The making of the will of self one with His will makes a whole attunement with Him...with the making of self in accord* [with Him] *and desiring* [the] *same,* [He will] *speak with thee* [saying] *"Be not afraid, it is I."*

In Matthew 7:21 the Master tells us that our entrance into heaven depends upon our doing the will of the Father: **Not every one that saith unto me, Lord, Lord, shall enter into the kingdom of heaven; but he that doeth the will of my Father, which is in heaven.** Reading 281-19 includes this verse: *Keep the heart singing. Be more joyous in thine service day by day. "Not every one that saith Lord, Lord, but he that doeth the will of the Father." Thou may aid in helping others to find the way. Be gentle, be kind, be meek.*

Here is a second reference to this verse from reading 262-121: *Put...thy trust in the Lord. For He is life, and health, and strength to those who put their trust in Him. Not everyone that saith "Lord, Lord," shall enter in, but he that doeth the will of the Father by just being patient, just being kind to others.*

John 21:15 says: **Jesus saith to Simon Peter, Simon, son of Jonas, lovest thou me? He saith unto him, Yea, Lord, thou knowest that I love thee. Jesus saith unto him, Feed my lambs.** In reading 262-51, Edgar Cayce was asked, "How may I make my will more in accord with His will, that He will speak with me?" Here is the answer: *As He has given to those to whom He spoke... "If ye love me, keep my commandments. If ye love me, feed my sheep. If ye love me, feed my lambs." So, in the experience of all that seek to know His biddings, do with* [thy] *might, that* [which] *opportunity presents to thee in each day's activity.*

Our last Bible verse is from what is known as the Lord's Prayer in Matthew 6:10: **Thy kingdom come. Thy will be done in earth, as it is in heaven.** This verse is referenced in reading 262-29: *Do ye become rebels? Do ye find fault one with another...Rather be in that humbleness of spirit, that His will "be done in earth as it is in heaven." Thus do we become the children of the Father, the door to the way, and joint heirs with Him in glory.*

Here is a second reference to this verse from reading 262-3: *... "Not as I will but thine will be done in earth as it is in heaven." Make thine self a channel of blessings to someone; so will His blessings come to thee...*

According to the Edgar Cayce readings WILL IS:
- an attribute of the soul
- the ability to choose
- the developer or the retarder in earth experience
- the greater influence in the experience of every soul

What we do is governed by the action of the will. Here are some words from an affirmation in reading 262-3: **Not my will but thine, O Lord, be done in and through me.** In order for our will to be attuned to that of the Father, it is helpful if our desires are His desires and in reading 262-60 we find this affirmation: **Father, let Thy desires be my desires. Let my de-**

sires, God, be Thy desires, in spirit and in truth.

Our final reference to Matthew 12:50 is from reading 262-87: *Whom did He say is thy father, thy mother, thy sister, thy brother? He that doeth the will of the Father in heaven...They that love* truth *rather than the...gratifying of* fleshly *desires. This does not indicate that no beauty, no joy, no happiness is to be in the experience of those who claim to seek to be the channel of blessings, or...inspiration to others! Who is the father of Joy...Happiness...Peace?...For he that is long-faced, he that is sorry for the world is sorry most for himself...*

38

QUALITIES TO CULTIVATE

In I Peter 3:11 we are instructed to avoid evil, do good, and seek peace: **Let him eschew evil, and do good; let him seek peace and ensue it.** Edgar Cayce includes reference to this verse in the following advice for a 48-year-old merchant in reading 1603-1: *It is not well that any soul or mind should be* satisfied, *for that indicates staleness, lack of growth. Be* content...know, *this is the whole law - to love God, eschew evil, and love thy neighbor as thyself!* Be content but not satisfied. Be happy with what you have. But, be active and continue to seek growth for yourself and others.

In I Peter 3:8 we are directed to be united in sympathy, love, and humility: **Finally, be ye all of one mind, having compassion one of another, love as brethren, be pitiful, be courteous.** Cayce refers to this verse in the following message for the Prayer Healing Group in reading 281-35: *...be of one mind, one purpose, one desire, by and through a common cause...[This] should bring - a unison of thought.* We are to be like-minded, compassionate, tenderhearted, humble-minded, and united in sentiment and disposition.

Being a follower of the Master involves more than listening. Here is Luke 8:21: **And he answered and said unto them, My mother and my brethren are these which hear the word of God and do it.** Reading 3645-1 for a 36-year-old lady mentions this verse: *...the universal consciousness...is a part of the entity's whole being. Let that love be without dissimilation. For who is the father, the mother, the brother? He that doeth the will of the Father, he may be thy brother...* It's good to be a doer. Doing the right thing is even better!

Matthew 5:5 states: **Blessed are the meek: for they shall inherit the earth.** In reading 262-25 Cayce discusses the importance of controlling anger saying, "This is patience, and love, and hope, and meekness, and pureness of heart." Then he refers to this verse as follows: *The meek shall inherit the earth, said He - the pure in heart shall see God. They are* [His] *promises! Believest thou Him?*

In Galations 5:22 Paul lists the fruit of the Spirit: **But the fruit of the**

Spirit is love, joy, peace, long suffering, gentleness, goodness, faith, meekness, temperance... Reading 254-68 includes reference to this verse: *As ye seek Him, so does like beget like. For, ye are co-laborers with Him, if ye have put on the whole of His love in thine own life. Feed, then, upon the fruits of the spirit. Love, hope, joy, mercy, long-suffering, brotherly love, and the contact, the growth, will be seen; and within the consciousness of the soul will the awareness come of the personality of...God in thee!*

The message of Luke 18:14 is to be humble: **I tell you, this man went down to his house justified rather than the other: for every one that exalteth himself shall be abased; and he that humbleth himself shall be exalted.** Being abased and exalted in life are referred to in the following portion of reading 262-58: *...as the love of the Father is manifested in the earth through the Son, so may self - become selfless in thy associations with those that...*[indulge in] *self-exaltation or self-glorification, for of such is it said, "Though ye may do wonders in the earth in my name, self may be abased." But those that glory in the love of the Father through the Son, in* selflessness, *may be exalted in the manifestations in the earth.*

John tells us in I John 1:4 that his purpose in writing is to bring joy: **And these things write we unto you, that your joy may be full.** Cayce refers to this verse in the following message for a member of the Prayer Healing Group in reading 281-61: *The way, the purpose, the aims and desires should ever be set in being of a purposeful helpfulness to others; that His joy in thee may be full.*

In Philippians 4:8 Paul tells us to think about things that are true, honest, just, pure, and lovely: **Finally, brethren, whatsoever things are true, whatsoever things are honest, whatsoever things are just, whatsoever things are pure, whatsoever things are lovely, whatsoever things are of good report; if there be any virtue, and if there be any praise, think on these things.** This verse is included in reading 3356-1: *Know that whatever is good, whatever is true, whatever has virtue, should be considered. Think on these things. For it is the purpose, the spirit with which an individual entity applies new knowledge in the earth, that governs whether such knowledge becomes good or bad.*

Based on these Bible verses here are some qualities to be cultivated:
- Be active
- Be contented but not satisfied
- Be compassionate
- Be courteous
- Be good (for something)
- Be faithful
- Be gentle
- Be honest

- Be humble
- Be joyous
- Be just
- Be lovely
- Be long suffering
- Be loving
- Be meek
- Be peaceful
- Be pure
- Be truthful

39

SIN

In this chapter on sin we will first look at five verses from the Old Testament. Genesis 4:7 tells us that if we do not do well sin is at our door: **If thou doest well, shall thou not be accepted? And if thou doest not well, sin lieth at the door. And unto thee shall be his desire, and thou shall rule over him.** Edgar Cayce mentions this verse in reading 262-114 for members of Study Group 1: *...the truth would make us free. Of what? Selfishness!...we should each know that the sin which lies at our door is ever the sin of selfishness, self-glory, self-honor. Hence as the Master has said, unless we become even as He, we may not in* any *wise enter in.*

God commanded Adam and Eve not to eat fruit from the tree in the center of the garden lest you die. In Genesis 3:4 the serpent tells Eve she will not die: **And the serpent said unto the woman, Ye shall not surely die.** Reference to this verse is included in reading 2784-1 for a 42-year-old man: *...there is a way that seemeth right to a man, but the end thereof may be death. For the law is, "in the day ye eat thereof...ye shall surely die." Only Satan...would...say, as he did, "Ye will not surely die"...by one man sin came into God's creation. By one man death came. By that same man death was overcome. Thus He is the way, the truth and the light...* Sin came with Adam, who progressed, and, incarnating as Jesus became The Way.

God asked Adam if he had eaten fruit from the forbidden tree. Adam offers this excuse in Genesis 3:12: **And the man said, The woman whom thou gavest to be with me, she gave me of the tree, and I did eat.** Reading 262-125 cites this verse as follows: *Sin...is willful disobedience...*[The Master said] *"Know ye not that I must be about my Father's business?" How different from that other, "The* woman *thou gavest me,* she *persuaded me, and I did eat?"*

Isaiah 14:12 says: **How art thou fallen from heaven, O Lucifer, son of the morning! how art thou cut down to the ground, which didst weaken the nations.** Edgar Cayce comments on the meaning of the term Lucifer in reading 262-89: *...the prince of this world, Satan, Lucifer, the Devil - as a soul - made those necessities...of the consciousness in materiality;* [so]

that man might - or that the soul might - become aware of its separation from the God-force. Hence the continued warring that is ever present in materiality or in the flesh, or the warring - as is termed - between the flesh and the devil, or the warring between those influences of good and evil. As the soul is…a portion of the Divine, it must eventually return to that source from which, of which, it is a part. Will thy *name be written there?* Let's hope so!

The last of our Old Testament verses on sin, Jeremiah 17:9, tells us that the heart (our feelings) are deceitful and wicked: **The heart is deceitful above all things, and desperately wicked: who can know it?** Reference to this verse is included in reading 281-44: *…how is it termed in the record? That the heart and purpose of man is to do evil! In the present when evil has taken hold, it forms itself into those influences which are called habits, or inclinations, or intents; and it is necessary to eliminate these from the purposes and aims and desires of individuals.*

In our first New Testament verse on sin, a woman found in adultery was about to be stoned to death but the words of Jesus saved her life. Here are His parting words to her in John 8:11: **…And Jesus said unto her, Neither do I condemn thee: go, and sin no more.** In reading 3292-1, a 47-year-old woman wanted to know how she had failed to use wisely what God had given her and why she was so confused about so many things. Cayce's reply makes reference to this verse: *Do not…feel that ye have failed. Do not judge self. You have not failed* yet. *You only fail if you quit trying. The trying is oft counted for righteousness. Remember as He has given, "I do not condemn thee." Go be patient, be kind, and the Lord will be with thee!*

Here is Matthew 5:29-30: **And if thy right eye offend thee, pluck it out, and cast it from thee: for it is profitable for thee that one of thy members should perish, and not that thy whole body should be cast into hell. And if thy right hand offend thee, cut it off, and cast it from thee: for it is profitable for thee that one of thy members should perish, and not that thy whole body should be cast into hell.** Reading 281-27 for the Prayer Healing Group includes reference to this verse: *Healing…is all of the same source. Whether it be in the application of those influences that would separate, as He hath given, "If thine eye offend thee, pluck it out. If thine hand offend thee, cut it off." What meaneth these? That there may be in the experience of individuals those influences that become necessary in the material world for the separation of those bodily forces that have become, as it were, entangled in the influences about the individual, the influences brought on by individual activity, influences magnified by associations in the…activities of an individual.* Just as physical surgery is sometimes required for health of the body, there may be times when surgery is required in terms of our association and activity with other people for our better mental and/or spiritual development.

II Corinthians 5:21 says: **For he hath made him to be sin for us, who know no sin; that we might be made the righteousness of God in him.** In reading 262-59 Cayce was asked to explain, "For he hath made Him to be sin who knew no sin." Here is his reply: *...though He were* without *sin yet He thought it not robbery to make Himself equal with God...when the spirit brought* in *spirit, that of condemnation or sin in manifested form in the earth, then the Son came* in *manifested form - or in sin - that through Him the earth, or the spirit of man, might have the advocate with the Father and through Him once for all be made free from sin through that activity of the Christ-Spirit in the earth. Hence that given, He became sin - or* in *sin, rather should be the translation - that those in sin, or in the earth...might know the Light and have Life, and...have it more abundantly...*

In John 17:12 it states: **While I was with them in the world, I kept them in thy name: those that thou gavest me I have kept, and none of them is lost, but the son of perdition; that the scripture might be fulfilled.** Cayce was asked to explain "and none of them is lost, but the son of perdition." Here is his reply in reading 262-93: *He* [Judas] *had chosen rather to seek his* own *ways and to deceive others into seeking to follow their own manner rather than that there should be credence or credit or loyalty or love shown to that source from which life, consciousness or manifestations emanated. Hence that spoken of him that rebelled against the throne of heaven, and manifested in the flesh in the one who betrayed Him. Then, all are sons of perdition - or allow that force to manifest through them - who deny Him, or who betray Him, or who present themselves to be one thing and...for personal gain, or for reasons of gratification - do otherwise; for they do but persecute, deny,* [and] *betray Him.*

We also must not cause someone else to sin, as mentioned in Romans 14:13: **Let us not therefore judge one another any more: but judge this rather, that no man put a stumbling block or an occasion to fall, in his brothers way.** Reading 262-91 includes reference to the creation of stumbling blocks for ourselves or others: *...Glory is that which is sought in the experience of each and every individual...Glory, is the natural expression also of every thing, condition,* [or] *circumstance that gives to man and his mind a concept of Creative Forces as they manifest in materiality. Hence* [glory] *is the natural seeking of man. Yet, as with* every *phase of man's experience with conditions that deal with the fellow man, this may be turned into that which may become a stumblingblock to self or to others.*

Here is Matthew 23:27: **Woe unto you, scribes and Pharisees, hypo-**

crites! for ye are like unto whited sepulchers, which indeed appear beautiful outward, but are within full of dead men's bones, and of all uncleanness. Edgar Cayce refers to this verse in reading 262-10: ... *"Not that which entereth into a man defileth him, but that which cometh forth. Many are as whitened sepulchers, beautiful without but within full of dead men's bones!" This* [refers] *to the activities of a physical being,* [but] *taking into consideration the activities of a physical body, a mental body,* and *spiritual body.* One *that lives to gratify the desires of the fleshly body* alone *may be beautiful without (and often is!), but within is as of those foul, that make for the belittling of the soul...*

John 15:22 states: **If I had not come and spoken unto them, they had not sin: but now they have no cloak for their sin.** Reference to this verse is included in reading 262-82: *...as the Master hath said, "Had I not come ye would not have known sin." Hence man in his awareness of sin,* [and] *of the Christ Spirit, of that which makes him...awakened...may become aware of God's destiny for the soul. Shall it return empty-handed or bearing thy name? ...the Destiny of the Soul is to return to the Giver, the Maker.*

The message of James 4:17 is similar to that found in the preceding verse: **Therefore to him that knoweth to do good, and doeth it not, to him it is sin.** Cayce refers to this verse in reading 262-65: *...each soul is a free-will agent in a material world, with the choice before it in its own experience. This you each will recognize as you meditate upon putting it into* activity. *To know to do good and to do it not, is what? He that had experienced same gave that it is sin.*

In Matthew 15:11 it says: **Not that which goeth into the mouth defileth, a man; but that which cometh out of the mouth, this defileth a man.** This verse is mentioned in reading 5401-1: *...as the Master gave, it is not that which entereth in the body, but that which cometh out that causes sin. It is what one does with the purpose, for all things are pure in themselves and are for the sustenance of man, body, mind, and soul, and remember - these must work together...*

Paul confesses his sin in I Corinthians 15:9: **For I am the least of the apostles, that am not meet to be called an apostle, because I persecuted the church of God.** The following reading, 262-126, includes Paul's persecution of the church: *To be sure, many are active as illustrated in that pronouncement of Paul, "I did in all good consciousness persecute the church." This to him was sin, yet - according to the consciousness - righteous sinning; for when he was aware of his error, through the call to service, he became...active in the defense of that...he had persecuted in all good consciousness. Then, one's consciousness - by* [its] *activity... may...make for those choices by the individual of that which to another would be...sin. To be sure, this is an approach only from the individual* *standpoint, the individual's activity; but considered in the light of those influences of statements which we have made here, ...one had best be active and in error than not doing anything at all.*

40

HEALING

The Edgar Cayce readings say that which we call God works through many fields, products and services to provide healing. In this chapter our focus is on spiritual healing. The healing verse most frequently quoted in the readings is Psalm 103:3: **Who forgiveth all thine iniquities; Who healeth all thy diseases?** In reading 281-3 a member of the Prayer Healing Group asked if they would ever be able to diagnose ailments, and, if so, what spirit would give this information to them. Here is Cayce's reply: *Will the body-consciousness intend or desire* [this], [then] *that may be a portion of the entity's work. This will be accomplished by a unison of cosmic or universal forces...This may be raised in anyone that so cleanses their own physical consciousness, or raises the vibrations of their own physical bodies, to that attunement that brings healings to others; for as has been given, "Who healeth all thine infirmities? Who bringeth the hope, the abounding forces of love, in thine life?"*

Here is Zechariah 4:6: **...Not by might, nor by power, but by my spirit, saith the Lord of hosts.** In reading 1125-1 a 56-year-old osteopath asked Cayce how she could always know the way for each individual's better healing. Cayce's reply includes reference to this verse: *By knowing that there must be aroused in the individual...that which* awakens *the Creative Forces within itself. "Not by might nor by power, but by my word, saith the Lord of hosts."...*[This] *awakens and loosens...the spiritual essence of life itself - for its greater, its better propagation.*

Luke 4:23 says: **...Physician, heal thyself...** In reading 281-12 for members of the Prayer Healing Group, Cayce says that healing for others must come first in self: *...those that would bring healing to others, the healing of every sort must come first in self* [so] *that it may be raised in another. This...healing in self* [aids] *that raising of the vision that may heal... others.*

In II Chronicles 7:14 it says: **If my people, which are called by my name, shall humble themselves, and pray, and seek my face, and turn from their wicked ways; then will I hear from heaven, and will forgive their sin, and will heal their land.** In reading 262-3 a member of Study Group 1 asked how they could best cooperate with and serve the group. Cayce includes a brief reference to this verse in his reply: *Do with all thy might what thy hand finds to do. Let* this *mind be in you as was in Him, "Not as I will but* Thine *will be done in earth as it is in heaven." Make thine self a channel of blessings to* someone; *so will His blessings come to thee, as an individual, as an integral part of the group. "They that seek my face shall find it."*

Mark 2:9 states: **Whether is it easier to say to the sick of the palsy, Thy sins be forgiven thee, or to say arise, and take up thy bed, and walk?** Reference to this verse is included in reading 281-9 for members of the Prayer Healing Group: *...prayer for others is* [a] *defense against influences that would hinder...prayer and meditation - and the unison of purpose for healing -* [work] *against an offense committed in the body* [which is] *to be overcome, or made every whit whole by His cleansing, forgiving* [and] *His lifegiving power. Hence the closer the union of purpose* [produces] *that* [which] *He* gave, *"Thy* faith *has made thee whole." Whether* [it's] *easier to say, "Thy sins be forgiven", or "Take up thy bed and walk?" The forgiveness, the cleansing, is in Him.*

Here is Luke 5:31: **And Jesus answering said unto them, They that are whole need not a physician, but they that are sick.** The following portion of reading 262-22, for members of Study Group 1, includes reference to this verse: *"Were there not ten healed? Where are the other nine?"...the healing was just as true for the nine as* [for] *the one. They that are whole need not the physician...in thy ministering be rather in that of* daring *to do even for those that would not understand, but doing rather for Him...*

Here is Luke 8:48: **And he said unto her, Daughter, be of good comfort: thy faith has made thee whole; go in peace.** This verse is cited in reading 264-50: *...* [Strive for] *less and less of self...of self indulgence...of self glory* [and] *more and more that the glory of the Father through the Son may be made manifest in the experiences of self...These must be an activity in self. For as hath been given, "By faith are ye healed and not of yourself."*

Revelation 22:2: **...On either side of the river, was there the tree of life, which bare twelve manner of fruits, and yielded her fruit every month: and the leaves of the tree were for the healing of the nations.** Reference to this verse is included in reading 262-78: *...the tree of life in the garden...its leaves are for the healings of the nations;* [These] *are the leaves that may fall from thy lips, from thy activities* [with] *thy fellow man...Why? Because of thine own self, because thou art grounded in the water of life itself...*

A woman suffering from hemorrhages for twelve years touched the fringe of the Master's clothes and was immediately healed. He comments on this in Luke 8:46: **And Jesus said, Somebody hath touched me: for I**

perceive that virtue is gone out of me. In reading 69-3 this question was asked: Is it necessary for one to feel vibration in helping others? Here is Cayce's answer: *Not necessary, unless there is felt within self that it must be a form of expression. If the results come, then it is known. How often gave He that "Virtue has gone out of me," or that the vibration by the touch of faith had required strength of Him? ...each in their* own *way and manner...*[know] *wherein the help cometh.*

A man lame from birth asks alms from Peter who responds in Acts 3:6: **Then Peter said, Silver and gold have I none; but such as I have give I thee: In the name of Jesus Christ of Nazareth rise up and walk.** In reading 281-7, for the Prayer Healing Group, Cayce was asked to define vibration in relation to healing. He refers to this verse in his reply: *Vibration is, in its simple essence...raising the Christ Consciousness in self to such an extent* [that] *it may flow out of self to him thou would direct it to. As, "Silver and gold I have none, but such as I have give I unto thee." "In the name of Jesus Christ, stand up and walk." That is an illustration of vibration that heals, manifested in a material world. What flowed out of Peter and John* [was that] *...received by knowing self in its entirety, body, mind, soul, is one with that Creative Energy that is LIFE itself!*

41

LIGHT

Four of the seven verses in this chapter on light are from the Gospel of John and two are from the First Letter of John. We begin with the remaining verse, Matthew 6:22, where the Master speaks of the eye as the light of the body: **The light of the body is the eye; if therefore thine eye be single thy whole body shall be full of life:** In reading 1442-1, a 14-year-old young man was concerned about apparent insanity in his father's family. He asked what he should do to avoid such influences in his own experiences. Edgar Cayce replies: *Keep the eye single to a service for* spiritual *understanding, and a mental aberration or a mental disturbance may not touch thee!*

Our second reference to this verse is from reading 1537-1: *Thy purpose...thy heart and thy life must be a* consistent *thing! For if thine eye be single...then thy* whole body *is full of light...But if ye are attempting to have thy physical body doing just as it pleases, thy mental body controlled by "What will other people say?" and thy spiritual body and mind shelved...*[then] *there* cannot *be other than confusion!*

Our last reference to Matthew 6:22 is from 262-85 where Cayce was asked to explain "If thine eye be single, thy whole body shall be full of light." Here is his response: *The I am, the I Self, the I Consciousness...the eye that hath looked on, the eye that hath observed, the eye that hath desired in the heart. That eye. If thine eye be single thine whole body is then full of light.*

I John 1:5 states: **This then is the message which we have heard of him and declare unto you, that God is light, and in him is no darkness at all.** Cayce refers to this verse in reading 262-115: *He came...when man was in the beginning of what we have recorded as...God brought light. What is Light, then, in that sense? In that city, in that place, there is no need of the sun, nor of the moon, nor the stars; for He is the light...and in Him is no darkness at all!*

Here is John 8:12: **Then spake Jesus again unto them, saying, I am the light of the world: he that followeth me shall not walk in darkness, but shall have the light of life.** In reading 2533-8 Cayce was asked to define

"The light that cannot fail." Here is a portion of his reply: *This is the Christ...And when that light enters, by the individual entity opening the consciousness of self to that abiding presence, the light has entered. What is light? That from which, through which, in which may be found all things, out of which all things come. Thus the first of everything that may be visible, in earth, in heaven, in space, is of that light* [and] *is that light!*

In John 9:5 it says: **As long as I am in the world, I am the light of the world.** Edgar Cayce refers to Jesus as the light of the world in reading 288-30: *...He is the light of the world. In Him is no darkness at all! Leave all in His hands, for He has appointed the way. Choose thou whom ye will serve. Those things that would make* [ye] *afraid, or those* [things] *that satisfy for the moment, or those* [things] *that build and build in the heart and soul to* life *everlasting in Him.*

John 12:46 says: **I am come a light into the world, that whosoever believeth on me should not abide in darkness.** The following reading, 288-30, mentions this verse: *...know in whom, in what, thou hast believed, and* believing - *in faith - give that* [into] *His keeping, and there will come, as has been promised in thine vision...through and by the way of the Cross...the light of His countenance made manifest in thine own life and existence; for in Him is life, and light, and He is the light of the world.*

Here is John 1:5: **And the light shineth in darkness; and the darkness comprehended it not.** Reference to this verse is included in reading 1716-1: *The...* [WORD] *dwelt among men, and men knew it not - for being blinded to the light, only those that choose to make themselves one with the whole, are given the introspective influence in their material phases.*

Finally, I John 1:7: **But if we walk in the light, as he is in the light, we have fellowship one with another...** In reading 262-67 the following reference is made to this verse: *Walk in the light, even as He is in the light. Let less and less of self enter into the desires of thy mind, of thy body,* [so] *that thy desire may be, "Have Thy way with me, O Lord. Be thou the guide. Let that Thou would have me do be the purpose of my life, the desire of my heart, and let me give the praise to Him that leads the way."*

42

LIFE/DEATH

In this chapter we will be looking at some Scripture and related Edgar Cayce readings dealing with the life transition experience called death. The readings say that as we come to a better understanding of that experience which we call death we will come to a better understanding of the experience known as life. Our first verse is II Corinthians 5:8: **We are confident, I say, and willing rather to be absent from the body, and to be present with the Lord.** Paul's message here is that when death separates us from our physical body we will be at home with the Father. In reading 1824 -1 Cayce refers to this verse in his comments to the son of an 82-year-old lady who was at death's door: *...there should not be sorrow and sadness in those periods when the physical turmoils and strifes of the body are laid aside, for the moment, for the closer walk with Him. For indeed to be absent from the material body is to be present with the Lord. Let those admonitions and those promises, then, fill thy life - and so determine within selves that ye will walk the closer with Him day by day. And then when the shadows, as here, begin to close about, and there is the meeting at the river, there will be indeed no sorrow when this barque puts out to sea.*

In Isaiah 38:1 the king is instructed to put his house in order: **In those days was Hezekiah sick unto death. And Isaiah the prophet the son of Amoz came unto him, and said unto him, Thus saith the Lord, Set thine house in order: for thou shalt die, and not live.** Reading 281-41 refers to setting our house in order: *...woe be unto thee - lest ye set thy house in order. For as has been indicated, there are physical contacts in thy own body with thy own soul, thy own mind. Does anyone have to indicate to you that if you touch a needle there is pain felt? Ye are told that such an awareness is an activity of consciousness that passes along the nervous system to and from the brain. Then, just the same there are contacts with that which is eternal within thy physical body. For there is the bowl that must one day be broken, the cord that must one day be severed from thine own physical body, and to be absent from the body is to be present with God.* Not a good time to let your insurance lapse!

Ecclesiastes 12:6 gives an esoteric explanation of what takes place internally when the soul leaves the body: (If) **ever the silver cord be loosed, or the golden bowl be broken, or the pitcher be broken at the fountain, or the wheel broken at the cistern** (death follows). The silver cord and its destruction is discussed in reading 262-20: *...that which gives more understanding of the relationship of self with the creative forces of a universal experience, rather than individual, makes for a closer walk with God, that from which the essence of life itself has its emanation. In the body we find that which connects the pineal, the pituitary, the lyden, may be truly called the silver cord, or the golden cup [which] may be filled with a closer walk with that which is the creative essence in physical, mental and spiritual life; for the destruction wholly of either will make for the disintegration of the soul from its house of clay.* And thus when the soul senses that physical death is imminent and unavoidable it may decide "I'm out of here."

In Matthew 20:16 it says: **So the last shall be first, and the first last...**Cayce was asked to explain these words in reading 262-39. Here is his response: *...when life ends it begins. The end is the beginning of the transposition, or the change. The first is last the last is first. Transposition.*

II Peter 1:5 states: **Moreover I will endeavor that ye may be able after my decease to have these things always in remembrance.** In reading 281-16, reference is made to this verse: *Remember, then, that Peter - chosen as the rock, chosen to open the doors of that known today as the church - had said to this companion [John], "I will endeavor to keep thee in remembrance; even after my demise I will return to you."*

Here is Revelation 14:3: **And I heard a voice from heaven saying unto me, Write, Blessed are the dead which die in the Lord from henceforth: Yea, saith the Spirit, that they may rest from their labors; and their works do follow them.** Reading 281-36 includes this verse: *...as He preached to those bound even in the shadows of death, [they] loosened that which made it possible for them to become again conscious of the opportunities for reconstructing...themselves...so blessed then are they who die in the Lord - for the body alone is bound [by death].*

Genesis 1:11 says: **And God said, Let the earth bring forth grass and herb yielding seed, and the fruit tree yielding fruit after his kind, whose seed is in itself, upon the earth: and it was so.** Reading 136-18 makes reference to this verse: *We find in a grain of corn or wheat that germ that, set in motion through its natural process with Mother Earth and the elements about same, brings forth corn after its kind...the germ being of a spiritual nature, the husk or corn, and the nature or physical condition, being physical forces...Then, as the corn dies, the process is as the growth* *is seen in that as expressed to the entity, and the entity expressing same...that death, as commonly viewed, is not that of the passing away, or becoming a non-entity, but the phenomenized condition in a physical world that may be understood with such an illustration...* The principle of continuity of life is not limited to humankind.

Mark 9:42 says: **And whosoever shall offend one of these little ones that believe in me, it is better for him that a millstone were hanged about his neck, and he were cast into the sea.** In reading 1175-1 Cayce was asked about suicide. His response makes reference to this verse: *No man liveth to himself, no man dieth to himself. No man hath been so low that* some *soul hath not depended upon, relied upon same for strength. Thus we find while there may be those experiences, these are rather of a selfish nature. But remember He gave, "Those that would offend one of these, my little ones, better that a millstone were hanged about his neck and he were cast into the depths of the sea." Then, when thine whole body and the purposes of thine mind...[is]* to do evil, [then it would be] *well that they be separated from the channel or the means of bringing offense.*

43

NATURE OF MAN

Our verses on the nature of man come from several sections of the Bible. We have three verses from Genesis, one from Proverbs, three from the Gospels, and we finish with two verses by Paul. Our first verse is Genesis 2:7: **And the Lord formed man of the dust of the ground, and breathed into his nostrils the breath of life; and man became a living soul.** Reading 262-63 includes the following reference to this verse: *As given in the Scripture, there was breathed into man the soul. Biologically, man makes himself as an animal of the physical; with the desires that are as the instinct in animal...*

Reading 281-53 also mentions this verse: *God breathed into man the breath of life and he became a living soul...with the first breath of the infant there comes into being in the flesh a soul - that has been attracted ...by all the influences and activities that have gone to make up the process through the period of gestation...*

As you may know Genesis includes two accounts of the creation of man. The previous verse is the second account. However, most believe it is the older of the two. Now we will look at Genesis 1:27: **So God created man in his own image, in the image of God created he him; male and female created he them.** Edgar Cayce refers to this verse in reading 3509-1: *...magnify the virtues...minimize the faults. It would be well for this to be thy policy, thy tenet. For there is none so bad nor yet so good that any can afford to judge or speak evil of the other. Ye may speak evil of evil things, but not of man. For he is in the image of his God and his God is eternal...man's soul is eternal. Then speak not evil of thy brother, lest ye condemn thine own self.*

Genesis 6:2 states: **The sons of God saw the daughters of men that they were fair, and took them wives of all which they chose.** In reading 262-119 Cayce was asked to explain the meaning of sons of God and daughters of men. Here is his reply: *...the influences of those souls that sought material expression pushed themselves into thought forms in the earth...When the Creative Forces, God, made...the first man - or God-man he was the beginning of the Sons of God. Then those souls who en-*

tered through a channel made by God - not by thought [forms], *not by desire, not by lust, not by things that separated continually - were the Sons of God* [and] *the Daughters of God. The Daughters of Men, then, were those who became the channels through which lust knew its activity; and it was in this manner...that the conditions were expressed as given of old, that the Sons of God looked upon the Daughters of Men and saw that they were fair, and* **lusted!** As you can see, the readings, here and elsewhere, give us a somewhat modified translation of the verse.

Here is Proverbs 27:19: **As in water face answereth to face, so the heart of man to man.** The following advice for a member of Study Group 1 in reading 262-7 makes reference to this verse: *Doubt not self nor self's abilities, for in* doing *does strength come. Keep that consciousness that answers to self, as face answers to face in the water, and this will bring the answer in self...*[that] *the Spirit of the Creative Forces bears witness with thine* own *spirit.*

In Matthew 19:17 it says: **And he said unto him, why callest thou me good? there is none good but one, that is God...** The following reference is from reading 262-128: *As indicated by Him, there is none righteous - save the Father. Thus all righteousness is bound in the attempt of individuals to make application of that* [which] *in the material* [is] *termed good. And yet good appears in varied forms to man's consciousness. Good being from the all-good, or as He gave there is none good save God - then that which would be good for* [one] *individual might not be* [good] *to another...and thus it would be sin to that individual. Thus Righteousness Versus Sin becomes...a personal application of the individual's awareness of God's purpose.*

Mark 2:27 says: **And he said unto them, The Sabbath was made for man, and not man for the Sabbath.** In reading 3976-21, Edgar Cayce was asked to comment on the true spirit of Thanksgiving. He refers to this verse in his discourse: *What...will* ye - *as servants...as children of a living God, of a living promise to thee -* do about *such a period, such a day? For the day itself is as nothing. Remember how He as the Teacher of teachers gave that the Sabbath was made for man,* not *man for the Sabbath! Then remember, Thanksgiving is thy* opportunity *to show thy appreciation to thy friend, thy home, thy mother, thy children...*[and] *most of all to thy God!*

Our next verse, John 17:16, is a portion of the Master's prayer on the evening before the crucifixion: **They are not of the world even as I am not of the world.** The disciples to whom Jesus refers are not ordinary men and will be given the aid and grace of God. In reading 1158-9 a 47-year-old housewife asked Cayce to comment on what she was to "endure" as related to an earlier reading. He refers to this verse in his reply: *...endure the* *unkind things that may be said about others. Endure that which is of the world. For as He said, "Ye are in the world but be not of the world, even as I am in the world but not of the world."...the imaginative forces...are then to be creative...*

Paul reminds us in I Corinthians 13:11 that it may be time to "grow up": **When I was a child, I spake as a child, I understood as a child, I thought as a child: but when I became a man, I put away childish things.** In reading 281-32 Cayce was asked to comment on the symbolic meaning of the four horsemen in the book of Revelation. He refers to the above verse in his reply: *...as put by another, "When I was a child I did as a child, when I was a man I did as a man," the same as in the beginning and the same as in the activities, or the same as in the relationships to all of these then as has been given heretofore - they must be as one, they must be compatible, they must be coordinate, they must be in the relative relationships one to another. These* [horsemen] *then become as destroying influences within the individual.* Thus, the horsemen in Revelation symbolize aspects of immaturity.

The next verse by Paul is I Corinthians 13:12; and he's still talking about "growing up:" **For now we see through a glass, darkly; but then face to face: now I know in part; but then shall I know even as also I am known.** In reading 262-9 Cayce was asked, "How may I learn to know self as I am known?" Here is his reply: *...literally, stand aside and watch self pass by! Take the time to occasionally be sufficiently introspective of that, that may happen in self's relation to others, to see the reactions of others...to that...done by self...as has been given, "Now we know in part, then shall we know even as we are known." Then, in Him so let thy life be in Him, in thought, in deed, that "Ye that have known me have known the Father also" may be truly said of self. Stand aside and watch self pass by!*

You might see if a friend would make a video tape, secretly, of course.

44

ANGELS/HOLY GHOST/SPIRITS

In this chapter we will look at five verses that speak of angels, two that speak of the Holy Ghost, one that speaks of the Comforter, and one that speaks of spirits. Our first verse is Psalm 8:5: **For thou hast made him a little lower than the angels, and hast crowned him with glory and honor.** Edgar Cayce refers to this verse in reading 262-31: *...let each individual...*[give] *forth* from *His presence that which would make known to those he meets...day by day* [a greater] *awareness of that presence...in their* own *lives; and how gently one...* [should] *look upon the shortcomings of his brother...for He hath made man a little lower than the angels, with that ability through his* (man's) *will to make himself equal with the Father, that* man *may even judge angels!*

Here is a second reference to this verse from reading 2172-1: *WILL* (is) *the factor which makes the human soul...different from all other creatures in the earth...For he, man, has been made just a little lower than the angels; with all the abilities to become* one *with him! not the whole, nor...lost in the individuality of the whole, but, becoming more and more personal in ALL of its consciousnesses of the application of the individuality of Creative Forces, thus, more and more at-onement with Him, - yet conscious of being himself.*

Hebrews 13:2 tells us to entertain strangers: **Be not forgetful to entertain strangers: for thereby some have entertained angels unawares.** Cayce refers to this verse in reading 262-40 for members of Study Group 1: *Be not unmindful that ye entertain strangers that come to thee in thine consciousness,* [which] *reaches to the inner self and to the cosmic spheres; for angels are often entertained. Then, clothe and feed them only upon the words and the activities of the spirit of truth, and through same may come those experiences that have been long sought...*

Here is a second reference to this verse from reading 520-3: *...be ye mindful in every association...when ye entertain strangers, for often ye entertain angels unawares. Those that may fit in the lowliest of circles* [or] *the highest of positions, whether in this or that sphere, may be just as needy. Then, do to each individual as ye would be done by* [them]...

In Genesis 28:12 Jacob dreams of a ladder from earth to heaven: **And he dreamed, and behold a ladder set up on the earth, and the top of it reached to heaven; and behold the angels of God ascending and descending on it.** In reading 281-19 Cayce was asked about a dream in which the person was climbing a ladder. He makes reference to this verse in his response: *...the ladder represents the Way...the ladder to heaven upon which there ascended and descended the angels of light...the voice ...came from above, when the self had made the way easier for those that would ascend by the experiences of self, that "I AM the way," knowing that He made of Himself no estate that others* through *Him might have the access to the Father.*

Psalm 91:11 tells us, **He shall give his angels charge over thee.** This verse was quoted in Chapter 13 on "Protection." Here we repeat this verse in order to introduce the following portion of reading 262-98: *Let the ideal of the Christ guide thee...*[Know] *thy Savior, as thy companion...*[Look] *not back but ever upward, onward, into the face, into the love of the Christ. And ye will find His presence giving thee strength...He hath given His angels charge concerning thee...the Christ has given, "I - even I - will be with thee."... this is indeed Knowledge.*

John, apparently, had frequent contact with those on the other side, as inferred in I John 4:1: **Beloved, believe not every spirit, but try the spirits whether they are of God: because many false prophets are gone out into the world.** In reading 262-85 Cayce was asked to explain the phrase "try the spirits." Here is his reply: *All force, all power, is of the one source...as was given by the Master when questioned by Pilate, "No power is given over me save from the Father." So in the experiences, as indicated oft, there are those activities from...outside of the physical body, through the mental, through the spirit of those...disincarnate influences or forces...*[try these] *as to whether there is the force or power of that constructive nature...They that deny that the Christ has come in the body are not of Him.*

John 14:16 says: **And I will pray the Father, and he shall give you another Comforter, that he may abide with you for ever.** Reading 1742-4 includes the following reference to John 14:16: *As the mental body is aware of the spiritual aptitudes, or the spiritual movements, so does the promise become manifest, that "I go to the Father, and if I go I will send my spirit and he will abide with thee always, even unto the end of the earth." So, as the spirit moves thee...let thy yeas and thy nays be governed by that...*

In Mark 13:11 Jesus tells his followers that the Holy Ghost will speak through them: **But when they shall lead you, and deliver you up, take no thought beforehand what ye shall speak, neither do ye premeditate: but**

whatsoever shall be given you in that hour, that speak ye: for it is not ye that speak, but the Holy Ghost. In reading 262-15 a member of Study Group 1 asked how to act in connection with a test to be faced in their life. Cayce refers to this verse in his reply: *As has been promised, "My grace is sufficient," and "Take no thought of what ye shall say in the hour of trial or test, for it will be given thee that as is necessary for the renewing of that spirit that makes for the understanding of 'His Spirit beareth witness with thy spirit.'" Then, meet each step as is shown thee, remembering that He has promised, "I am with thee always..."*

In Luke 1:35 Mary is told that the Holy Ghost will come to her: **And the angel answered unto her, The Holy Ghost shall come upon thee, and the power of the Highest shall overshadow thee: therefore also that holy thing which shall be born of thee shall be called the Son of God.** In reading 262-59 Cayce was asked to explain this verse: *"The Holy Ghost shall make that within thee alive." This is the body of the mother becoming aware of the spirit of truth being made manifest into materiality, or the spirit of the Father making aware through conscious forces active in* [the] *material body that the* body *is then moved or acted upon by the Spirit of the Father - or the Holy Spirit active in material force.* Mary thus became aware both mentally and physically of the activity of the Holy Spirit within her body.

Luke 2:19 tells us of Mary's response to the angelic messages and other events surrounding the birth of Jesus: **But Mary kept all these things and pondered them in her heart.** Reference to this verse is included in reading 262-46: *...through the glorying in Him, and not in self...we become conscious of that He would accomplish* through *us...as was said of her of old, "She pondered these and kept them in her heart," knowing that there would be revealed...that* [which] *each soul may need for the stimulation of* its...*broader, better service in His name.*

As we reflect upon and ponder the spiritual events in our life, God reveals what we need to do.

45

KINGDOM OF HEAVEN

In this chapter we will be looking at six Bible verses that deal with heaven. Our first verse is Matthew 18:3: **Verily I say unto you, Except ye be converted, and become as little children, ye shall not enter into the kingdom of heaven.** Our first reference to this verse implies that heaven is a state of consciousness. Here is a portion of reading 262-114: *...as the Master has said, unless we become even as He, we may not in* any *wise enter in. Enter to what? To the consciousness that our Father would...*[have us enter and become].

Here is a second reference from reading 1223-9: *...read...study...analyze how the Master treated children, young people, during His ministry in the earth, it will be seen how oft He used children, the young people, as the hope of the world...unless each individual puts away those selfish desires which arise and becomes as little children, one may never quite understand the simplicity of...Christ-like faith...Christ-like forgiveness, Christ-like love, Christ-like helpfulness to others.*

A third reference to Matthew 18:3 is from reading 5747-1: *...as He gave... "Unless ye become as little children ye shall not enter the kingdom of heaven." Be able...to be one* with *them in* their *problems, for in the tot that has just begun to think* their *problems to them are as great as thine own, yet how easily are they forgotten -* [just] *as yours should be!*

Our next verse is I Corinthians 15:50: **Now this I say, brethren, that flesh and blood cannot inherit the kingdom of God; neither doth corruption inherit incorruption.** Reading 281-7 includes this reference: *...as this body* [Edgar Cayce] *takes up life from period to period, through the laying aside of the all physical consciousness* [so] *does the body, in conquering death,* enable *the mental, the physical, to overcome those powers that would hinder it from* being *one* with *Him. "Flesh and blood may not inherit eternal life. Corruption shall put on incorruption." So, as the mind becomes attuned, clarified, cleansed, as to relationships either in the mental or material plane, so do these influences overcome that force that would separate the soul from the material, for material puts on immortality...*

Here is a second reference to this verse from reading 1567-2: *In the be-ginning, when there was the creating, or the calling of individual entities into being, we were made to be the companions with the Father-God. Now flesh and blood may not inherit eternal life; only the spirit, only the pur-pose, only the desire may inherit same.*

On that first Easter morning Mary Magdalene sees Jesus and we come to our next verse, John 20:17, which does not contain the word heaven but Jesus speaks of ascending to the Father: **Jesus saith unto her, Touch me not for I am not yet ascended to my Father: but go to my brethren and say unto them, I ascend unto my Father, and your Father; and to my God, and your God.** Edgar Cayce was asked about this verse in reading 262-88. Here is a portion of his reply: ... *"I have not yet ascended to my Father" would to some indicate that the heaven and the Father are some-where else - a place of abode, the center about which all universal forces, all energies must turn or give off from. Hence "up" may be rather from within, or to the within - of which each soul is to become aware. For heaven is that place, that awareness where the Soul - with all its at-tributes, its Mind, its Body - becomes aware of being in the presence of the Creative Forces, or one with same. That is heaven.*

In reading 262-87 the question was asked, why did Jesus, in this verse, tell Mary Magdalene not to touch his body. Here is the response: ...*the vibrations to which the glorified body was raised would have been the same as a physical body touching a high power current. Why do you say not touch the wire? If* [you are]...*not in touch with the earth* [grounded], *it doesn't harm; otherwise, it's too bad!*

In reading 294-15 Cayce was asked, "Where do entities recede to after leaving earth's plane?" His answer refers to John 20:17: *As was given... "Touch not, for I have not yet ascended unto my Father." In the separation of the soul and spirit from an earthly* [body], *each enter the spirit realm. When the entity has fully completed its separation, it goes to that...*[to] *which the entity merits* [by its activity while] *upon the earth's plane...*[It goes to] *the various spheres, or...elements,* [that have] *been prepared for its...development...*[This] *sojourn is taken, until the entity is ready for again manifesting* [in] *the flesh...the will MUST be made one with the Father,* [so] *that we may enter into that realm of the blessed, for, as has been given, only the true, the perfect, may see God, and we* must [become] *one with Him.*

Luke 20:35 tells us that marriage does not exist in heaven. **But they which shall be accounted worthy to obtain that world, and the resurrec-tion from the dead, neither marry, nor are given in marriage.** Edgar Cayce comments on this verse in reading 262-86: *As He gave in answer to the question, "Whose wife will she be?" In the heavenly kingdom ye are nei-*

ther married nor given in marriage; neither is there any such thing as sex; ye become as one - *in the union of that from which,* of *which, ye have been the portion from the beginning!*

A second reference to this verse is from reading 254-92: *...do not consider for a moment...that an individual soul-entity passing from an earth plane as a Catholic, a Methodist, an Episcopalian, is something else because he is dead! He's only a dead Episcopalian, Catholic or Methodist. And such personalities and their attempts are the same...For all are under the law of God equal...*[What] *did He say...respecting the home? "They are neither married nor given in marriage in the* heavenly *home but are* one!

In II Corinthians 5:1 Paul refers to a building of God which is eternal in the heavens: **For we know that if our earthly house of this tabernacle were dissolved, we have a building of God, an house not made with hands, eternal in the heavens.** In reading 262-60 Cayce was asked to explain this verse: *Would that each soul might grasp that truth that, though the soul may not be seen, that* [which] *it doeth* [is the] *growth it makes...*[The soul] *body, must dwell in that house not made with hands, eternal with the Father. For...life* is *the spirit of the soul, it is God eternal, however it may manifest itself in that we know as materiality or matter...*[Eternal] *things are not made with hands,* [but] *rather by the deeds done,* [by] *that expended; and...the* [deeds], *as the light itself, shineth on and on...*

We started this chapter with Matthew 18:3 where the Master says we must become like children to enter the kingdom. In Luke 18:16 He instructs the disciples to permit the children to come to Him. The readings say He truly loved the company of children. **Jesus called them unto him, and said, Suffer little children to come unto me, and forbid them not: for of such is the kingdom of God.** Reading 281-7 mentions this verse: *...raise in self that beauty of spirit as expressed in Him, "Suffer little children to come unto me, for of such is the kingdom of heaven." In raising...the consciousness of self that kingdom is being manifested, expressed, in the body. Though not seen or understood by us...His will* [is] *being accomplished,* [so] *that this entity...may be one with Him in that kingdom.*

In reading 1992-1 Cayce was asked, "Should I continue my work with children?" He replied: *By all means...For, as He taught... "Suffer little children to come unto me" is indeed the greater promise to the earth. For unless we become as children we cannot enter in; unless we learn as they. No faults, no hates remain in their experience, until they are taught to manifest such. Hence these may give thee greater insight into the meaning of it all.*

46

DIVINE ASSISTANCE

In this chapter we will look at seven Bible verses that touch on some form or aspect of divine assistance available to each of us. This assistance is not represented as being an unconditional gift. Our first verse is II Corinthians 12:9: **He said unto me, my grace is sufficient for thee: for my strength is made perfect in weakness. Most gladly therefore will I rather glory in my infirmities, that the power of Christ may rest upon me.** Cayce refers to this verse in some general words of advice for members of Study Group 1 in reading 262-73: *...as ye seek to become that channel through which there may come to others those blessings, those experiences that are thy very own, know that - if ye have chosen...the Christ, the consciousness of His Presence abiding in thee - there is that strength, that grace [which is] sufficient for ye in every trial, in every blessing, in every shadow, in every light.*

Here is a second reference to this verse from reading 303-6: *...His grace is sufficient unto the end. He that endureth the cross shall wear the crown; not he that gives up, that cries "Enough" and is ready to quit, but they that press on even when there apparently is no way out.*

Our last reference to II Corinthians 12:9 is from reading 702-1: *...His grace is sufficient unto thee, and will keep and sustain thee even in those conditions that overwhelm thee at times, and [will] bring thee to a greater knowledge and understanding in the light of that service He would have thee render in His vineyard.*

John 12:32 says: **And I, if I be lifted up from the earth, will draw all men unto me.** Reference to this verse is included in reading 262-31: *...as He gave "And I, if I be lifted up, will draw all men unto me. I will* not *leave thee comfortless, I will* come *and abide with thee." Then be not afraid to declare thyself* [in] *any and* all *experiences.* When you need assistance, "declare thyself."

Our second reference to this verse is from reading 262-3: *They that seek God may find Him...for "As ye lift Me* in *thine life, so shall* ye *be lifted in...life here, now, and hereafter."*

Here is Matthew 16:19: **I will give thee the keys of the kingdom of** heaven: and whatsoever thou shalt bind on earth shall be bound in heaven: and whatsoever thou shall loose on earth shall be loosed in heaven. This verse is included in reading 3504-1: *...the spirit is willing if ye are in soul and purpose ready to accept the Christ-Consciousness that taketh away sin...if sin is removed in purpose, in desire, and is replaced by hope, determination and the living of* [these] *in the daily life...so may it be unto thee... "Whatsoever ye shall ask in my name, believing; ye shall have in the body. What ye shall bind on earth shall be bound in... heaven."...to attain one must first believe that He is, and that He is able to keep all promises...*

In Isaiah 61:2 it states: **To proclaim the acceptable year of the Lord...To comfort all that mourn.** The following portion of reading 694-2 concludes with the opening words of this verse: *Learn that quiet first within self, from within, through those applications not only of the material things but from the counsel and meditating from within self; and ye shall stand approved unto Him, wherein there may be the peace and harmony and joy of a life lived in...active service for not only thy fellow man but -* forgetting *self - pressing on to the mark of the higher calling set in Him, to that day when ye shall stand as a light to many, as a guide to those in the dark ways, and* proclaim *the acceptable year of thy Lord!*

Numbers 16:48 says: **And he stood between the dead and the living; and the plague was stayed.** Reading 281-60 for members of the Prayer Healing Group includes this verse: *All are aware that selfishness causes many to be downtrodden, living in hovels; that greed, as is being manifested, would make slaves of thy fellow man. Yet each individual as an individual, and as a group, may fulfill those words, "He stood between the living and the dead and the plague was stayed."*

Our second reference to this verse is from reading, 3976-27, for the A.R.E. Congress in 1942, during W.W.II: *What can you do, then, as individuals, that this plague of war, this injustice to man be taken away - this plague of death and fear of destruction?* Ye may stand - even as He - Between the living and the dead! *Let those that die have that purpose even as He, "It shall* not be in vain!" *Let those that live* live *unto God; magnifying, spreading the fruits of brotherly love, kindness, patience; that this plague of war may be stayed...Only as ye* use *that birthright, that purpose, that* will *within thine own consciousness to do justice, to do right, to love good, to eschew evil, may ye as individuals, as a group, as a nation, stand between the living and the dead - and* stay *the sin that maketh man make war - of any nature - against his brother.*

Here is John 4:32: **But he said unto them, I have meat to eat that ye know not of.** Reading 281-13 includes this verse: *...properly done* [meditation] *makes one* stronger *mentally* [and] *physically, for has it not been* *given? He went in the strength of that meat received for many days? Was it not given by Him who has shown us the Way, "I have had meat that ye know not of?"*

Our second reference to this verse is from reading 281-29 in response to a question as to how the Lord's Prayer could be used in meditation to open the seven spiritual centers: [By] *feeling...the flow of the meanings of each portion of same throughout the body-physical. For as there is the response to the mental representations of all of these in the* mental *body, it may build into the physical body in the manner as He, thy Lord, thy Brother, so well expressed in, "I have bread ye know not of."* Divine assistance is greatly enhanced by both prayer and meditation.

Proverbs 18:24 says: **There are friends who pretend to be friends, but there is a friend who sticks closer than a brother.** Reading 1610-2 for a 34-year-old man Cayce refers to Jesus, the Christ, as being the kind of friend described in this verse: *He is thy friend. And as ye journey through the material experiences, ye will find indeed what it means to have a friend in Him, who has promised that as ye take hold on Him, He is able then to give that strength, that courage, that purpose for the activity in which ye may find yourself engaged. Only in Him may ye find extremes meeting, yet ye will find whether in joy, in sorrow, in disappointment, in exaltation, in whatever may be thy lot or thy activity, that He is thy friend.*

Knowing, without question, that He is truly our closest friend may be the key to our greatest source of divine assistance.

47

HIS WAY

In this final chapter on Bible quotations in the Edgar Cayce readings, we will look at seven verses which disclose something about His Way. We start with John 2:19: **Jesus answered and said unto them, Destroy this temple, and in three days I will raise it up.** In reading 1598-1 a writer and missionary asked if he should study and try to develop psychic ability. Here is Edgar Cayce's response: *It is well to study same...in those ways that are in keeping with Him who is thy Ideal! Not, then, by communion with those only of discarnate entities - or souls! but rather with that direction which comes from within. For how has He given? "Destroy this temple and in three days I will raise it again."...thy body is indeed the temple of the living God.* There *He has promised to meet thee, to commune with thee.* There *is the psychic development, the psychic phenomena that ye seek!*

A second reference to this verse is from reading 262-88: *Mind ever is the builder; hence, man in the mental sphere, man in the material sphere, must* [seek] *that experience where the Body and the Mind are as one and not warring one with another...the consciousness of the Spirit of Truth is ever the motivative influence in the experience of the individual...in the hour of trial, of temptation...He gave the lesson as to how...even though the body would be destroyed...it would be raised again.*

Here is Psalm 19:1: **The heavens declare the glory of God; and the firmament sheweth his handiwork.** Our first reference to this verse is from reading 2117-1: *...the heavens declare the glory of God and the firmament showeth His handiwork...they that study nature...find their closer relationships to the better things, the purposeful things, the things with meaning...*

Our next reference is from reading 818-1: *...there should be the realization by all that matter in any form is of the spirit, whether...[it's an] atom in a corpuscle in the body, or...any of those systems* [stars] *seen about the earth and described by the psalmist, "The heavens declare the glory of God, the firmament showeth His handiwork..."*

Our last reference to Psalm 19:1 is from reading 2454-4: *From the advent of the souls of man into materiality, laws were initiated; such as is evidenced by the psalmist, "The heavens declare the glory of God, the fir-mament showeth his handiwork"...Man's destiny lies within his indi-vidual grasp,* [if] *he takes hold upon those laws, those self-evident truths. Applying them in his relationships one to another there may come the knowledge that He walketh and talketh with those who would, who do, exalt and glorify His name in the earth.*

In times of stress we need to remember the words of the Master, Peace, be still, as mentioned in Mark 4:39: **And he arose, and rebuked the wind, and said unto the sea, Peace, be still. And the wind ceased, and there was a great calm.** In reading 540-3, a 32-year-old lady asked Cayce to com-ment on the roaring sound in her right ear during meditation. He refers to this verse in his response: *Thou hast heard...the voice of Him* [coming] *as the rushing of mighty waters; and that injunction which came with same, "Peace be still."For it is not only in the storm, nor the rocks, but rather the still small voice that comes after same. Hence thou hast drawn, and do draw, nigh unto the brink of a greater understanding. Hold fast to His hand, that leads the way!*

Luke 2:14 says: **Glory to God in the highest and on earth peace, good will toward men.** In a Christmas season reading, 262-103 for Study Group 1, Cayce makes reference to this verse as follows: *Only...to those that sought could such a message come, or could there be heard the songs of the angels, or that music of the spheres that sang, "Peace on earth - good will to men!" For this, then, is in* every *birth - the possibilities, the glories, the activating of that influence of that entrance again of god-man into the earth that man might know the way.*

In Colossians 3:16 Paul tells us to sing with grace in our heart: **Let the word of Christ dwell in you richly in all wisdom; teaching and admon-ishing one another in psalms and hymns and spiritual songs, singing with grace in you hearts to the Lord.** In reading 262-37 a member of Study Group 1 was encouraged to keep singing: *Be joyous in thy service day by day. Let not trouble bar thee from knowing the peace, the happiness, the joy in the Lord...Keep the heart singing. Keep the glory of Him before thee.*

Some words of encouragement for a member of the Prayer Healing Group are found in reading 281-19: *...keep the heart singing - and the expectancy for great things to be accomplished in His name. And there will come those...experiences, that make the...present more and more worthwhile.*

In Matthew 17:1-3 it states: **And after six days Jesus taketh Peter, James, and John his brother, and bringeth them up unto an high mountain apart, And was transfigured before them: and his face did shine as the sun and his raiment was white as the light. And behold, there appeared unto them Moses and Elijah talking with him.** Cayce was asked about communion with Spirit. He refers to these verses in reading 262-87: *"...and after six days he taketh with him Peter, James and John and goeth apart into the mountain and there was transfigured before them?" What saw they? A glorified body? The glory of the body brought what? Communion of saints? For who appeared with Him? Moses [who] to those present meant a definite undertaking which set them apart from other peoples, [who had]...communication direct with...God...And [they saw] Elijah (or John the Baptist); representing that they, too, would become messengers to a waiting world...*

Following the events described in the preceding verses Peter, James, and John hear a voice out of a "bright cloud." Was it round? Here is Matthew 17:5: **Behold, a bright cloud overshadowed them: and behold a voice out of the cloud, which said, This is my beloved Son, in whom I am well pleased; hear ye him.** Reference to this verse is included near the end of reading 262-82 for members of Study Group 1: *...the Son entered into the earth throughout the ages...there was the growth [which] made for...purposefulness...[Of] shortcomings many there were, yet tempted in all...He presented His body before the Throne of grace and mercy (as is the promise of every man) and offered it up - without question...[and became] pure. So does every soul that offers its body, its mind for a cleansing, become pure...He [went] through all [and] grew to where [the Voice said] "This is my beloved son; hear ye him," for He hath the words of life.*

48

BIBLE STUDY

The Edgar Cayce readings recommend study of the Bible in its entirety. In addition, for a large number of people, the readings suggested study of specific sections of the Bible.

Members of Study Group 1 asked Cayce what parallel material should be studied along with his readings. In his reply Cayce recommended Deuteronomy 30 through 34; Psalms 1, 2, 23, 24, 67, 91, 150; John 14, 15, 16, 17; III John; Jude; Revelation.

Listed in Appendix A, immediately following this chapter, is a tabulation of all the Bible study recommendations contained in the readings.

The section of the Bible most frequently recommended for study is John 14, 15, 16, and 17. This portion of the Gospel of John was recommended 129 times. The readings say that these four chapters sum up the message of Jesus Christ. This was the Master's last discourse to His disciples.

The section of the Bible with the second highest number of study recommendations, eighty-four, is chapter thirty of Deuteronomy. The verses most frequently quoted from this chapter tell us that the "word" is "in our heart" and that we must make choices.

Study of the 23rd Psalm was recommended eighteen times and the 24th Psalm was recommended thirteen times. Just reading either of these Psalms will help give the reader a feeling of the immanent presence of the Lord.

The thirteenth chapter of I Corinthians was recommended ten times. This is Paul's discourse on love which is patient and kind, does not insist on having its own way. It believes all things, hopes all things, endures all things, and never ends.

Study of the book of Revelation was recommended sixteen times. Edgar Cayce gave a series of twenty-four readings in which he provides a metaphysical interpretation of this book. His interpretation is unique. The readings encourage regular periods of prayer and silent meditation. The central message of Revelation is that we can find the way to our Source through prayer and meditation. The difficulty is that this message is hidden under a large amount of symbology involving angels, dragons, cities, beasts, and jewels. For example, the seven churches in Revelation symbolize the seven endocrine glands. And, just as these seven churches were meeting places for the early Christians, our seven endocrine glands are meeting places in the body where mind and spirit come together.

Study of the fifth verse of the nineteenth chapter of Exodus was recommended twenty-two times. The key point in this verse is to "obey my voice." Perhaps each of these twenty-two people needed to think carefully about the ways in which they ignore their own inner guidance. If they read Exodus 19:5 and, in reflection, come to this conclusion on their own, it could be far more effective than the reading telling them, point blank, to pay closer attention to their inner guidance.

Psalm 91 was recommended nine times. This Psalm assures us of the abiding presence and protection of God. Psalm 1 was recommended eight times. It praises those who delight in the law of the Lord and promises them prosperity. Psalm 150 was recommended seven times. This is a Psalm of praise which begins and ends with "Praise ye the Lord."

Study of the twelfth chapter of Romans was recommended twelve times. This chapter includes lots of good advice. The verse most frequently quoted is 12:3 which tells us not to think of ourselves more highly than we ought to think.

One thing to keep in mind as we study the recommended books, chapters, and verses from the Bible is their meaning for us personally, at this particular time of our life. To do this, we should read only a sentence or two at a time, and then reflect on its meaning. Doing this for ten or fifteen minutes a day would be more helpful than just reading the verses at our usual pace. Of course, reading the Bible at your normal speed would be better than simply not reading it!

Appendix A

BIBLE STUDY

Book	Chapter	Verse	Number of Times Recommended
Acts	1-2	all	2
I Corinthians	13	all	10
Daniel	12	all	1
Deuteronomy	all	all	1
	4	all	1
	30	all	84
	30-31	all	1
	30-34	all	2
	31	all	2
Exodus	19	5	22
	20	all	5
Genesis	1	1-6	1
	1	3	2
	1-3	all	1
	30	all	1
	30-33	all	2
Habakkuk	all	all	1
Hebrews	7	all	1
	11	all	1
James	all	all	3
John	all	all	6
	1	1-10	1
	3-8	all	1

Book	Chapter	Verse	Number of Times Recommended
John	14	all	9
	14	2-4	1
	14-15	all	5
	14-16	all	4
	14-17	all	129
	14	1-8	1
John	15	all	2
	15-17	all	1
	17	all	2
I John	all	all	6
II John	all	all	9
III John	all	all	4
Joshua	4	all	1
	5	all	1
	6	1-7	1
	7	all	1
	14	all	1
	24	all	2
Jude	all	all	4
Judges	5	all	1
Luke	all	all	1
	2	36-38	1
	7	19-35	1
	24	all	1
Mark	all	all	2
	14	all	1
Matthew	5	all	1
	5-7	all	1
	6	9-15	1
Nehemiah	6-8	all	1

Book	Chapter	Verse	Number of Times Recommended
New Testament	all	all	1
Philemon	all	all	1
Proverbs	all	all	1
Psalms	all	all	2
	1	all	8
Psalms	1-2	all	1
	2	all	2
	4	all	1
	22	all	1
	23	all	18
	23-24	all	1
	24	all	13
	27	all	1
	42	all	1
	57	all	1
	67	all	1
	90	all	1
	91	all	9
	119	all	1
	150	all	7
Revelation	all	all	16
Romans	all	all	5
	1-6	all	1
	3	all	1
	7	all	1
	12	all	12
Ruth	all	all	1
I Samuel	all	all	1
Titus	all	all	1
Entire Bible	all	all	8

Appendix B

VERSES INTERPRETED

Verse	Page	Text
Gen. 6:2	156	The sons of God saw the daughters of men that they were fair.
Gen. 49:10	32	The scepter shall not depart from Judah.
Exod. 20:5	5	God visits the iniquity of the parents on the third and fourth generation of those who reject him.
Exod. 20:12	107	Honor your father and your mother so that you may enjoy longevity.
Ps. 51:6	56	Thou desirest truth in the inward parts.
Ps. 91:1	120	He that dwelleth in the secret place of the Most High shall abide under the shadow of the Almighty.
Ps. 111:10	55	Fear of the Lord is the beginning of wisdom.
Jer. 17:9	144	The heart is deceitful and desperately wicked.
Hag. 2:7	13	I will shake all the nations.
Matt. 5:3	114	Blessed are the poor in spirit.
Matt. 5:4	115	Blessed are they that mourn.
Matt. 6:14-15	74	Forgive us our debts, as we forgive our debtors.
Matt. 12:36	14	We must give account for every idle word we speak.

Verse	Page	Text
Matt. 20:16	154	The last shall be first, and the first last.
Matt. 24:34	132	This generation will not pass away until all these things have taken place.
Mark 4:11-12	27	Jesus taught in parables so that those "outside" would not understand and "be forgiven."
Mark 4:25	113	He that hath not, from him shall be taken that which he hath.
Mark 16:15	108	Go into all the world and preach the gospel.
Luke 1:35	161	The Holy Spirit will come upon you (Mary) and the Most High will overshadow you.
Luke 21:8	100	Do not be deceived for many shall come saying I am the Christ.
John 14:30	36	Jesus says the ruler of this world is coming but he has no power over me.
John 17:12	145	I kept them thou gavest me and none is lost but the son of perdition.
John 20:17	163	Jesus says, I have not yet ascended to my Father.
John 20:17	163	Jesus says, Touch me not.
Acts 9:5	99	Do not kick against the pricks.
I Cor. 15:51	131	We shall not all sleep, but we shall all be changed.
II Cor. 5:1	164	If our body is destroyed, we have a building from God eternal in the heavens.
II Cor. 5:21	145	He made him to be sin who knew no sin.
Heb. 9:22	75	Without the shedding of blood, there is no forgiveness of sin.

Verse	Page	Text
Heb. 9:28	42	Christ will appear a second time to save those eagerly waiting for him.
I John 4:1	160	Believe not every spirit but try the spirits to see if they are from God.
Rev. 20:2	49	An angel binds Satan for a thousand years.
Rev. 21:1	131	I saw a new heaven and a new earth.
Rev. 21:2	131	I saw a new Jerusalem coming down from heaven.
Rev. 22:13	16	I am Alpha and Omega.

Appendix C

QUESTIONS OF SPECIAL INTEREST

Appendix D

BIBLE QUOTATIONS

Chapter & Verse	Times Quoted	Key Message	Page
Gen. 1:1	2	In the beginning God created the heaven and the earth.	49
Gen. 1:11	5	God said, "Let the earth put forth vegetation of every kind with seed in it."	154
Gen. 1:26-27	9	God created humankind in his image; male and female he created them.	156
Gen. 1:28	51	God blessed them and said to them, "Be fruitful and multiply, and fill the earth and subdue it; and have dominion over every living thing."	63
Gen. 2:7	13	God breathed in the breath of life and man became a living soul.	156
Gen. 2:17	7	Of the tree of the knowledge of good and evil you shall not eat, for the day that you eat of it you shall die.	122
Gen. 3:4	2	But the serpent said to the woman, "You will not die."	143
Gen. 3:10	1	He said, "I heard the sound of you in the garden, and was afraid because I was naked and I hid myself."	123

Chapter & Verse	Times Quoted	Key Message	Page
Exod. 19:5	43	If you obey my voice and keep my covenant, you will be my treasured possession.	12
Exod. 20:5	4	God visits the iniquity of the parents on the third and fourth generation of those who reject him.	5
Exod. 20:8	1	Remember the Sabbath day, and keep it holy.	91
Exod. 20:12	9	Honor your father and your mother.	107
Exod. 23:13	2	Be attentive to all that I have said to you.	108
Lev. 26:12	84	I will be your God and you shall be my people.	12
Num. 6:24-26	7	The Lord bless you and keep you: the Lord make his face to shine upon you, and be gracious to you; the Lord lift up his countenance upon you, and give you peace.	104
Num. 16:48	3	God stood between the dead and the living and the plague was stopped.	166
Num. 20:24	1	Aaron SHALL NOT ENTER the land that I have given to the Israelites, BECAUSE HE REBELLED against my command at the waters of Meribah.	123
Deut. 4:29	1	Seek the Lord your God and you will find him if you search after him with all your heart and soul.	119
Deut. 6:4	123	The Lord our God is one Lord.	39
Deut. 11:9	10	Keep God's commandments so that you	45

Chapter & Verse	Times Quoted	Key Message	Page
		may prolong your days in the promised land.	
Deut. 30:11-14	90	It is not who will go up to heaven or beyond the sea to bring a message; for, your answer is in your heart.	77
Deut. 30:14	3	The word is very near to you; it is in your heart.	78
Deut. 30:15	127	I have set before you TODAY life and prosperity, death and adversity.	43
Deut. 30:19	13	I have set before you life and death, blessings and curses. Choose life.	45
Josh. 24:15	188	Choose this day whom you will serve. As for me and my household, we will serve the Lord.	43
I Sam. 16:7	60	Mortals look at the outward appearance, but the Lord looks on the heart.	12
I Kings 19:12	72	After the earthquake a fire, and after the fire, a still small voice.	78
I Chron. 22:16	21	Arise and be doing. (Begin the work NOW.)	85
II Chron. 7:14	5	If my people humble themselves, pray and seek my face, I will forgive and heal.	148
Job 3:25	16	The thing that I fear comes upon me.	110
Job 14:14	1	If people die will they live again?	101
Job 19:25	33	I know that my redeemer lives.	70
Job 21:22	1	Will any teach God knowledge?	13

Chapter & Verse	Times Quoted	Key Message	Page
Ps. 1:1	3	Blessed are they who do not follow the advice of the ungodly nor sit in the seat of the scornful.	115
Ps. 1:2	3	They delight in the law of the Lord and they meditate on it.	26
Ps. 1:3	2	They are like trees planted by streams of water, which yield fruit. In all that they do they prosper.	91
Ps. 8:5	13	God made human beings a little lower than the angels.	159
Ps. 11:4	12	The Lord is in his holy temple.	48
Ps. 19:1	10	The heavens declare the glory of God.	168
Ps. 19:2	14	Day unto day pours forth speech and night unto night declares knowledge.	64
Ps. 19:7	98	The law of the Lord is perfect.	48
Ps. 19:14	35	Let the words of my mouth and the meditations of my heart be acceptable to you, O Lord.	80
Ps. 24:1	69	The earth is the Lord's and all that is in it.	12
Ps. 27:14	15	Wait for the Lord; be strong, and let your heart take courage; wait for the Lord.	118
Ps. 37:25	19	I have not seen the righteous forsaken or their children begging bread.	10
Ps. 46:1	3	God is our refuge and strength, a very present help in trouble.	94
Ps. 46:10	9	Be still and know that I am God.	104

Chapter & Verse	Times Quoted	Key Message	Page
Ps. 50:10	33	The cattle upon a thousand hills are his.	9
Ps. 51:6	1	You desire truth in my inward being, therefore teach me wisdom in my secret heart.	56
Ps. 51:10	8	Create in me a clean heart, O God, and put a new and right spirit within me.	82
Ps. 82:6	9	You are gods and children of the Most High.	61
Ps. 84:10	4	Be a doorkeeper in the house of God.	46
Ps. 84:11	28	The Lord God bestows favor and honor, and no good thing will be withheld from those who walk uprightly.	9
Ps. 90:4	2	A thousand years in your sight are like yesterday when it is past.	49
Ps. 91:1	1	He that dwells in the secret place of the Most High shall abide under the shadow of the Almighty.	120
Ps. 91:11	40	He shall give his angels charge over thee.	94, 160
Ps. 102:2	25	O Lord, incline your ear to me and answer me speedily when I call.	81
Ps. 103:2	3	Bless the Lord, O my soul, and do not forget all his benefits.	114
Ps. 103:3	37	The Lord heals all your diseases.	148
Ps. 111:10	7	The fear of the Lord is the beginning of wisdom; all those who practice it have a good understanding.	55

Chapter & Verse	Times Quoted	Key Message	Page
Ps. 139:8	11	If I ascend up to heaven you are there. If I make my bed in hell you are there.	119
Prov. 4:7	21	With all your getting, get understanding.	10
Prov. 7:15	3	I came forth to meet thee, diligently to seek thy face, and I have found thee.	119
Prov. 14:12	46	A way which seems right to a person can become the way to death.	98
Prov. 15:1	16	A soft answer turns away wrath, but a harsh word stirs up anger.	58
Prov. 18:24	2	Some play at friendship, but there is a friend who is closer than a brother.	167
Prov. 23:5	8	Riches make themselves wings and then fly away.	11
Prov. 23:7	54	As one thinks in their heart, so are they.	90
Prov. 24:12	13	If you say, "Look, we did not know this" - does not He who weighs the heart perceive it?	55
Prov. 26:11	6	A fool reverts to his folly.	122
Prov. 27:19	13	As in water face answers to face, so the mind of a person reflects that person.	157
Prov. 29:18	1	Where there is no vision, the people perish.	2
Eccles. 9:8	1	Let your garments always be white.	108
Eccles. 9:10	52	Whatever your hand finds to do, do it with your might.	84

Chapter & Verse	Times Quoted	Key Message	Page
Eccles. 11:3	25	Where the tree falls, there it will lie.	5
Eccles. 12:6	9	If the silver cord is snapped, death follows.	154
Isa. 1:18	9	Come now, let us reason together.	59
Isa. 1:18	9	Though your sins are like scarlet, they shall be made as white as snow.	75
Isa. 6:8	9	Then I said, "Here am I; send me."	85
Isa. 11:1	9	There shall come forth a Rod out of the stem of Jesse, and a branch shall grow out of his roots.	129
Isa. 14:12	1	How you are fallen from heaven, O Day Star, son of Dawn! How you are cut down to the ground, you who laid the nations low!	143
Isa. 25:8	1	God will wipe away the tears from all faces.	33
Isa. 28:10	110	Precept upon precept, precept upon precept; Line upon line, line upon line; Here a little and there a little.	24
Isa. 38:1	11	Set your house in order says the Lord.	153
Isa. 43:5	1	Fear not, for I am with you.	110
Isa. 55:6	63	Seek the Lord, now, while he is near.	54
Isa. 59:1	12	The Lord's hand is not too short to save you.	13
Isa. 61:2	3	Proclaim the year of the Lord's favor.	166
Jer. 17:9	1	The heart is devious above all else; it is perverse -who can understand it.	144

Chapter & Verse	Times Quoted	Key Message	Page
Ezek. 20:37	17	I will cause you to pass under the rod and I will bring you within the bond of the covenant.	28
Dan. 1:8	1	Daniel resolved that he would not defile himself with the royal food or wine.	124
Hos. 6:6	18	I desire steadfast love and not sacrifice, the knowledge of God rather than burnt offerings.	81
Mic. 4:4	1	They shall sit under their own vines and fig trees, and no one shall make them afraid.	110
Mic. 6:8	5	What does the Lord require of you but to do justice, and to love kindness, and to walk humbly with your God.	2
Hab. 2:2	6	Write the vision and make it plain so that a runner may read it.	65
Hab. 2:20	20	The Lord is in his holy temple; let all the earth keep silence before him.	13
Hag. 2:7	1	I will shake all the nations, so that their treasure shall come, and I will fill this house with splendor, says the Lord of hosts.	13
Hag. 2:8	67	The silver and the Gold are mine says the Lord.	9
Zech. 4:6	24	Not by might, nor by power, but by my spirit, says the Lord.	148
Mal. 3:10	11	Bring the full tithe into the storehouse and I will open the windows of heaven and pour down an overflowing blessing says the Lord.	9

Chapter & Verse	Times Quoted	Key Message	Page
Matt. 4:4	11	One does not live by bread alone.	64
Matt. 5:3	4	Blessed are the poor in spirit for theirs is the kingdom of heaven.	114
Matt. 5:4	2	Blessed are those who mourn for they will be comforted.	115
Matt. 5:5	11	Blessed are the meek for they will inherit the earth.	140
Matt. 5:8	5	Blessed are the poor in heart for they will see God.	28
Matt. 5:15	9	A lamp is placed on a lampstand so that it may give light to all in the house.	82
Matt. 5:16	52	Let your light shine before others so that they may see your good works and give glory to God.	1
Matt. 5:17	5	I have come not to abolish the law or the prophets but to fulfill them.	107
Matt. 5:18	12	Not one letter will pass from the law until all is accomplished.	5
Matt. 5:28	5	Everyone who looks with lust has committed adultery in their heart.	122
Matt. 5:29-30	7	If your eye causes you to sin, tear it out, and if your hand causes you to sin cut it off.	144
Matt. 5:40	7	If a person takes away your coat then give them your cloak as well.	19
Matt. 5:44	26	Love your enemies and pray for those who persecute you.	19

Chapter & Verse	Times Quoted	Key Message	Page
Matt. 5:45	10	God's sun rises on the evil and the good - His rain falls on the just and the unjust.	51
Matt. 5:46	8	If you love only those who love you what reward do you have.	135
Matt. 5:48	12	Become perfect, as your heavenly father is perfect.	22
Matt. 6:3	16	When you do a kindness, do it secretly.	106
Matt. 6:6	16	When you pray, go into your room and shut the door - your Father will reward you.	81
Matt. 6:8	15	Your Father knows what you need before you ask him.	81
Matt. 6:10	3	Thy will be done in earth as it is in heaven.	138
Matt. 6:19	20	Do not store up for yourself treasures on earth.	88
Matt. 6:21	18	Where your treasure is, there your heart will be also.	3
Matt. 6:22	25	If your eye is healthy your whole body will be full of light.	151
Matt. 6:24	20	No one can serve two masters.	44
Matt. 6:27	24	Can any of you add to your span of life by worrying.	110
Matt. 6:33	59	Seek first the kingdom of God and righteousness then material things will be given to you as well.	90
Matt. 6:34	33	Let today's troubles be sufficient for the day.	109

Chapter & Verse	Times Quoted	Key Message	Page
Matt. 7:2	207	The measure you give will be the measure you get.	4
Matt. 7:3	7	Why do you see the speck in your neighbor's eye but do not notice the log in your own eye?	121
Matt. 7:6	29	Do not throw your pearls before swine.	87
Matt. 7:12	289	In everything do to others as you would have them do to you.	57
Matt. 7:14	29	The gate is narrow and the road is hard that leads to life.	63
Matt. 7:16	33	You will know false prophets by their fruits.	6
Matt. 7:21	8	Only those who do the will of the Father will enter the kingdom of heaven.	138
Matt. 8:22	7	Follow me and let the dead bury their own dead.	45
Matt. 8:26	2	He said, "Why are you afraid, you of little faith?" He got up and rebuked the winds and the sea and there was a dead calm.	111
Matt. 9:29	10	According to your faith let it be done to you.	71
Matt. 9:37	10	The harvest is plentiful but the laborers are few.	85
Matt. 10:8	13	You received without payment - Give without payment.	11
Matt. 10:19	21	Do not worry about what you are to say for it will be given to you.	54

Chapter & Verse	Times Quoted	Key Message	Page
Matt. 10:24	3	The disciple is not above his master.	16
Matt. 10:28	7	Do not fear those who can kill the body but fear that which can destroy both soul and body.	110
Matt. 10:41	14	Whoever welcomes a prophet in the name of a prophet will receive a prophet's reward.	6
Matt. 11:28	23	Come to me all of you that are weary and are carrying heavy burdens and I will give you rest.	32
Matt. 11:29	36	Learn from me for I am gentle and humble in heart.	25
Matt. 11:30	23	My yoke is easy and my burden is light.	25
Matt. 12:25	15	A house divided against itself will not stand.	58
Matt. 12:30	26	He that gathereth not with me scattereth abroad.	135
Matt. 12:36	9	You will have to give an account for every careless word you utter.	14
Matt. 12:45	17	The last state of a person seeking a sign may be worse than the first.	99
Matt. 12:50	40	Whoever does the will of my Father in heaven is my brother and sister and mother.	137, 139
Matt. 13:23	3	One who hears the word and understands it bears fruit. Some yield a hundred fold, some sixty and some thirty.	65
Matt. 13:46	5	The kingdom of heaven is like a merchant	107

Chapter & Verse	Times Quoted	Key Message	Page
		never enter the kingdom of heaven.	
Matt. 18:19	8	If two of you agree and ask, it will be done for you by my Father in heaven.	82
Matt. 18:20	18	Where two or three are gathered in my name, I am there among them.	117
Matt. 18:22	4	Forgive not seven times, but seventy times seven.	127
Matt. 19:17	3	Jesus said, Why do you call me good. There is none good but one, that is God.	157
Matt. 20:16	8	The last will be first and the first will be last.	154
Matt. 20:22	15	Jesus asked, Are you able to drink from my cup and they answered, We are able.	44
Matt. 20:23	9	To sit at my right hand is not mine to grant but my Father's.	28
Matt. 21:22	17	Whatever you ask for in prayer with faith, you will receive.	71
Matt. 22:14	6	Many are called but few are chosen.	46
Matt. 22:21	13	Give to the emperor the things that are the emperor's and to God the things that are God's.	29
Matt. 22:37	12	You shall love the Lord your God with all your heart and with all your soul and with all your mind.	15
Matt. 23:11	153	The greatest among you will be your servant.	67

Chapter & Verse	Times Quoted	Key Message	Page
Matt. 23:27	8	Many are like whitewashed tombs, which on the outside look beautiful but inside are full of the bones of the dead.	145
Matt. 24:34	3	This generation shall not pass away until all these prophesied changes take place.	132
Matt. 24:36	5	No one except the Father knows the day and hour of these prophesied changes.	132
Matt. 25:21	80	You have been trustworthy in a few things, I will put you in charge of many things.	9
Matt. 25:40	418	Just as you have done things to those of least importance you have done them to me.	18
Matt. 26:40	4	Could you not stay awake with me one hour.	123
Matt. 26:41	85	The spirit is willing but the flesh is weak.	121
Matt. 27:22	1	What shall I do with Jesus?	47
Matt. 27:46	8	Jesus cried out, My God, my God why have you forsaken me.	99
Matt. 28:18	2	Jesus said, All authority in heaven and on earth been given to me.	37
Matt. 28:20	56	Jesus said, I am with you always, to the end of the age.	117
Mark 1:3	10	Prepare the way of the Lord; make his paths straight.	65
Mark 1:17	2	Jesus said, Follow me and I will make you fishers for men.	86

Chapter & Verse	Times Quoted	Key Message	Page
Mark 2:9	5	Is it easier to say, Your sins are forgiven, or to say, Stand up, take your mat and walk.	149
Mark 2:27	2	The sabbath was made for humankind and not humankind for the sabbath.	157
Mark 4:11	1	To you has been given the secret of the kingdom of God but for those outside everything comes in parables.	27
Mark 4:25	10	To those who have more will be given.	113
Mark 4:39	4	Jesus said to the sea, Peace, be still.	169
Mark 7:37	26	He (Jesus) has done everything well.	35
Mark 9:23	1	All things are possible for one that believes.	71
Mark 9:29	7	Some unclean spirits can be driven out only through prayer.	83
Mark 9:41	29	Whoever gives you a cup of water will not lose the reward.	112
Mark 9:42	12	If any of you put a stumbling block before one of these little ones, it would be better for you to be thrown into the sea.	155
Mark 10:21	3	Jesus looking at him, loved him.	135
Mark 10:27	6	With God all things are possible.	51
Mark 10:44	124	Whosoever will be the chiefest, shall be servant of all.	27
Mark 10:45	17	The son of man came not to be served but to serve and to give his life, a ransom for many.	69

Chapter & Verse	Times Quoted	Key Message	Page
Mark 12:31	11·	You shall love your neighbor as yourself.	134
Mark 13:11	3	Say what is given, for it is not you who speak, but the Holy Spirit.	160
Mark 13:31	64	Heaven and earth will pass away but my words not pass away.	129
Mark 13:33	6	Beware, keep alert for you do not know when the time will come.	107
Mark 16:15	3	Go into all the world and proclaim the good news.	108
Luke 1:35	1	The Holy Spirit will come upon you and the Most High will overshadow you.	161
Luke 2:7	3	She laid him in a manger because there was no room in the inn.	37
Luke 2:11	1	To you is born a Savior which is Christ the Lord.	37
Luke 2:14	4	Glory to God in the highest heaven and on earth peace and good will among all.	169
Luke 2:19	17	Mary treasured the messages and pondered them in her heart.	161
Luke 2:49	9	Did you not know that I must be in my Father's house.	36
Luke 3:17	1	He gathers the wheat into the granary but will burn the chaff.	29
Luke 4:23	6	Physician, heal yourself.	148
Luke 5:31	3	Those who are well have no need of a physician.	149

Chapter & Verse	Times Quoted	Key Message	Page
Luke 6:28	21	Bless those who curse you and pray for those who abuse you.	19
Luke 6:29	18	If anyone strikes you on the cheek, offer the other also.	19
Luke 6:37	129	Do not judge and you will not be judged. Do not condemn and you will not be con-demned.	4
Luke 6:37		Forgive and you will be forgiven.	74
Luke 6:39	15	If the blind lead the blind will not both fall into the ditch.	121
Luke 6:45	12	It is out of the abundance of the heart that the mouth speaks.	2
Luke 8:21	17	My mother and brothers are those who hear the word of God and do it.	140
Luke 8:46	3	Someone touched me for I noticed that power had gone out from me.	149
Luke 8:48	3	Your faith has made you well; go in peace.	149
Luke 9:62	22	No one who puts a hand to the plow and looks back is fit for the Kingdom of God.	88
Luke 10:7	32	The laborer deserves to be paid.	10
Luke 10:20	3	Rejoice because your names are written in heaven.	115
Luke 10:27	117	Love God with all your heart, soul, strength and mind; and your neighbor as yourself.	62
Luke 10:42	5	Mary has chosen the better part which will	46

Chapter & Verse	Times Quoted	Key Message	Page
Luke 18:13	3	The tax collector prayed, "God be merciful to me a sinner."	83
Luke 18:14	7	All who exalt themselves will be humbled, but all who humble themselves will be exalted.	141
Luke 18:16	12	Let the little children come to me, for it is to such as these that the kingdom of God belongs.	164
Luke 19:8	2	Zacchaeus said, "If I have defrauded anyone of anything I will pay back four times as much."	76
Luke 19:40	6	Jesus said, "If my disciples were silent these stones would shout out."	86
Luke 20:35	4	Those resurrected from the dead neither marry, nor are given in marriage.	163
Luke 20:38	17	He is God not of the dead, but of the living; for to him all are alive.	51
Luke 21:8	1	Do not be lead astray for many will come in my name; but do not follow them.	100
Luke 21:19	108	In patience you possess your soul.	125, 127
Luke 22:32	7	When you have been converted, strengthen your brothers and sisters.	29
Luke 22:42	33	Father, please remove this cup: Yet not my will, but yours be done.	80
Luke 23:34	16	Father, forgive them; for they do not know what they are doing.	75
Luke 23:43	3	Today you will be with me in Paradise.	76

Chapter & Verse	Times Quoted	Key Message	Page
John 4:32	3	I have food to eat that you do not know about.	166
John 5:39	9	Eternal life is found in Christ.	41
John 8:11	24	Neither do I condemn you. Go your way and from now on do not sin again.	144
John 8:12	10	I am the light of the world. Whoever follows me will never walk in darkness but will have the light of life.	151
John 8:28	67	I do nothing on my own, but I speak these things as the Father instructed me.	53
John 8:32	95	You will know the truth and the truth will make you free.	53
John 8:36	4	If the Son makes you free, you will be free indeed.	114
John 9:3	2	Neither this man nor his parents sinned; he was born blind so that God's work might be revealed in him.	5
John 9:4	7	We must work while it is day for night is coming when no one can work.	86
John 9:5	9	As long as I am in the world, I am the light of the world.	152
John 10:1	47	Anyone who does not enter the sheepfold by the gate but climbs in by another way is a thief and a bandit.	34
John 10:3	14	The gatekeeper calls his own sheep by name and leads them out.	15
John 10:10	46	I came that they may have life and have it more abundantly.	2

Chapter & Verse	Times Quoted	Key Message	Page
John 10:27	9	My sheep hear my voice and follow me.	65
John 10:30	2	The Father and I are One.	41
John 11:35	3	Jesus wept.	37
John 12:32	3	When I am lifted up I will draw all people to myself.	165
John 12:46	9	I have come as light into the world.	152
John 13:34	18	Love one another, just as I have loved you.	134
John 14:1	39	Do not let your hearts be troubled.	109
John 14:2	47	In my Father's house there are many dwelling places. I go to prepare a place for you.	27
John 14:3	10	I will come again and take you to myself, so that where I am, there you may be also.	113, 129
John 14:4	11	You know the way to the place where I am going.	82
John 14:6	232	I am the way, the truth and the life.	34
John 14:7	4	If you know me you will know my Father also.	51
John 14:9	4	Whoever has seen me has seen the Father.	36
John 14:10	11	The Father who dwells in me does his works.	60
John 14:11	10	I am in the Father and the Father is in me.	85
John 14:12	10	The one who believes in me will also do the works that I do, and, in fact, will do greater works than these.	10

Chapter & Verse	Times Quoted	Key Message	Page
John 14:13	57	I will do whatever you ask in my name.	112
John 14:14	18	If, in my name, you ask me for anything, I will do it.	113
John 14:15	13	If you love me, you will keep my commandments.	64
John 14:16	8	The Father will give you another Advocate to be with you forever.	160
John 14:18	52	I will not leave you comfortless: I will come to you.	103
John 14:20	69	You will know that I am in my Father and you in me and I in you.	39
John 14:23	64	Those who love me will keep my word and my Father will love them and We will make our home with them.	14
John 14:26	75	The Holy Spirit whom the Father will send in my name, will teach you everything.	53
John 14:27	65	My peace I give to you, but not as the world gives.	102
John 14:30	8	The ruler of this world is coming, but he has no power over me.	36
John 15:2	11	My Father removes every branch in me that bears no fruit. He prunes to make this true vine bear more fruit.	26
John 15:5	2	I am the vine, you are the branches.	26
John 15:7	4	If you abide in me, and my words abide in you; ask for whatever you wish and it will be done for you.	114

Chapter & Verse	Times Quoted	Key Message	Page
John 15:11	1	I have said these things to you so that my joy may be in you, and that your joy may be complete.	115
John 15:12	85	This is my commandment, That you love one as I have loved you.	57
John 15:13	3	No one has greater love than this, to lay down one's life for one's friends.	134
John 15:16	48	I chose you and appointed you to go and bear fruit that will last.	80
John 15:22	3	If I had not spoken to them, they would not have sin, but now they have no excuse.	146
John 16:33	24	Take courage; I have conquered the world.	98
John 17:5	17	Father, glorify me with the glory that I had before the world existed.	40
John 17:12	1	I guarded them that you gave me, and not one of them was lost except the one destined to be lost.	145
John 17:16	18	They do not belong to the world, just as I do not belong to the world.	157
John 19:11	8	You would have no power over me unless it had been given you from above.	51
John 20:17	5	I am ascending to my Father and your Father, my God and your God.	163
John 21:15	18	Jesus said, Do you love me? Feed my sheep.	138
Acts 1:11	6	Jesus who was taken up into heaven will come in the same way as you saw him go.	130

Chapter & Verse	Times Quoted	Key Message	Page
Acts 2:17	5	Your sons and daughters shall prophesy, your young men and women shall see visions, and your old men and women shall dream dreams.	130
Acts 3:6	1	I have no silver or gold but what I have I give you; in the name of Jesus Christ stand up and walk.	150
Acts 7:49	3	Heaven is my throne and earth is my footstool.	52
Acts 9:5	18	I am Jesus whom you are persecuting.	99
Acts 10:34	78	God shows no partiality, but in every nation anyone who fears him and does what is right is acceptable to him.	14
Acts 10:38	25	Jesus went about doing good and healing all who were oppressed.	35
Acts 17:28	134	In God we live and move and have our being.	50
Acts 20:35	4	Support the weak - it is more blessed to give than to receive.	26
Rom. 5:3	2	We rejoice in our sufferings, knowing that suffering produces patience and endurance.	127
Rom. 7:21	6	When I want to do what is good, evil lies close at hand.	100
Rom. 8:16	164	The Spirit bears witness with our spirit that we are children of God.	39
Rom. 8:28	18	All things work together for good for those who love God.	113

Chapter & Verse	Times Quoted	Key Message	Page
Rom. 8:31	22	If God is for us, who can be against us.	32
Rom. 8:38	60	Nothing in all creation can separate us from the love of God - (except self).	31
Rom. 12:1	70	Present your bodies as a living sacrifice, holy and acceptable to God.	2
Rom. 12:3	34	Do not think more highly of yourself than you ought to think.	87
Rom. 12:9	21	Let love be genuine - hold fast to that which is good.	3
Rom. 12:10	19	Love one another with mutual affection; outdo one another in showing honor.	133
Rom. 12:15	22	Rejoice with those who rejoice and weep with those who weep.	106
Rom. 12:16	12	Live in harmony with one another - associate with the lowly; do not claim to be wiser than you are.	89
Rom. 12:19	26	Never avenge yourselves - vengeance is mine, I will repay says the Lord.	87
Rom. 12:20	11	If your enemies are hungry, feed them and thus heap coals of fire on their head.	20
Rom. 12:21	23	Do not be overcome by evil, but overcome evil with good.	106
Rom. 14:7	10	We do not live to ourselves, and we do not die to ourselves.	16
Rom. 14:8	6	We live to the Lord and we die to the Lord.	3
Rom. 14:12	31	Each of us is accountable to God.	14

Chapter & Verse	Times Quoted	Key Message	Page
Rom. 14:13	7	Never put a stumbling block or hindrance in the way of another.	145
Rom. 14:16	82	Do not let your good be spoken of as evil.	21
I Cor. 1:27	1	God chose what is foolish in the world to shame the wise.	101
I Cor. 2:2	11	I have decided to speak of Jesus Christ and his death on the cross.	35
I Cor. 2:9	5	No eye has seen nor ear heard nor the human heart conceived, what God has prepared for those who love Him.	113
I Cor. 3:6-7	110	God gives the growth, the increase.	30
I Cor. 5:6	43	A little yeast leavens the whole batch of dough.	68
I Cor. 6:19	323	Your body is the temple of the Holy Spirit within you.	60
I Cor. 7:38	5	He who marries does well and he who refrains will do better.	46
I Cor. 9:22	36	I have become all things to all people that I might by all means save some.	84
I Cor. 10:13	155	God will not let you be tested beyond your strength, but with the testing he provides a way out.	93
I Cor. 12:29	13	Are all apostles, prophets, teachers or healers?	64
I Cor. 12:31	13	Strive for the greater gifts and I will show you a more excellent way.	55

Chapter & Verse	Times Quoted	Key Message	Page
I Cor. 13:1	13	If I speak in the tongues of angels but do not have love, I'm just making noise.	133
I Cor. 13:4	8	Love is patient and kind - it is not envious, boastful or arrogant.	133
I Cor. 13:7	5	Love bears all things, believes all things, hopes all things and endures all things.	133
I Cor. 13:11	5	When I was a child I spoke and thought like a child. When I became an adult I put an end to childish ways.	158
I Cor. 13:12	6	Now we see in a mirror dimly, but then we will see face to face. Now I know in part, but then I will know fully.	158
I Cor. 14:40	28	All things should be done decently and in order.	91
I Cor. 15:9	1	I am the least of the apostles because I persecuted the church of God.	146
I Cor. 15:22	5	All will be made alive in Christ.	130
I Cor. 15:45	8	The first man Adam became a living being; the last Adam (Jesus) became a life-giving Spirit.	25
I Cor. 15:50	9	Flesh and blood cannot inherit the kingdom of God; nor does perishable inherit the imperishable.	162
I Cor. 15:51	2	We will not all die, but we will all be changed.	131
I Cor. 16:13	14	Stand firm in your faith, be courageous, be strong.	71

Chapter & Verse	Times Quoted	Key Message	Page
II Cor. 3:6	39	The letter kills, but the Spirit gives life.	90
II Cor. 5:1	19	If the earthly tent we live in is destroyed, we have a building from God, a house not made of hands, eternal in the heavens.	164
II Cor. 5:8	32	We have confidence and would rather be away from the body and at home with the Lord.	153
II Cor. 5:21	1	He made Him to be sin, who knew no sin, so that in Him we might become the righteousness of God.	145
II Cor. 6:2	16	Now is the acceptable time - now is the day of salvation.	85
II Cor. 6:14	3	Do not be mismatched with unbelievers - what partnership or fellowship is there between light and darkness.	47
II Cor. 9:7	5	God loves a cheerful giver.	32
II Cor. 10:12	5	When people measure themselves by themselves and compare themselves among themselves they are unwise.	89
II Cor. 12:7	1	A thorn was given me in the flesh to keep me from being too elated.	123
II Cor. 12:9	16	My grace is sufficient for you; my power is made perfect in weakness.	165
Gal. 5:22	10	The fruits of the spirit are love, joy, peace, patience, kindness, generosity, faithfulness, gentleness and self-control.	140
Gal. 6:2	8	Bear one another's burdens.	69

Chapter & Verse	Times Quoted	Key Message	Page
Gal. 6:7	310	You reap whatever you sow.	4
Gal. 6:9	71	Let us not grow weary in doing what is right, for we will reap at harvest time, if we do not give up.	96
Eph. 2:18	13	Through Him we have access in one Spirit to the Father.	15
Eph. 4:5-6	1	There is one Lord, one faith, one baptism, one God and Father who is in all of you.	41
Eph. 4:11	18	He gave that some would be apostles, some prophets, some evangelists, some pastors and teachers.	44
Eph. 4:26	16	Be angry but do not sin; do not let the sun go down on your anger.	19
Eph. 5:15	4	Be careful how you live, not as unwise people but as wise.	58, 108
Eph. 6:13	29	Take up the whole armor of God.	21
Phil. 2:5	61	Let the same mind be in you that was in Christ.	40
Phil. 2:6	31	Jesus thought it not robbery to be equal with God.	22
Phil. 2:7	17	Jesus made himself of no reputation - taking the form of a servant.	35
Phil. 3:14	51	Press toward the mark for the prize of the high calling.	97
Phil. 4:7	60	The peace of God which surpasses all understanding will guard your hearts and your minds in Christ.	103

Chapter & Verse	Times Quoted	Key Message	Page
Phil. 4:8	5	Beloved, whatever is true, honorable, just, pure, pleasing, commendable, excellent or worthy of praise, think about these things.	141
Col. 3:16	13	With gratitude in your heart sing praises to God.	169
I Thess. 5:21	61	Test everything; hold fast to what is good.	96
I Thess. 5:22	23	Abstain from all appearance of evil.	22
I Tim. 2:6	16	Jesus gave himself a ransom for all.	35
I Tim. 5:8	14	Whoever does not provide for relatives, especially family members, has denied the faith.	97
I Tim. 6:17	4	Command the rich not to be haughty, or to set their hopes on the uncertainty of riches, but rather on God who richly provides us with everything for our enjoyment.	89
II Tim. 1:12	193	I know the one in whom I have put my trust, and I am sure that He is able to guard until that day what I have entrusted to Him.	70
II Tim. 2:15	638	Do your best to present yourself to God as one approved by Him, a worker who has no need to be ashamed, rightly explaining the word of truth.	1
II Tim. 2:19	27	The foundations of God stand firm - the Lord knows those who are his.	50
II Tim. 4:7	5	I have fought the good fight, finished the race and kept the faith.	72

Chapter & Verse	Times Quoted	Key Message	Page
Heb. 5:8	56	Although he was a Son, he learned obedience through what he suffered.	24
Heb. 9:22	10	Under the law almost everything is purified with blood. (By Christ life)	75
Heb. 9:28	1	Christ will appear a second time to those who are EAGERLY waiting for him.	42
Heb. 11:1	10	Faith is the assurance of things hoped for, the conviction of things not seen.	71
Heb. 11:6	34	Whoever would approach God must believe that he exists and that He rewards those who seek Him.	84
Heb. 11:10	2	He looked for a city with foundations whose architect and builder is God.	66
Heb. 12:1	16	Let us run with patience the race that is set before us.	125, 126
Heb. 12:2	28	Look to Jesus, the pioneer and perfecter of our faith who for the joy that was set before him endured the cross.	34
Heb. 12:6	41	The Lord disciplines those whom he loves and chastises every child whom he accepts.	31
Heb. 12:29	1	Our God is a consuming fire.	52
Heb. 13:2	8	Show hospitality to strangers, for by doing that some have entertained angels without knowing it.	159
Heb. 13:8	26	Jesus Christ is the same yesterday and today and forever.	34

Chapter & Verse	Times Quoted	Key Message	Page
James 1:12	12	Blessed is anyone who endures temptation. They will receive the crown of life.	26
James 1:17	200	Every good and perfect gift comes from the Father.	8
James 1:22	9	Be doers of the word and not merely hearers.	85
James 1:27	336	Keep yourself unstained by the world.	21
James 2:19	1	You believe that there is one God and you do well. The devils also believe and tremble.	72
James 4:8	6	Draw near to God and He will draw near to you. Cleanse your hands and purify your heart.	119
James 4:17	11	Anyone who knows the right thing to do and fails to do it commits sin.	146
James 5:8	1	Be patient. Strengthen your heart for the coming of the Lord is near.	127
James 5:12	100	Let your yes be yes and your no be no.	106
I Pet. 3:8	18	Have unity of spirit, sympathy, love for one another, a tender heart and a humble mind.	140
I Pet. 3:11	30	Turn away from evil and do good; seek peace and pursue it.	140
II Pet. 1:15	1	I will endeavor that after my death you will have these things always in remembrance.	154
II Pet. 3:9	189	The Lord is patient with you not wanting any to perish but all to come to repentance.	30

Chapter & Verse	Times Quoted	Key Message	Page
Rev. 7:17	1	The Lamb will guide them to the springs of the water of life and God will wipe away every tear from their eyes.	27
Rev. 13:8	1	All that dwell upon the earth shall worship Him.	16
Rev. 14:13	2	Blessed are the dead which die in the Lord.	154
Rev. 21:1	2	I saw a new heaven and a new earth.	131
Rev. 21:2	2	I saw the holy city, the new Jerusalem, coming down out of heaven from God.	131
Rev. 21:4	1	There will be no more death, sorrow, crying or pain for the first things have passed away.	131
Rev. 21:15	1	The angel had a golden rod to measure the city.	42
Rev. 22:2	3	The leaves of the tree of life are for the healing of the nations.	149
Rev. 22:13	12	I am the Alpha and the Omega, the first and last, the beginning and the end.	16
Rev. 22:17	36	Let anyone who wishes take the water of life freely, as a gift.	117

A.R.E. PRESS

The A.R.E. Press publishes quality books, videos, and audiotapes meant to improve the quality of our readers' lives—personally, professionally, and spiritually. We hope our products support your endeavors to realize your career potential, to enhance your relationships, to improve your health, and to encourage you to make the changes necessary to live a loving, joyful, and fulfilling life.

For more information or to receive a free catalog, call

        1-800-723-1112

Or write

        A.R.E. Press
        215 67th Street
        Virginia Beach, VA 23451-2061

DISCOVER HOW THE EDGAR CAYCE MATERIAL CAN HELP YOU!

The Association for Research and Enlightenment, Inc. (A.R.E.®), was founded in 1931 by Edgar Cayce. Its international headquarters are in Virginia Beach, Virginia, where thousands of visitors come year round. Many more are helped and inspired by A.R.E.'s local activities in their own hometowns or by contact via mail (and now the Internet!) with A.R.E. headquarters.

People from all walks of life, all around the world, have discovered meaningful and life-transforming insights in the A.R.E. programs and materials, which focus on such areas as holistic health, dreams, family life, finding your best vocation, reincarnation, ESP, meditation, personal spirituality, and soul growth in small-group settings. Call us today on our toll-free number

1-800-333-4499

or

Explore our electronic visitor's center on the
INTERNET: http://www.are-cayce.com

We'll be happy to tell you more about how the work of the A.R.E. can help you!

A.R.E.
215 67th Street
Virginia Beach, VA 23451-2061